TAKING THE HARD ROAD

Life Course in French and German Workers'

Autobiographies in the Era of Industrialization

TAKING THE HARD ROAD

MARY JO MAYNES

THE UNIVERSITY OF NORTH CAROLINA PRESS

CHAPEL HILL AND LONDON

Mary Jo Maynes is professor of
history at the University of
Minnesota. She is author of
*Schooling in Western Europe: A
Social History* and coeditor of
*Interpreting Women's Lives:
Feminist Theory and Personal
Narratives.*

99 98 97 96 95
5   4   3   2   1

Library of Congress
Cataloging-in-Publication Data
Maynes, Mary Jo.
    Taking the hard road : life course in French
and German workers' autobiographies in the era
of industrialization / by Mary J. Maynes.
        p. cm.
    Includes bibliographical references and index.
    ISBN 0-8078-2187-x (alk. paper). —
ISBN 0-8078-4497-7 (pbk. : alk. paper)
        1. Working class — France — History — 19th
century. 2. Working class — Germany — History —
19th century. I. Title.
HD8430.M29   1995   94-27197
205.5′62′094409034 — dc20   CIP

To Kathryn and Robert Maynes

and Louise and Charles Tilly

CONTENTS

Illustrations follow pages 53 and 180.

TABLES, FIGURES, AND MAPS

Tables

Figures

Maps

ACKNOWLEDGMENTS

I have been working on this book for many years, and during those years important methodological and theoretical discussions have been reshaping the writing of working-class history. I am keenly aware of how much my thinking and writing owes to the many people who have been participating in this broad discussion. I cannot imagine having written this book without help from and conversations or even arguments with many individuals and groups who have worked with me on one aspect or another of it over the past decade. I thank first those who read the entire manuscript (in some cases, more than once) — Barbara Laslett, Eric Weitz, Mark Traugott, Ron Aminzade, Allen Isaacman, and John Gillis, as well as three anonymous reviewers. These readers will, I trust, recognize their stamp upon this book (even if I did not make *all* the changes they asked for). Many others provided timely and important feedback on conference papers or other earlier drafts of chapters, among them Birgitte Soland, Sara Evans, Barbara Hanawalt, Geoff Eley, Louise Tilly, George Steinmetz, William Sewell, Michael Hanagan, Susan Cahn, and Liz Faue. The members of the Personal Narratives Group affiliated with the Center for Advanced Feminist Studies at the University of Minnesota contributed in many ways; this project really emerged from my working with them. Members of the History and Society Program, also at Minnesota, and the European Fertility Decline Working Group, the interdisciplinary audiences who have commented on parts of this project over the years at meetings of the Social Science History Association, and, most recently, participants in Minnesota's Comparative Women's History Workshop all deserve acknowledgment, as do the students who have given me feedback on chapters in history department seminars over the past half-dozen years. Birgitte Soland and Matt Sobek were there when it started, as invaluable research assistants. For helpful suggestions and correspondence early on, my thanks go to Daniel Bertaux and Philippe Lejeune. Finally, sometimes the right conversation at a decisive moment has been the key to my resolving a challenging problem; for such conversations, I thank in particular Barbara Laslett, Ann Waltner, Ulrike Strasser, Gianna Pomata, Ron Aminzade, and Liz Faue.

Institutional support has also been critical to the project. I am grateful to the staffs of the Friedrich Ebert Stiftung in Bonn-Bad Godesberg, the International Social History Archives in Amsterdam, the Bibliothèque nationale in Paris, and the Interlibrary Loan Section of the Wilson Library at the University of Minnesota for providing me with the texts on which the book is based. The staff of the Minnesota History Department has provided cheerful and competent assistance. For particular help on my research program, I'd like to thank Sue Haskins, who always makes sure that I get my grant applications in on time, and Kathy Donahue, who keeps track of complicated budgetary matters. The College of Liberal Arts and the Graduate School at the University of Minnesota have offered generous support over the years for the project. The American Philosophical Society helped me to get started with an early grant as well. The staff at the University of North Carolina Press has been very helpful; in particular, my thanks go to Lewis Bateman for his support for the project and his patience in waiting for its completion.

I've already thanked Ron Aminzade for his intellectual contributions to the project. I want to thank him for all the other stuff as well, and thank our kids Daniel and Elizabeth Maynes-Aminzade basically for being terrific, but also for helping me to understand childhood and parenthood. My last word goes to the people to whom this book is dedicated. I want to express my deep and lasting gratitude to my parents, Kathryn and Robert Maynes, who got me started, and to Louise and Charles Tilly, who served as early guides on the roads I still travel.

St. Paul, Minnesota
April 12, 1994

TAKING THE HARD ROAD

It was not my intention to speak about myself, my own life, in these memoirs . . . It's not a special life; just as I've lived and worked, so have thousands of other working girls of my time lived and worked. (Ottilie Baader, 11)[1]

ONE

SURVEYING THE TERRAIN

AUTOBIOGRAPHY, LIFE COURSE, AND

THE HISTORY OF CLASS IDENTITIES

IN NINETEENTH-CENTURY EUROPE

In 1921 the German seamstress and socialist organizer Ottilie Baader published her autobiography with the encouragement of her Social Democratic Party comrades. In her autobiography she told how she had become a socialist and what her accomplishments in the movement were. Her book was one of the dozens of German working-class-life narratives to appear during the epoch of the growth of socialism from the early 1890s through the 1920s.

Writing an autobiography had by Baader's lifetime become something of a commonplace for politically active German workers. If hers marks the flowering of the genre of workers' autobiography, the memoirs of Valentin Jamerey-Duval marked the emergence of it. Born in 1695 into a French peasant family, Jamerey-Duval had become a learned man, a court librarian, by the time he wrote his memoirs between 1733 and 1747. He wrote his memoirs at the request of an aristocratic patron, and his story recounts his transformation from illiterate peasant to scholar. It is one of the earliest autobiographical accounts by a European of lower-class origins.

Writing stories about growing up poor or working class echoed other expressions of European working-class consciousness. The genre flourished during the decades bracketed on one end by the innovative, often clandestine, and illegal organization of workers in the period before 1848, and on the other end by the decade of the 1930s when fascist and antifascist movements dramatically reshaped European working-class political organization. Later, in the era of complacence after World War II, when working-class identity had become the subject of mass-media nostalgia (in the West) or party line (in Eastern Europe), institutional and political support for the circulation of published workers' life stories was undermined. The voices diminished until "history from below" sought to revive them beginning in the 1960s.[2]

This book addresses the question of what these stories reveal about the experience of growing up in the working class in Europe during the transition to industrial capitalism. Its focus is on the autobiographical construction of class identity in childhood and youth. These subjective and personal sources have a great deal to add to history, for they allow us to view and assess historical transformations from the perspective of people who lived through them. The subjectivity of autobiographical accounts provides a place from which to interrogate and refine the categories through which the past is understood. The autobiography's personal emphasis, moreover, points to the significance of private life in history — a significance that historians are only beginning to appreciate. Such "personal matters" as family life, taste in clothing, and sexual experiences were all important dimensions of the history of class relations and class identities.

The ninety autobiographers whose works are the focus of this study wrote from positions widely ranging in time and space. The earliest mem-

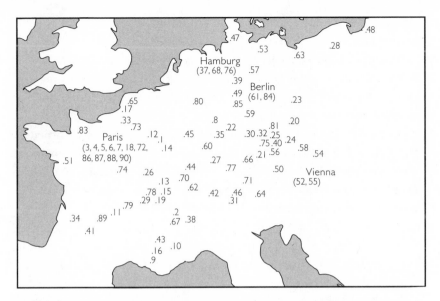

Map 1. Birthplaces of Autobiographers. Numbers correspond to those assigned each author in part 1 of the bibliography. They are ordered chronologically by birthdate of author.

oirist was born at the end of the seventeenth century and wrote in the middle of the eighteenth. The latest were born at the beginning of the twentieth century and wrote in the post–World War II era. They wrote in French or German, and their birthplaces were scattered across Western and Central Europe (see map 1). Most of the stories were written by men, but a substantial minority of the authors — nearly a third — were women. They came from milieux where livelihoods were based on labor. Some worked in factories or on large farms, some in craft industries, some in cottage industries or sweatshops, others in small family-owned businesses or farms.

Their accounts simultaneously recorded and contributed to the construction of class identities. They illuminate how social position, or location in social hierarchies, was internalized as identity. This did not happen automatically by virtue of birth alone or by the act of working. Rather, the autobiographies record identity taking shape through very complicated interactions with parents, grandparents, and fosterparents; siblings, lovers, spouses, aunts, and uncles; neighbors, midwives, and nurses; teachers and clergymen; masters, bosses, and coworkers; political organizers and uplifters; shopkeepers, peddlars and booksellers; policemen and overseers of the poor; writers, actors and even strangers in the street. Just as this subjectivity — this sense of identity — cannot be separated from the complex social experiences and the institutions in which it was rooted, neither can the historical record of this subjectivity — the autobiographies — be divorced from the contexts that spawned them.

The history of identities that these texts record might seem idiosyncratic indeed, as well as very elusive, to historians accustomed to analyses based on records created by parliaments, or census takers, or trade union councils. But the construction of identity that occurs and is recorded in these autobiographies, while it is the product of individual imagination, is also very clearly marked by the social, economic, political, and cultural institutions that shaped the authors' lives. These institutions also influenced how and which subjectivities found expression in autobiography. These autobiographies thus demonstrate the fluidity of the boundary between the individual and the social. As vividly as they document individuality, they also nevertheless illustrate, in their very patterning, how individuals came to understand and define their innermost selves in ways that reflected their position in time and place and in the hierarchies defined by class and gender.

Autobiographical sources open ways of understanding the past that are often barred by more usual modes of inquiry, but they do demand their own methods and cautions.[3] Autobiographers were not typical workers. In fact one of them, Sebastien Commissaire, declared in the preface to his autobiography that "workers don't write memoirs" (iv). This might seem paradoxical, or tongue-in-cheek, for Commissaire was for much of his life a silk weaver, certainly a worker. On the other hand, he had also become a political leader, a deputy in the French Parliament. So he was not *merely* a worker. His class ambiguity is, in fact, typical of worker autobiographers.

The autobiographers whose life stories form the basis of this book are distinctive in many respects — their commitment to the written word, their tendency to militancy, their likelihood to have come to self-identity through one of a set number of channels (for example, in a workers' movement or through self-help). Other peculiarities emerge in comparing aspects of the lives recalled with those of the broader working population. Thus, for example, it turns out that working-class autobiographers were disproportionately likely to have been firstborn, and the German authors were more likely than the general population to have lost one or both parents before adolescence. Observations like these, it should be emphasized, are meant to contextualize but not to discredit the autobiographical testimony. The peculiar characteristics of authors of personal narratives do not invalidate their testimony. But the selectivity that affected *whose* memories were recorded in autobiographies needs to be an intrinsic part of the history told from them.[4]

Beyond their selectivity, the historian's distrust of autobiography stems as well from the possibility of deception and the probability of distortion of the experiences remembered and recounted. Oral historians long ago discovered that informants rarely "get the facts right" — and they can check their sources to an extent that is impossible in the case of auto-biographers of centuries past. The authors themselves were aware of their audience's suspicions. Wilhelm Kaisen was most forthright: "Some-body once said to me," he wrote, "that he really loved reading memoirs because people tell such wonderful lies in them. What I'm now about to relate, he would certainly reckon among these" (32).

Certainly in some cases, historians can compare autobiographical ren-ditions of events with other sources. In his recent edition of the auto-biography of Jacques-Louis Ménétra, Daniel Roche has done a meticu-lous job of tracking down references in the text to events or acts that could be verified through external sources. In this particular case, Mén-étra's memory proved to be startlingly sound and accurate. Michele Per-rot noted with surprise the degree of precision with which certain phe-nomena are recalled in workers' autobiography (especially such details as wages and hours worked). Moreover, in a newly or marginally literate culture, feats of memory that now seem unlikely must have been more commonplace.[5] Still, however much we may be inclined to trust certain autobiographical testimony, it is important to avoid too literal a reading of it. The rich potential of these sources lies more in the insights they provide into subjectivities, more in the clues they offer about how people made sense of and reconstructed the course of their life, than in the information they provide about particular aspects of working-class expe-rience. On these latter details, they can be tantalizing but indeterminate. For the task here, however — tracing the construction of class identities — recorded memories are pertinent evidence indeed even where their factual base is suspect or impossible to assess.[6]

The question of lying or forgetting is not insignificant for the reader of autobiography, but the work of oral historians who are attentive to method suggests how even suspect accounts are telling. For any rendition of the past has to be seen in the context of its present motives, its symbolic power, its contextual framing. In other words, to use autobiography and other personal narrative evidence well, it cannot be taken at face value; it must be read in a context and be interpreted. Luisa Passerini put it well in discussing her Italian working-class informants' accounts of life under fascism: "All autobiographical memory is true. It is up to the interpreter to discover in which sense, where, for which purpose."[7]

Like oral histories, autobiographies are not transparent representations or objective reconstructions. Their evidence must be interpreted through careful contextualization and with sensitivity to their nature as particular kinds of texts. Throughout the book, I will be making comparisons of one story to another and comparing the stories to evidence external to them, not so much to check for accuracy as to understand why authors write what they do (or, in some cases, choose not to write about some things). These are texts, and as such they follow rules and logics inherent to genres of texts. But they can also be assessed through reference to information about the institutions and practices that shaped their authors' lives. Plotting and unconscious rules of genre surely fed into every episode, but information about the author's context often can illuminate why certain rules were followed or defied, why one story was told and not another. No reading can be seen as definitive; further contextualization can certainly alter or even reverse a meaning previously understood.[8] Still, far from being random or idiosyncratic reflections of their authors' individual trajectories, autobiographies are products of collective social, political, and cultural historical processes to which they offer privileged access.

My concern for context led me to limit the kinds of texts upon which this book focuses to those autobiographies written for publication. These particular writings were generally intended to enter into public discourse, to contribute to the open exchange of views. Moreover, concentrating primarily on published texts permits me to address questions about how the auspices of publishing influence the flavor of the autobiographical testimony available to historians. I sometimes refer to adjacent genres — fictionalized autobiographies, autobiographies not written for publication, and autobiographical novels — but my primary concern is that set of texts written as true life stories with a "public" audience in mind, and with the broad conversation and possibility of response or even refutation that publication suggests.[9]

Reading these autobiographical texts has to be framed by characteristics of the stories themselves, by what can be deduced about the authors' aims in writing and their sense of what a life story was supposed to look like. Comparisons among subsets of the ninety texts — grouped by type of story, or by the gender, nationality, or era of the author — highlight the effects of all of these influences. To underscore the literary self-construc-

tion entailed in writing autobiography and to keep in view the dual moment inherent in each autobiographical account (that is, the initial experience and the later memory and interpretation of that experience), I
distinguish between the autobiographer as author and as subject by using
the first name to indicate the recalled hero or heroine of the autobiographical account and the last name to refer to the author, the persona
the autobiographer has in the interim become.

The Set of Autobiographies

This book is based on a set of ninety French- and German-language
autobiographies by lower-class authors. Because its main interest is the
phenomenon of "growing up working class" in the era of European
industrialization, it focuses on texts that devote attention to the years of
childhood and to those written by authors whose childhoods occurred
before the First World War. I selected this set from among about four
hundred French- and German-language workers' memoirs that I have so
far identified. (See the first section of the bibliography for a complete list
and description of the set.)

Comparison between texts written by French- and German-speaking
authors is an important analytical device throughout. Including texts in
two languages and from the different countries where those languages
were spoken (France, the German states, Switzerland, and German-
speaking areas of the Austrian Empire) allowed the examination of variations stemming from important differences in national cultural and political histories. Certain aspects of working-class childhood and its representation in autobiography look very different in French and German texts;
in other respects, differences between men and women, or across types of
story, seem far more compelling than national differences. Although it is
perhaps unusual to have chosen linguistic rather than strictly political
boundaries in constructing my comparison, good justifications exist for
having done so. First, political boundaries changed considerably over the
long period the book addresses. From the middle of the eighteenth century through the First World War, Central European political boundaries
altered dramatically both during the Revolutionary-Napoleonic era and
during the period leading up to the unification of the Second German
Empire in 1871. Second, the cultural traditions that shaped popular
experiences in Europe were a composite of highly localized and national
or transnational experiences. Because language is a prime vehicle for the

transmission of familial and political culture, I was interested in comparing both across languages and across strictly political boundaries that did not represent linguistic frontiers.

The set of autobiographies was structured not randomly but rather to include examples of the different sorts of texts, and hence life trajectories, that isolate particular phenomena. Because I am very interested in analyzing gender differences in the construction of class identity, I followed leads to virtually every woman's autobiography because they are so rare; I was more selective with the men's stories. (For example, for men I followed leads to stories from underrepresented regions or occupations since I found many more men's stories than I could analyze.) Unfortunately, French working women's autobiographies are especially scarce; their paucity makes it difficult to characterize them as a subgroup, and their variations are often more noticeable than their commonalities. This means that discussion of them must be more cautious; however, the very scarcity of women's stories relative to men's, especially in French, is itself a telling by-product of the institutional and cultural history of the working classes.

The set was also constructed with an eye toward broad occupational variation. Occupational boundaries were often fluid in this era of massive structural shift. Especially in the early to mid-nineteenth century, moving between agricultural and industrial employment in one lifetime, one year, or even one day was quite common. Of course such patterns varied regionally, and, over time, the number of workers whose entire life was spent in industrial employment increased. But it seemed useful to cast the net widely rather than narrowly by defining as a "worker" anyone who came from the milieux of manual labor and thus to include autobiographical texts by authors from a great range of occupations, including agrarian ones.[10]

More specifically, the autobiographers' families lived from skilled and unskilled manual labor in either industry or agriculture. Autobiographers of peasant origins are rare but represented; artisans and factory workers are well represented; even waitresses and domestics, miners and agricultural laborers, itinerant peddlars and railroad workers have their place. (The first section of the bibliography includes information about the occupations of the autobiographers and their parents.) The set includes not only the writings of core proletarians of the industrial era, such as miners, factory workers, and railroad workers, but also upwardly or downwardly mobile artisans, service workers who proliferated in the growing cities, and agricultural wage workers. Mothers' as well as fathers' occupations figure into the analysis. The vast majority of autobiographers described their mothers as having done paid work routinely; moreover, mothers' work and identities figured as keenly in the authors' self-definition as fathers'.

The parents of the autobiographers in the German sample were more often factory workers than in the French; agricultural families were more prevalent among the French. In other words, the population of autobiographers is not occupationally identical for both languages. This difference certainly helps to account for some of the contrasts among the stories, but these occupational profiles also reflect (though they exaggerate) differences between French- and German-speaking regions in the nineteenth century that are related to the specific character and pace of industrialization and working-class formation in France and Central Europe.

The subgenres, or formal categories, into which these stories fall — the kind of story the author was telling — also figure into the analysis in important ways. I made a point of including both a substantial number of militants' texts (often recounting socialist or trade union activities) as well as examples of those rarer texts by authors who pointedly were not politically affiliated or who chose to pursue success through self-improvement and individual social mobility. I will refer most frequently to these two subgenres — militants' tales and success stories. But a few texts that fit into neither category have been included in the analysis, particularly at moments when the testimony of these more marginal or "accidental" autobiographers hints at both the boundaries of the genre and the ways in which the selectivity of authors colors the kinds of stories (and subjectivities) that come to be preserved in autobiography.

Such comparisons between the set of autobiographers and the broader population of French and German workers help situate the particular social perspectives the stories tap into, but these stories cannot be taken to mirror somehow the working-class populations of France and Central Europe. After all, only a restricted group of people came to write these autobiographies. Moreover, generalizations based upon these stories, however large their number, can always be contradicted in individual cases and even ultimately overturned as an increasing number of texts come to light. I cannot claim that these autobiographies provide us with direct access to a forgotten past nor that they preserve *the* authentic voice of the European working class. Although the stories corroborate one another in some regards, their variety also breaks down many simple generalizations. The authors' frequent attention to the ways in which they felt themselves to be distinctive makes it impossible to see them simply as workers who happened to leave autobiographies. Nevertheless, bringing their voices into the history of class identity, while hardly a straightforward task, is a compelling one. Working-class autobiographers offer unparalleled perspectives on questions of deep historical significance, and they write with a degree of intelligence, eloquence, and insight that commands attention and respect.

Autobiography, Life Course, and Working-Class History

What did it mean to be working-class in industrializing Europe? How did people acquire and understand class identities? There was a time when social historians thought they had figured out the meaning of class divisions and their importance in history. Often following the lead of Karl Marx, they looked in the standard places — in the workshops, factories, and union halls of Europe and North America during the growth of industrial capitalism, between the late eighteenth and the mid-twentieth centuries. Studying the workers they found in these places, they looked for evidence of their development into what Marx had called a "class for itself" — a class-conscious proletariat whose political organization in the socialist movement pushed forward the struggle with capitalist employers.

But historical research on the history of working people in the West has broadened the agenda and called into question many of the initial categories of analysis. Of course, the enormous global changes that have framed historical study since the emergence of "history from below" in the 1960s have also played their part. Historians are always writing history from the perspective of their own time as they try to bring the present into dialogue with the past. This changing present — the constantly moving *end* of the human story — has forced a continual refreshening of our understanding of the story's beginning and its middle.

The political and economic collapse of Eastern European socialist societies, the persistence and even increase of inequalities within and across the world's regions, the late twentieth-century crisis of unionism, and the feminist struggle to include women in contemporary institutions and in analyses of the past have pushed historians to keep revising their story lines. In terms of working-class history, that story line has become more complex and interesting. Research on family and women's history has demonstrated how much was left out when attention was restricted to the adult male labor force, the workplace, and organized political movements.[11] Feminist criticism of traditions of class analysis has emphasized the problematic relationship of women to all class categories and the inadequacy of simply adding them into theories that were constructed without regard to them.[12] Neomarxist critics have pointed to the importance of national and local political cultures for the changing conditions and fates of workers under different political regimes. Cultural studies have begun to reconstruct the world of workers from sources closer to the grass roots and often quite distinct from the official culture of organized workers' movements.[13] This study of nineteenth-century European workers' lives builds on all of these developments. But its main contribution will be to explore the varied and changing experience of growing up working class as recorded in the highly subjective and personal source of workers' autobiography.

BECAUSE THE autobiographies and their interpretation are the core of this analysis, the book begins with a closer look at them. Chapter 2 recounts the history of the genre of workers' autobiography and describes the particular milieux from which the authors emerged. This chapter also builds an institutional context for understanding why the autobiographers wrote when they did and what they did.

Subsequent chapters are organized around critical moments in the life course as these autobiographers portrayed them. The life course perspective — that is, the examination of successive phases of development through which individuals move chronologically as they mature — provides a useful frame for several reasons. First, it reflects to some extent the narrative categories that the autobiographies themselves employed. The stories typically include chronologically organized episodes centered on childhood, schooling, and various aspects of "coming-of-age."[14] The autobiographical plot often traces the process by which these successive phases of life contributed to the author's adult sense of identity and purpose. Second, the authors were also often quite interested in questions that a life course perspective addresses; they reflected upon how their childhood experiences echoed in later life and how their expectations and decisions shaped their future. Finally, examining the autobiographical testimony through the categories of life course analysis allows one to place those very categories in historical context and highlights the variations in how they were experienced. The autobiographers often used such terms as "childhood" or "apprenticeship" only to tell why their lives did not match normative understandings of these experiences. Workers' lives, to paraphrase one author, often "didn't turn out the way they were expected to,"[15] and this experience of life as counternormative — as not the way it was supposed to be — is one of the richest and most persistent leitmotifs of the genre. In workers' autobiographies, life course categories are simultaneously affirmed and questioned.

Childhood and Class in Nineteenth-Century Europe

Chapter 3 explores the origins of class identity in childhood experiences. Carolyn Steedman has recently posed a pertinent question: "What becomes of the notion of class consciousness when it is seen as a structure of feeling that can be learned in childhood, with one of its components a proper envy, the desire of people for things of the earth?"[16] Like Steedman, these working-class autobiographers often rooted their class identities in childhood experiences, and many workers represented their childhood as lacking, as wrong somehow, as different. Remembering herself at age ten, the autobiographer Adelheid Popp remarked, "I didn't think of myself as a child" (10). Her comment, simple as it is, highlights an important dimension of the history of childhood. The subjective experience of a life phase, both as lived through and as subsequently reconstructed in memory, is affected by both what actually "happens" and what is supposed to happen. These stories emphasize the need to be alert to the not-always-predictable interplay between norms and experiences.

Historians of the western family have long been concerned with recounting the social and cultural processes that shaped modern norms about childhood. Philippe Ariès permanently recast notions about childhood when he published his pathbreaking book *L'enfant et la vie familiale sous l'Ancien Regime* in 1960.[17] Ariès suggested that childhood, far from being a universal experience with common characteristics in all times and places, was significantly restructured during the early modern epoch. The new western understanding of childhood paid close attention to the characteristics of specific ages and to the effects of childhood experiences on adult character. The early modern era brought new institutions dedicated to child socialization, the sentimentalization of the bond between parents and young children, and the segregation of young children and adolescents from each other and from their elders. Ariès argued that this "discovery" of childhood, which occurred between the sixteenth and the eighteenth centuries, was connected to the emergence of the modern nuclear and privatized family, which became the special preserve of emotion.

Critics have pointed to limitations of Ariès's thesis. For example, the demographic basis for the new notions of childhood—lowered infant and child mortality that encouraged both emotional closeness to and material investment in children—applied only to elite populations before the nineteenth century. Moreover, the evidence upon which Ariès relied so heavily—pictures, diaries, and school plans—was both heavily skewed toward upper-class experiences and prescriptive rather than descriptive.[18]

If we accept a more limited version of Ariès's thesis—that new understandings of childhood and family life and new family practices came to predominate in the elite classes of Western Europe in the early modern epoch—we are left with a puzzle. Many of these practices bore little relation to childrearing habits in lower-class milieux even at the beginning of the twentieth century. When and under what conditions did popular notions of childhood change? How did the temporalities affecting the conditions of children vary regionally? And what difference did this variety of notions of childhood make to the generations who grew up under regimes of childhood that varied from what the dominant norms prescribed?

Recent research on the history of childhood in more popular milieux suggests some of the most significant departures from the model Ariès described. In the first place, segregating children from the adult world of work was inconsistent with the family economy of peasants and industrial workers in the nineteenth century. Children worked alongside adults and were central to their economic activities; young children disappeared from the European labor force only between the third quarter of the nineteenth century and the first quarter of the twentieth century at a pace that varied regionally.

The transition to industrial capitalism affected patterns of family work and changed the demand for male, female, and child labor. The demand for child labor may well have intensified in some areas before it eventually diminished. In particular, it seems likely that where entrepreneurs relied upon the common practice of "putting out"—that is, the hiring of laborers who worked at home on mass-marketed goods—labor demands on all members of the household engaged in this form of work intensified.[19] If by the middle of the nineteenth century schools were drawing an increasing proportion of children out of work activities and into age-segregated classrooms for at least part of the day, schooling did not eradicate either the persistent view of children as family workers or the need of most families for their children's labor. Indeed, only with the success of the "male-breadwinner" norm and increasing real wage levels was it possible for families even to imagine living without the supplemental wages of children or mothers. This possibility was won first among the so-called labor aristocracy in Great Britain as a result of increasing productivity and the unionization struggles of the 1860s; one-earner families became a possibility on the Continent only during the last quarter of the nineteenth century, and then only for the highest-paid echelons of the working class.[20] For the vast majority of working-class families, women and children provided important and necessary contributions to the family wage even at the end of the nineteenth century.

Demographic conditions also worked against the emergence of a child-centered family in popular milieux in most of Europe before the late nineteenth century. The new notions of childhood — centered on increased attention to a smaller number of children — made most sense when birth rates and infant and child death rates were low. With the exception of peasant and petit bourgeois France, where fertility had declined by the early nineteenth century, family size among the European popular classes remained high until the very end of that century. High levels of infant and child mortality among the poor also persisted despite the overall mortality decline. In Germany at least, demographic differentials between classes widened before they converged. For example, in Prussia between 1880 and 1900 mortality rates for the infants of civil servants dropped from 180 to 153 per thousand, while during the same two decades mortality rates for infants whose fathers were unskilled workers rose from 216 to 237 per thousand. Even wider differentials were evident between upper-class and working-class city neighborhoods.[21]

Though less commonly noted, adult mortality also affected the possibilities that new patterns of childhood would emerge. For the parent-child (and especially mother-child) bond to replace the more diffuse supervision of earlier eras, parents had to survive long enough to raise their children. Demographic evidence suggests that mothers could expect to survive past their offsprings' maturation in some areas of Europe by the second quarter of the nineteenth century. Life expectancy was on the rise generally and probably increased by as much as five years throughout much of Western Europe over the course of the nineteenth century.[22] But there were also temporary and regional setbacks in adult life expectancy, especially where urban and industrial diseases such as cholera and tuberculosis took their toll. Rough estimates from regional life tables suggest that parents' survival to a child's twentieth birthday could not be taken for granted even in the second half of the nineteenth century.[23] Scattered direct evidence on parental survival shows dramatic

contrasts between the demographic fates of poorer and wealthier populations during the epoch of demographic transition. For example, in the
French industrial town of Mulhouse in the 1850s, children of artisans
and wage earners were three times more likely than children of *patrons*
(employers) and white-collar workers to have lost their fathers by late
adolescence. German demographic evidence shows that the mortality
rates of younger adults were especially high in the rapidly growing industrial cities. Within cities, wide differentials in adult mortality across neighborhoods marked socioeconomic boundaries. As with child mortality,
these social differentials in adult mortality rates in Germany only began
to converge in the early twentieth century.[24] What was becoming a common experience in healthier and better-fed upper-class populations by
the eighteenth century — the survival of children to adulthood and of
parents to their children's maturity — was still uncertain for working-class
families before the beginning of the twentieth century.

The eventual withdrawal of children from the labor force, along with
the decline of child and adult mortality throughout Western Europe,
permitted the diffusion of some of the features of middle-class childhood
throughout the population. But childhood's various contours — demographic, emotional, economic, educational — moved according to
rhythms that varied by region and social class. During the nineteenth
century a variety of norms, expectations, and rationalities coexisted and
often clashed. And these clashing experiences of childhood did not go
without notice. As Chapter 3 will show, workers' awareness of how class
differences mattered dated to early childhood, which left an imprint that
lasted a lifetime. Autobiographical accounts of working-class childhoods
joined representations in fiction, art, parliamentary inquiries, and other
media of childhoods far different from those prescribed in the child-
centered family of middle-class imagery. Writing autobiographical accounts provided working-class authors with both an occasion for working
through the psychological residues of a "deficient" past and a powerful
political forum for an appeal to recognize and rectify damages resulting
from deprivations experienced in early childhood.

Schooling

The political dimension of accounts of the early years of life becomes
even more explicit in the elementary school stories explored in chapter
4. In the classroom, in the person of the teacher, the young child first encountered extrafamilial political authority most directly. Memories of

schooling once again reveal how the meanings associated with phases of childhoods are both patterned and historically specific. Both gender differences and significant differences in the political cultures of nineteenth-century France and Central Europe fed into accounts of schooling and colored autobiographers' perceptions of the impact of schooling on their later lives.

School reforms in the German states beginning in the late eighteenth century had dramatic consequences for lower-class children. School enrollment was pushed toward universality at a very early date: by the mid-nineteenth century children routinely attended school for at least part of the legally mandated period (generally from age six to thirteen or fourteen). Schooling had become virtually inescapable for all school-age children by roughly the 1880s — earlier in Germany than anywhere else. The autobiographies provide cultural documentation of what school enrollment figures suggest: by the second half of the nineteenth century children knew they had to be enrolled in school during the legally prescribed ages, and the few who escaped before the official *Schulentlassung*, with its certificate, did so only with permission from school authorities.

Moreover, with few exceptions, children were routed into institutions based on their social position. Peasants' and workers' children attended the *Volksschulen* from age six or seven to age thirteen or fourteen. Middle- and upper-class children attended separate public or private schools with more ambitious curricula and longer periods of schooling.[25] In smaller communities in many regions elementary schools were coeducational. But in the cities, which supported many schools, and in the Catholic South, separate schools, and to some extent different curricula, were typically provided for girls and boys. Official curricula prepared boys for futures as laborers and soldiers and girls to be housewives and part-time workers.[26] Religious texts were at the center of instruction.

The political character of the state-supervised elementary schools varied among the different German states over the course of the nineteenth century. Throughout Central Europe, state authorities had developed a precocious interest in and control over the schools, generally through the state-church bureaucracies. The influence of this state control varied, however, with the political climate and particular state policy. In Prussia, the largest of the German states, there were several moments of political contest over the school system, most notably during the French Revolution and the reform era that followed Prussia's defeat by Napoleon in 1806, again around the epoch of the 1848 revolts, and after German unification in the anti-Catholic *Kulturkampf* era of the 1870s. During these periods, traditional pedagogy and classroom relations deemed so crucial for building the character of future citizens came under scrutiny. But, in contrast with France, the liberal critique of the disciplinarian classroom had little impact in Prussia until the end of the century. The neohumanist movement of the early part of century was forgotten in the emphasis on strict discipline and rote learning of religious texts. The defeat of the 1848 revolt also had pedagogic repercussions as the emphasis of educational policy throughout the second half of the nineteenth century rested upon the teaching of discipline, piety, and civic loyalty above all else.[27] Teachers trained during these repressive periods dominated in the classrooms of Prussia until the century's end.

In contrast with pedagogic theory developed in other European countries by the early nineteenth century, law and practice in Prussia continued to rest on the maintenance of the teacher's authority through the use of corporal punishment. Historians of education have pointed to the persistent place of corporal discipline in Prussian school regulations well into the era of organized capitalism. Jürgen Reulecke, for example, noted that "in 1898 a Royal District Court confirmed in finest official German that 'moderate welts on the seat' and 'mild headaches' were manifestations 'that could result from corporal punishments that to some extent accomplished their goal of physical displeasure and pain without the level of permissible punishment being overstepped.' There were even exact guidelines for the instrument of discipline: it should be 'a pliant, smooth stick which was not more than 1 cm. thick.' "[28]

Prussia, of course, was not all of Germany. But several other German states followed suit. In Bavaria, the second-largest German state, the political reaction of the 1820s followed a logic similar to what prevailed in Prussia. Bavarian teachers found themselves under pressure to be agents in the state's quest to teach piety and obedience. The reaction of the 1850s also paralleled the Prussian reactionary reforms. According to a historian of this era, "A solid moral accomplishment which alone would preserve the untutored orders from the dangers of scientific education" was more important for teachers than a solid general education. Behind this caution lay a fear of mass mobilization through education.[29]

More liberal traditions took root in other German states, and educational policy reflected a different perception of the proper character of classroom relations. In Baden, for example, where an activist teaching corps was part of the relatively liberal and anticlerical coalition behind reform, school policy bore a far less conservative stamp than elsewhere. Even more dramatically, in Bremen and Hamburg, which as large city-states evolved according to a different political dynamic and where active workers' movements existed early on, classroom politics could be very different indeed. Schoolteachers were even among the earliest recruits of socialist movements in these localities.[30] Still, they appear as islands of benignity in a sea of classroom authoritarianism. The teacher as tyrant, the pedagogy of suppression, seems to have held as the dominant German model long after the inauguration of the industrial capitalist order. Efforts at teaching reform in the later decades of the nineteenth century were further stymied by adoption of a prostatist position by Prussian liberals in the era of the *Kulturkampf*.[31]

The political history of schooling in France presents a different picture. By the beginning of the Third Republic (founded in 1870), the public elementary schools of France had become key institutions forming the basis of a new political consensus around a radical-liberal program. In the narrative of the Third Republic triumphant, the battle over the schools was portrayed as a century-long struggle between reactionary, clerical darkness and enlightenment for the masses. A faith in liberation through knowledge and the opportunity for improvement through education open to all Frenchmen was one of the founding myths and supporting pillars of the Third Republic.

This philosophy had roots in the epoch of the Enlightenment and the French Revolution. Throughout the various moments of contention over the French state that punctuated the period from 1789 to 1871, debates over schooling held a prominent place in political discussion.[32] After decades of conflict, schools were made free, obligatory, and lay once the liberal government of the Third Republic had cemented its control over state policy. The school administrators of the Third Republic aimed to integrate working-class children into the vision of interclass solidarity and cooperation that underlay the government's political strategy. The *instituteurs* and *institutrices* sent out to teach in public schools in cities and villages all over France were recruited and trained to embody the spirit of the Third Republic. And they did so with a remarkable consensus behind them. The schools were contested strenuously only by opposition from the right. What little opposition they encountered on the left tended to be sporadic and unsystematic anarchist assaults on any but familial education.[33]

School authorities in France during the Third Republic also had a clear agenda regarding gender relations. Historical research has shown that educational planners who concerned themselves with girls' education did so primarily out of fear that the ideological split between women educated by nuns and men educated in the secular state schools endangered the unity of the family. It is also clear that the institutions they created to educate girls were designed to contain inappropriate female ambitions and buttress the male-headed family.[34] The conservative views of gender roles behind this policy resemble those of German educational administrators of the period, but they flowed from different political concerns; ironically, official concern about girls' education in France, in the context of a desire to combat the Catholic Church's influence over women, may have brought unanticipated consequences for girls. If for the sake of the unity of the family girls needed to be educated in secular state institutions, they came increasingly to be taught by well-educated public schoolmistresses with ideas of their own about female education. Schooling in France and in the German states thus served quite specific and different political agendas. These differences, as chapter 4 will suggest, fed into the experiences, memories, and assessments of the ultimate effects of schooling that autobiographers recounted.

Transition to Adulthood

Chapter 5 takes on autobiographical discussions of what was perhaps the most determinant moment of growing up working class — namely, the cluster of experiences at the onset of what is now termed early adolescence, around age thirteen or fourteen. The stories suggest that this moment took on greater significance in the course of the nineteenth century because it came to mark the end of obligatory schooling in a working-class family economy still dependent upon the work of the younger generation. This double transition — out of school and into full-time work — was often reinforced by religious ceremonies that provided rituals of coming-of-age. But here again the autobiographies express the same tension between what was and what was supposed to have been that provided the critical edge to their accounts of childhood. More than in their accounts of earlier life episodes, however, autobiographers recalled this moment as a choice point; their own choices, or more typically those of the adults who held custody of them, began to seem definitive. They recalled becoming aware of their destiny and the constraints that surrounded them because of their poverty. What they wanted to become or might have become got lost in what others required of them. But in contrast with their generally more passive self-portraits as young children, many autobiographical heroes and heroines moved into more active roles at this moment in the life course. Here, too, the stories of men and women clearly part ways. Systematic differences begin to emerge between male and female autobiographers in their recollections of how occupational choices were imagined and recounted, how new relations with the family were defined.

How did young people get slotted into occupations when these auto-biographers were growing up? How did routes to careers shift with the massive transformation of the European economy in the nineteenth century? The simplest answer is that at the beginning of the nineteenth century most Europeans probably expected to do what their parents did to earn a living, and by the end of the century that traditional pattern was no longer taken for granted. In the peasant and handicraft milieux of preindustrial Europe, the skills and capital it took to set up a new genera-tions' family economy was part of the patrimony. Family strategies some-times dictated switches for "surplus" sons or daughters who could not be accommodated through the family plot, credit, dowry, or apprenticeship. Moreover, in areas where merchant capitalists had already set into mo-tion a market for wage labor in putting-out industries (and thus outside the auspices of the peasant community or guild) new patterns of family formation and work often followed. The lives of these protoindustrial workers, many historians argue, provided a glimpse into the familial and cultural patterns that became increasingly common as the wage labor force grew. Young people with little capital and few skills could begin to earn wages in their late teens and often were at their earning peak in their early twenties. As many authorities complained, they seemed "out of control" because their families no longer exercised the kind of author-ity over them that would have been more typical in a peasant or artisanal setting.[35]

Although older patterns of occupational inheritance still pertained to some degree among peasants and artisans in Western Europe even in 1900, for many families conditions had changed. With the rapid develop-ment of first protoindustry and later industrial capitalism, important shifts in the occupational structure created new circumstances for an increasing number of families. First, the proportion who worked solely in agricultural occupations declined. Europe still had a predominantly agrarian economy as late as the first half of the nineteenth century, but things were clearly changing. If the rhythms of growth were slow and still determined by agricultural production everywhere but in England, glimpses of the future were at hand throughout Europe. Pursuing a liveli-hood through a combination of a small farm and some part-time indus-trial work, so characteristic of the European countryside of the protoindustrial era, was becoming more difficult. The growth of an international market in agricultural products and land spelled the ruin of marginal small producers and even "inefficient" large farms, as the agricultural crises of the 1820s, 1840s, and 1870s brought home.

The introduction of new sources of power and new transportation networks brought more work into urban agglomerations and undermined those putting-out industries that had helped Europe's peasants stretch their agricultural income. A growing proportion of those who worked on farms worked for wages and produced goods that were offered for sale in distant markets. Marx was perceptive in his observations of the growth of the proletariat, but it was growing outside the industrial cities as well as within.[36]

If the trends all over pointed to a decreasing proportion of the workforce in agriculture, important regional distinctions persisted and suggested that Europe's different national economies were following somewhat different paths to industrial capitalism. The English model — surprisingly complete and early conversion of the countryside to a market system as the economy industrialized — was not reproduced elsewhere. French economic development was less destructive of the family farm sector. The growth of urban industry occurred more dramatically in Central Europe, with recurrent signs of an agrarian economy that was both diminishing in importance and languishing. The relatively rapid decline of agricultural employment in many areas of Central Europe in the late nineteenth century meant that both occupational and geographic mobility were the hallmarks of working-class experience, in contrast with the relative stability of the French labor force.[37] Mid-nineteenth-century occupational censuses of France and Prussia (the largest of the German states) show that 52 percent and 55 percent of their respective workforces were still employed in the agrarian sector. But in France the proportion fell only gradually in the second half of the century; it stood at 42 percent of the workforce in 1901, whereas the Prussian figure had dropped to 34 percent.[38]

Even more striking was the different role of migration. In France, a substantial migration took place from rural to urban areas, especially to Paris, and from less to more developed regions.[39] While this movement was certainly substantial, during the period of industrialization the French rarely migrated overseas. In contrast, rates of both regional and overseas migration were high in nineteenth-century Germany; moreover, as the distances covered were longer, the disruptions to family life were more profound.

The French economy also kept a more secure place for its small industrial producers than the English model would have predicted. As several studies have shown, capitalist development often revolved around the reorganization of the highly skilled artisanal trades as well as the introduction of the newer industrial forms in some regions of northern and eastern France. The special place of French luxury trade goods on the world market insured the continuance of older artisanal models of work even if many industries were either undermined or drastically transformed by industrial capitalism.[40]

In Central Europe, too, the persistence and redefinition of small industrial producers were important parts of the history of class formation. If many industrial occupations fought a losing battle against mass-produced goods, it is also true that such artisanally organized sectors as baking actually grew as a result of new conditions. Moreover, in contrast with both England and France, in many German states artisans retained their legal rights to guild organization — at least into the era of reform that began with Napoleon's victories — and in some cases these rights were restored in the conservative regimes that took over later in the century.

Studies of intra- and intergenerational mobility are beginning to suggest some of the occupational routes through which people moved. Deskilling, proletarianization, and market risk undermined the traditional power of a peasant or artisanal paterfamilias to set up his sons with a livelihood and his daughters with a dowry. Sending children into wage labor probably looked like a failure to these families. For other families, the expansion of the tertiary sector brought the possibility of setting up children in jobs like schoolteaching or office work that smacked of improvement. Access to such jobs often required skills acquired through schooling, even though investment in education could hardly guarantee such triumph.[41]

All of these developments echo in the autobiographical accounts of "coming-of-age" in chapter 5. Most autobiographers had some sense of rules that were supposed to govern this transition, but they also recalled much insecurity and contention over them. Who had the right to decide what job they would take at age fourteen? What, if any, difference did personal inclinations or talents play? Who controlled wages? While it might be tempting to regard these struggles as simply "typical" of early adolescence and the convention of establishing independence from parents, to do so misses a lot. These accounts record recollections of a historical struggle to redefine this moment of life, to reshape its contours under new circumstances. The individual struggles eventually fed into a larger battle for different familial conditions, for the expansion of options for working-class children. Behind the memories of the unfairness of a family economy that pushed its children to work too early was a vision of a world where such a practice would no longer be necessary.

The traditional links between economic and sexual coming-of-age were also disrupted with the transformation of the family economy. Characteristically late marriage, associated with the acquisition of a farm or shop, had for centuries left Western European youth facing a comparatively long hiatus between puberty and marriage. But changing norms about the relationship between love and marriage — especially the claim that affection and attraction between spouses was crucial to a successful marriage — and the possibility of earning money outside the family economic enterprise weakened parental control over children's marital decisions. Arranged marriages were by the early nineteenth century gradually giving way to more choice on the part of young people, opening up what some adults saw as sexual dangers for courting adolescents.[42] Sexual as well as economic coming-of-age took on new meanings.

Nineteenth-century discussions of sexuality were clearly informed by understandings of social class differences. Reports and statistics on illegitimacy, prostitution, slum crowding, and moral decay brought a new kind of problem to the attention of governments, moral authorities, and the reading public and suggested that the lower orders were victims of their uncontrolled passions. Working-class profligacy, which the middle class viewed as the product of the uninhibited pursuit of biological inclinations, served as a foil for the sexual discipline so central to middle-class character in this era.

Different sexual norms and behaviors apparently did obtain in the lower classes, but how sexuality was understood and how it was constructed remains open to question. As chapter 6 will argue, sexual identity was a very important dimension of social identity for worker autobiographers. A surprisingly large number of working-class autobiographers saw fit to describe sexual encounters that were part of their story of growing up. These episodes serve a variety of narrative functions, but they were very closely connected to the authors' evolving class identity in virtually every case. And, perhaps not surprisingly, here more than in earlier life episodes the stories clearly distinguish the history of female working-class identity from its male counterpart.

Class Identities and Political Organization

Historians of the working class have long been interested in the relation between class interests and political organization. They have hypothesized that the social and economic changes that accompanied the growth of industrial capitalism resulted in a reorganization of politics around class interests. A growing number of historical studies emphasize, however, how the very notions of class that people applied to themselves and others were in crucial ways as much the outcome as the cause of political organization. Certainly, important changes in the organization of work must be central to any understanding of the changing conditions of working people. But these changes do not automatically produce predictable political consequences. Studies of workers' organizations, political parties, and informal political culture suggest the extent to which notions of class are very much shaped by particular local and national political traditions and institutions.[43]

Moreover, many historians now emphasize that industrial capitalism could flourish under a wide range of political regimes. David Blackbourn and Geoff Eley demonstrate that accommodation between state authorities and entrepreneurial and landowning classes in Germany allowed the maintenance of an authoritarian style of labor discipline and the development of new modes of political incorporation without jeopardizing the growth of capitalism. Peter Stearns also has noted a contrast between paternalistic and authoritarian styles of labor discipline among the entrepreneurial classes of France and Germany, respectively, and has argued that these divergent styles could each be effective under certain circumstances.[44] The political alliances upon which state formation rested in France and Germany took quite different turns in the nineteenth century, differences that held consequences for the forms of worker organization that evolved and for militants' careers in different periods and regions.

In France, the Revolution that began in 1789 established a framework that continued to shape political development in the nineteenth century. The Revolution was initiated by a broad coalition that included reformist aristocrats as well as legal, professional, and administrative men of bourgeois origins. They mostly envisioned creating a more limited monarchial rule, not a democratic form of government. But the Revolution opened up the political process to an unprecedented degree. Assemblies to write complaints and petitions, political and neighborhood clubs, and direct actions in the streets brought ordinary men and even women into new forms of political action during different phases of the Revolution. Older organizations such as the journeymen's *compagnonnages* or municipal councils took on new roles. Even though most of this grass-roots activity was shut down in the later phases of the Revolution (revolutionary liberals had early on outlawed guilds, *compagnonnages*, and other forms of workers' organizations) and brought to a halt by the conservative Restoration monarchy that came to power following the defeat of Napoleon in 1815, the ideological and organizational legacy of the Revolutionary years left its mark on working-class culture.

Each of the periods of political and constitutional conflict that punctuated the nineteenth century in France — the overthrow of the Restoration government in 1830, the establishment of the Second Republic in 1848 and its replacement by the Second Empire in 1851, the defeat of the empire in 1870, the temporary rule by radical urban communes, and the establishment of the Third Republic — involved renegotiating the question of political representation that the Revolution had first posed. If middle-class reformers played key roles in all of these insurrectionary movements, it is also clear that they relied on, worked with, and often betrayed working-class allies during important moments of contest. Workers, for their part, pursued varying strategies of cross-class alliance and autonomous action at different moments during these contests for power.[45]

Involvement in the struggle for political power brought with it the development of workers' organizations in the 1830s and 1840s, even though most forms of combination remained illegal until the 1860s. Typically these organizations — such as the *compagnonnages*, brotherhoods, secret societies, cooperatives, and mutual benefit societies — were aimed at both economic and political improvements in workers' conditions. Various movements such as Icarian communism, Fourierism, and Republican socialism that flourished in the decades before 1848 fought for democratization of the government and the workplace. Workers' visions were strongly shaped by work experiences in the small shops that still dominated French industry. For members of some of these movements, reforms of family life were also high on the agenda, and efforts were made to incorporate women workers. Others, steeped in the more misogynist traditions of artisanal culture, excluded women as a matter of course and argued for suffrage only for male workers. Workers' memoirs first flourished in France as an outcome and record of this early mobilization. The identity of the worker militant took shape and was first institutionalized in the creative political actions of the 1830s and 1840s. Becoming a militant was as likely to follow attending an evening lecture or working for a newspaper as it was to follow a strike or a battle on a barricade.

The defeat of the Second Republic in 1851 ushered in a period of intense political repression by the police state set up under the Emperor Louis Napoleon. Not until the last years of the empire would workers once again be allowed to form organizations, but the liberalization of rights of association beginning in the late 1860s did launch an era of intensive worker organization.[46] The new organizations looked very different from their predecessors. Many workers aimed their activities primarily toward the shop floors of large workplaces. Militant male workers were the core of dramatic and often highly successful mass strike actions that reached a crescendo in the decades leading up to the First World War. Syndicalists saw unions as the real center of the workers' movement and had an uneasy relationship with the more electorally oriented radicals and socialists who also were involved in organizing efforts in the last decades of the nineteenth century. Moreover, neither syndicalists nor socialists, interested in heavy-industry shops or the ballot box, respectively, placed much value on organizing women workers. Both the new styles of organizing and the new rhetoric marginalized women or offered them only "apolitical" family roles. Many of the later French autobiographies emerged from and reflect these altered organizational forms. The militant identity was masculinized and identified with either workplace radicalism or, to a lesser extent, electoral triumph. French working women, as chapter 7 will argue, must have had a difficult time seeing themselves as activists under these circumstances.

Meanwhile, the successive governments of the Third Republic relied to varying degrees on strategies designed to lure workers into cooperation with the state and to demobilize more radical opposition. Solidarism, as this strategy was termed, rested on a belief in cross-class cooperation, technological progress, and heightened rationality. The state's role was to educate workers to become self-disciplined and productive, to encourage limited advancement for the highly talented, to facilitate cooperation between employers and workers. From the solidarist perspective, class conflict was unnecessary and counterproductive. On the other hand, outright suppression, the exercise of undue or inhumane discipline, or other abuses of power were also incompatible with the solidarist's optimism about reconciling capitalist labor practices with Republican political principles. Moreover, state concern over the declining birthrate fed into welfare programs to ameliorate some of the impact of poverty on working-class mothers and children.

Political development followed a different historical course in Central Europe in the nineteenth century. The western German states felt the impact of the French Revolution directly; "sister republics" were established in several of the states bordering France during the 1790s. More dramatically, the eventual conquest of Germany by Napoleon brought political consequences. Supporters of political and social reform saw the failure of the Prussian army to stave off Napoleon's forces as evidence for their cause. Eventually, important reforms including the emancipation of peasant serfs, the revitalization of municipal government, and restructuring the army did follow. But, in contrast with France, these reforms came as a result of administrative decree and did not involve significant popular mobilization.[47] As in France, however, reformist urges were cut short with the restoration of conservative monarchies after 1815.

Compared with the lively and varied organizational initiatives taken by French workers in the pre-1848 period, German workers were relatively quiet. Guilds continued to survive legally in many German states, but they functioned more often as vehicles of small-town administration run by master artisans and small shopkeepers than as bases for worker insurgency. In this era of intense police repression of newspapers and regulation of traffic across the many borders that divided the German states from one another, political experimentation and insurgent ideas tended to remain localized and marginal. The largely middle-class movement that advocated various forms of national unification and constitutionalism did, however, begin to recruit a popular base in the 1840s. There is some evidence of grass-roots organization in the years immediately preceding the revolutions of 1848, especially in the large cities and in the more liberal states and provinces of western Germany. In some regions the vision of a "social and democratic republic" that inspired organization resembled in many respects workers' movements across the Rhine. As in France, workers' programs appeared that coupled political with economic reform efforts. There was even an occasional call to rethink gender relations, although there is little evidence in Germany of the kind of radical experimentation in the arenas of gender relations, family life, and sexuality that could be found in France and England in the decades before 1848.[48] Nascent organizations, with the important exception of workers' education associations and self-help groups, were virtually destroyed in the repression that followed the defeat of the insurgent movement by the Prussian army in 1849. As in France, much of the leadership of democratic, populist, or socialist tendency ended up dead or exiled.

When German unification was forged under the impetus of the Prussian state in 1871, the empire so created embodied a vision different from the populism that had inspired the "springtime of peoples" in 1848. The constitution provided for a very authoritarian style of rule — few independent powers were granted to the imperial parliament or Reichstag. The first Chancellor, Bismarck, did take a calculated risk in granting universal manhood suffrage in elections to this parliament, but state suffrage continued to be quite restricted until the end of the empire.

As in France, workers' organizations slowly developed beginning in the 1860s; many early union and socialist militants emerged from the workers' education movement that had survived the repression of the 1850s. After 1875, the newly organized German Social Democratic Party, which would grow to become the largest and best-organized workers' party in Europe by the time of the First World War, was the focus of most union and electoral organization by German workers. Bismarck's gamble with universal suffrage (which had worked fairly well for Louis Napoleon in France) backfired in the dawning era of mass politics and Social Democratic growth. The very first national gathering of Reichstag deputies included a tiny contingent of socialists, and their strength continued to increase thereafter. Eventually Bismarck outlawed the Social Democratic Party for a period of twelve years (1878–90); the government's rhetoric of polarization around "enemies" and "friends of the state," which held sway in the German Empire during the formative years of the socialist movement, certainly contrasted with the more conciliatory rhetoric of solidarism in France. Illegality did not stop the growth of the German socialist movement, though it certainly affected its character. The drama and danger of the outlaw years favored some activities (for example, electoral) over others (grass roots) and some styles of militancy (including smuggling of banned newspapers) over more routine activities. During these years, involvement in socialist activities brought high risk of imprisonment or exile. It was only with the legalization of the Social Democratic Party that less heroic activities came to be associated with militancy, which, among other consequences, seems to have allowed for the easier incorporation of women into the movement. As chapter 7 will suggest, militants' lives and their memoirs reflect the changing historical circumstances under which they joined the workers' movement and changing forms of militancy.[49]

The explicitly political terms in which autobiographers understood their life courses influenced their rendition of many individual moments. Chapter 7 addresses the particular question of how workers recalled getting involved in politics and what their recollections reveal about the formation of specifically political aspects of militant class identities. By way of contrast, the chapter also examines the processes whereby the autobiographers who were not militants decided to set a different course for themselves (centered, in particular, around upward mobility). National contrasts among militants are far more striking than among authors of success stories. But political struggles that the autobiographers witnessed helped to shape their self-images no matter what their particular political stance was. Chapter 7 also points to important differences between men's and women's accounts of "setting a course." Gender differences turn out to be significant in both French and German memoirs, reflecting the role of gender in workers' organizing strategies and ultimately in available models for becoming militant, or, for that matter, a success.

Finally, chapter 8, while hardly a definitive conclusion, will weave together threads of the history of working-class identity spun through the different chapters of the book. How did autobiographers understand the role of active choice in determining the path they eventually follow? Did they see themselves more as victims of fate or as historical actors? How did their self-perceptions vary over time, between men and women, and in different regions? Although autobiographers by and large appear to be firm believers in human agency (perhaps as an artifact of the source itself), they were nevertheless also highly sensitive to the external constraints that shaped their lives (perhaps an artifact of their modest social origins). And in their narratives, they attribute most of these external constraints to class position.

Regardless of the author's specific political identity and of the path described, regardless of the profound differences that distinguish men's stories from women's, or French from German, worker autobiographers were uniformly and acutely aware of class as a meaningful category through which to interpret their life experiences. The autobiographers saw themselves and the social world around them in terms of class differences, whether or not they were formally predisposed to do so through ideological and organizational links with trade unions or socialist parties. Class awareness was rooted in more than political ideology precisely because of its origins in the prepolitical institutions of family life and in the primal time of childhood as it was experienced in societies deeply structured by class difference. Family life was shaped by political as well social and cultural manifestations of class, and family experience was in turn politicized to varying degrees in workers' recollections of it.

This "European working-class identity" — with its variations — evinces a distinct chronological development. Already apparent in popular milieux by the middle of the nineteenth century, self-understanding through class analysis continued to make sense to many workers throughout the latter part of the nineteenth century and even longer — certainly into the 1930s and in some milieux into the postwar era. At the current historical moment when class identities, while hardly without meaning, are nevertheless quite unstable, it seems particularly useful to consider the process whereby such identities are constructed and transformed. It would be inappropriate to apply the *particular* notions of class we find in these texts — notions rooted in specific political cultures and specific encounters with emergent industrial capitalism in the context of nineteenth-century Europe — to other times and places. It is nevertheless useful to note the resonance of notions of class in the subjectivities that workers' autobiographies reveal; these texts, indeed, suggest ways of historicizing rather than abandoning historical class analysis. It is to the meanings and experiences of class — with all of their chronological, geographic, gender, life course, and milieu-specific variations — that this book will continually return.

The memoirs that I've sketched out bristle with truths that the sensibilities of our age will tolerate only when time will have softened them and taken me to that fatal end where the pride and pomp of the Great and the humiliation of the Small blend together in the same dust. (Valentin Jamerey-Duval letter to Dom Calvet, published in 1981 edition of the Mémoires, 407–8).[1]

Two

NOTEBOOKS FROM THE ROAD

HOW WORKERS BECAME

AUTOBIOGRAPHERS

The memoirs of Valentin Jamerey-Duval tell the story of the wandering life of a young peasant boy who in his travels through ancien regime France encounters the world's irrationality. When he was first confronted as a young man with the knowledge of war, he wrote, "My incredulity was equal to my ignorance. It is true that this martial and murderous glory, which immune to justice and reason had placed the Alexanders and Caesars among the demi-gods, was at that time completely unknown to me. Nature, which teaches nothing foreign to her, had given me no notion of that science whose simple theory is offensive to her, at least when its goal is not our own defense or that of our country" (124–25). His ironic account of himself as young was part of a distancing strategy to suggest how far he had traveled intellectually since the time he recalled.

The History of a Genre

Valentin Jamerey-Duval's memoirs are a rare early example of lower-class autobiography, but by the late nineteenth century a growing number of authors from the lower classes were publishing autobiographical works. The history of how and why workers came to write autobiographies provides crucial context for the stories their autobiographies tell and is therefore an essential starting point for an exploration of the texts.[2]

Histories of autobiography in Europe often start with such writers as Jean-Jacques Rousseau (1712–78) and Johann Wolfgang von Goethe (1749–1832), men of letters who each wrote an autobiography that subsequent generations deemed to be a landmark and imitated widely.[3] Their self-portraits were personal and secular. Unlike the generations of memoirists and spiritual autobiographers that had preceded them, each of these men wrote an autobiography that centered on the development of a personality.

Social historians have noted connections between middle-class identity and the emergence of autobiography as a genre. Rousseau and Goethe were not merely creative individuals. By writing autobiography, each gave literary form to a new kind of social consciousness. Despite the fact that neither lived a typically middle-class life, the autobiographical form they pioneered has been viewed as the genre par excellence of the emergent bourgeoisie. It is a literary expression of the individualism so central to liberal economic and political philosophy of the late eighteenth and early nineteenth centuries. By describing the process of becoming an individual, by deeming this story worth telling, these authors and the genre they helped to shape became part of the broader historical creation of the Western bourgeois personality.[4]

But the search for a sense of self is not restricted to a single class or gender. Feminist and class analysis of the history of autobiography suggests that the genre should not be viewed exclusively as an expression of "bourgeois individualism." Autobiographies vary depending on the kinds of people who manage to write and publish them, and the history of the genre is enriched by taking these differences into account. Feminist literary critics have asked how women's autobiographies fit into the standard history of autobiography. Not in any simple fashion, it appears. Estelle Jelinek, for example, points to differences in the chronology of male and female autobiographical writing in her discussion of the evolution of American autobiography. The historical epochs and generational experiences that motivated male autobiography — the Civil War, for example — were not the same ones that led women to write.[5] Furthermore, men and women autobiographers have often constructed their life stories following different literary models.

Recent interest in working-class autobiography has also brought revisions; autobiographers who have emerged from popular or proletarian milieux have often defied the conventions of the genre just as women autobiographers do.[6] If our vision is enlarged to incorporate a wide variety of autobiographical texts, the history of the genre and its meaning begin to shift. For one thing, as Wolfgang Emmerich and others have pointed out, equating successful autobiography with the progressive unfolding of an individual personality breaks down. Emmerich argues that the kind of developmental model so common in the German tradition of middle-class autobiography was not adequate for proletarian accounts. The plotting of a human life course along an "ascending line" could not capture the experience of people who struggled to stay afloat and were beset by the chronic insecurity, poverty, illnesses, accidents, and family tragedies so common in working-class existence.[7]

Nevertheless, workers did write autobiographies and did have some basis in the self from which to write, even if that self differed in key ways from dominant notions. For example, working-class autobiographers often denied their individuality and emphasized how ordinary their story was. Like Ottilie Baader they claimed that their lives were like "thousands of others." The collective identity that working-class authors often assumed in their texts was both a rhetorical device to establish links between author and audience and an effort to contradict the individualism presumed to be at the core of personality. More deeply, in their formal structures, workers' autobiographies also often defy the linear development and heroic self-presentation thought to characterize Western notions of the autobiographical self. These works demonstrate that autobiography can emerge from a variety of impulses and follow a variety of models.

Models for Lives and Life Accounts

The way autobiographers understood and constructed their life stories was informed by available models of what a life was supposed to be like.[8] What shape did working-class autobiographical narratives take, and what are the models that informed them? One thing is fairly clear — only a few worker autobiographers seem to have read either Rousseau's *Confessions* or Goethe's *Dichtung and Wahrheit*, although some did, and among the more educated workers, particularly in France, a familiarity with Rousseau was not uncommon.[9] Not all Europeans inhabited the same cultural world; the cultural chasm that separated "the people" — and later "the proletariat" — from their social superiors was deep. The cultural historian Peter Burke has characterized the epoch of the emergence of bourgeois autobiography as the period during which educated Europeans came to see "the people" as distinct from themselves and either to denigrate or romanticize them as exotic or natural.[10] This view, Burke argues, coincided historically with the solidification of certain cultural class barriers. Some aspects of Western European culture had been broadly shared in earlier eras, but by the end of the eighteenth century the emergent class society was also building class-specific subcultures. By the beginning of the twentieth century, working-class culture was centered in distinctive neighborhoods, institutions and lifestyles.[11] So the cultural models embedded in working-class autobiographies must be read with an eye toward their relationship to these distinctive class cultures, even if, as I will argue, most working-class autobiographers were cultural ambassadors who deliberately moved across the formidable but not impermeable cultural boundaries between classes.

Picaresque: A Road to Nowhere?

One of the indications of the rootedness of workers' autobiographies in modes of popular culture is their use of formal models and patterns of language drawn from such genres as picaresque, fairy tales, and sermons. Road metaphors permeate both Western notions of life course and Western autobiographical writing. Georges Dumoulin titled his autobiography *Carnets de routes*, or *Notebooks from the Road*; Ottilie Baader's title for her memoirs — *Ein Steiniger Weg* — literally translates as "a stony path."[12] There are certainly Christian roots to this tradition, and the Christian pilgrim is a commonplace in the literary canon as well as in more popular works. But the road metaphor has other cultural roots and resonances as well. Two in particular seem important as models for popular autobiography — the picaresque and the fairy tale. Many workers' autobiographies resemble these narrative forms, which had developed through generations of oral storytelling, cheap published editions, and reading aloud. Several early workers' autobiographies have a particular affinity with picaresque stories and poems — those comic, often parodic epics whose wandering heroes like Don Quixote or Simplicissimus had entertained Europeans of all classes for centuries.[13] Striking early examples of this form in popular autobiography include the eighteenth-century works by Jacques-Louis Ménétra and Ulrich Bräker and continue through the mid-nineteenth-century accounts by Norbert Truquin and Claude Genoux. Each of these men traveled widely and constructed autobiographies around the variety of individuals and experiences encountered on their "journey through life."

The window maker Ménétra's autobiography is a long series of often humorous anecdotes. Ménétra's life story proceeds from encounter to encounter. His defiance of norms of propriety and his anticlerical humor emerged from isolated adventures; there is little sense of linear development. Also significant is the explicitly sexual character of many of the anecdotes and his reliance on them for humor, a trait that distinguishes Ménétra's autobiography from most bourgeois autobiography and links it to both contemporaneous fictional forms and later working-class autobiography. For example, Ménétra described an encounter with a woman whose husband had, on good grounds, suspected her of having an adulterous affair with Jacques-Louis: "Time passes I had even almost forgotten [the encounter] when one Sunday leaving my apartment I meet mother Pinard a book under her arm She stares at me I say hello She tells me she is going to mass I respond that I had heard a good sermon from her husband She tells me that it is by no means necessary to listen to it that she does what she wants and is the mistress of her will Good I tell her if that's the way it is would you like to come and refresh yourself in my room . . . She comes up We accommodate ourselves She is pleased promises to come often and hear the mass in this manner" (189).

Many of the earlier popular autobiographers were, like Ménétra, inveterate storytellers or the descendants of storytellers. Many seem to have had the prodigious memories that often accompany such habitual storytelling. Indeed, although the earliest workers' autobiographies were produced in an epoch when popular literacy was on the rise, several of the autobiographers only learned to read and write at a fairly advanced age.[14] Reading played a conspicuous role in the lives of most working-class autobiographers, but there were nevertheless a number who lived lives altogether on the margins of literate culture.

The best example is perhaps Norbert Truquin. Truquin dated his memoirs 1887, when he was fifty-four years old. By this time he had obviously learned to write, but there are indications throughout the book that reading and writing came late in his life. Although his dating was imprecise, he implied that he was still illiterate in his late twenties and could barely read and not yet write at the time of his imprisonment for political activities in 1870. (He would have been thirty-seven at the time.) Nevertheless, by the early 1850s (when he was in his twenties) he had become an active propagandist for Utopian socialism, had developed his own elaborate plans for socialist colonization, and had attempted to win converts to his system by the use of pointed storytelling and parables. Thus his illiteracy neither cut him off from the popular political culture of his times nor prevented his subsequently becoming an autobiographer. But it did shape the telling of his story. His autobiography, like that of many other working-class autobiographers, is a series of adventures and pointed anecdotes, of memories and stories bearing scant likeness to the conventional "ascending line" of literary autobiography.

Some popular autobiographers used aspects of the picaresque form — in particular the structuring journey — to a different end. The *Mémoires* of Valentin Jamerey-Duval read like the adventures of a real-life Candide.[15] His account, that of a peasant who left his class of origin to become a scholar and librarian, mixed picaresque episodes with linear plotting devices more typical of middle-class male autobiography.

Among women, a parallel form persisted even longer, encompassing such early accounts as Suzanne Voilquin's — whose memoirs of her later life center on her travels around Saint-Simonien "stations" in France and eventually in Egypt — as well as later autobiographers such as Marie Sans Gène or Madeleine Henrey — whose lives were constructed around picturesque encounters close to home in Danzig and Montmartre, respectively. The public, political storytelling Truquin documented appears to have been a predominantly male institution. Nevertheless, proletarian autobiographies are filled with women storytellers, even if their narrations occur in less open settings. Mothers and grandmothers often played the role of informant by their telling of family histories. Alternatively, the "gossip" in which, for example, Madeleine Henrey's otherwise timid mother loved to indulge is clearly the source of her rich account of her own childhood and the neighborhood in which it occurred: "I was born on 13th August 1906 in Montmartre in a steep cobbled street of leaning houses, slate-coloured and old, under the shining loftiness of Sacre-Coeur. Matilda, my mother, describing to me later this uncommodious but picturesque corner which we left soon after my birth, stressed the curious characters from the Auvergne and from Brittany who kept modest cafes with zinc bars" (1). Henrey's narrative, like that of Truquin, is structured around isolated events she lived or heard recounted. Her life account does not exactly go anywhere, although there are occasional hints about her eventual destination. It is rather a sequence of things that happen to and around her.[16] In these kinds of life stories, each encounter bears a moral and a sense of completeness of its own, while the heroine's long-term development is relegated to subplot.

Fairy tales, another popular narrative form, echo in popular autobiography, but they do not seem to have influenced plotting in the same essential way that picaresque narrative has. Traces of fairy tale imagery are reflected, for example, in Anna Altmann's allusion to "Father Sorrow and Mother Need" who stood "by the cradle of the proletarian child" (23), in the repetition in the German stories that "bei uns Schmalhans Küchenmeister war" (roughly, "our cupboard was always bare"),[17] or in Claude Genoux's rendition of his appeal for alms as an eight-year-old chimney sweep: "My father died last year. My good mother, who has many children to care for, told me the good Lord will take care of me" (5).[18] Claude, in fact, was one of many autobiographical heroes who, like those of fairy tales, sought his fortune on the road. But the autobiographies are much too realistic to rely heavily on the more magical fairy tale plot devices. As chapter 7 discloses, even the women who succeeded by marrying above their class defied certain conventions of the fairy tale by emphasizing the mundane actions they took on their own to transform themselves into princesses. Madeleine Henrey offered her revision of this model in recalling the advice of a neighbor: "What you want in life you must ask for. . . . If you have read Grimm, you will know that fairies always asked little girls what they wanted" (183).

Success Stories and Upward Climbs

Jamerey-Duval's autobiography is one of the earliest examples of a form that was later repeated—that of the "success story." These lives *did* go somewhere, however circuitous the upward route. Later success narratives include Jean Guehenno, who went from a shoemaker family to the Académie française, and Bruno Bürgel, the German worker turned astronomer. Both, like Jamerey-Duval, used their autobiographies to display their intellectual accomplishments even as they recounted, for the benefit of intellectuals born to the class, the trials and tribulations they faced en route.[19] These stories may have been a lower-class version of the *Bildungsroman*, a German fictional form similar to autobiography: they document progress through personal development but are attuned to its social and psychic costs as well. Several working-class success stories reveal their authors' ambivalence toward the selves they eventually became and an affection for their former identity that interrupts any formal linearity. Guehenno, for example, confessed this ambivalence toward the beginning of his autobiography: "It's necessary that I come to terms with this last man that I've become, this seeker after wisdom, this man of books, seated in his easy chair. I doubt that I will ever completely succeed. To tell the truth, I often feel the dull anxiety of a sort of treason" (15).

This kind of success story, with its broken linear structure, is once again largely a male form. With the exception of the occasional work such as Angela Langer's *Stromaufwärts*, a fictionalized autobiography depicting the social and intellectual ascent of a servant,[20] success stories by women autobiographers generally entail either marrying up or becoming a professional writer. Either of these routes could be and often was followed without a conscious plan of self-improvement that would then subsequently structure the life account. In other words, if the fairy tale plot did not really work for women authors, neither did that of social ascent, although their stories sometimes turn on subplots involving careful strategy on the part of the heroine. Women authors, whatever the particular story they wanted to tell, often found themselves struggling to redesign narrative models that did not quite fit.

Conversion Stories

Many socialist autobiographies of the later nineteenth century followed a form that, like the success story, is a variant on the theme of improvement. Following the suggestion of the scientific socialism then current, these autobiographies were intended as accounts of the transition from helpless object of history to active subject through socialist militancy. While not centered on the evolution and exaltation of individual personality and intellect, these stories nevertheless underscore the role of enlightenment or education in the broadest sense for a decisive transformation in the author's life. Sometimes these stories recount steady and plodding development, punctuated by reversals and obstacles. For example, the autobiography of the Austrian socialist Adelheid Popp recounts successive stages of enlightenment and optimism despite her constant struggles, and that of Jeanne Bouvier, an active French syndicalist, is a long account of her laborious and dedicated self-education under the most trying of circumstances. Often, however, the plots of militants' stories turn at a climax point where absorption into the movement, or identification with class destiny, is marked dramatically as a conversion.[21] These authors thus picked up on an old Christian motif and redefined it for new purposes. The formal characteristics of the large number of workers' autobiographies that recount paths to political militancy — whether through arduous training or sudden conversion — accentuate the connectedness of form and purpose. The authors' aims in recounting their life stories helped to determine the form the story took, even as their political activity offered a motive to recount their life stories.

The Autobiographical Impulse

The ability to read and write was a prerequisite for writing an autobiography, and so the contours of popular literacy obviously shaped the emergence of workers' autobiography. Still, if literacy was necessary, it was not sufficient. People had to believe they had a story to tell. The chronology of workers' autobiography points to the genre's embeddedness in particular historical developments that provided both plots and motives for writing.

The most striking feature of the history of workers' autobiography is its synchronization with the history of working-class political and labor organization. If middle-class autobiography appeared as the genre par excellence of the individual, working-class autobiography was usually enmeshed in collectivity. Political militants wrote more than half of the several hundred workers' autobiographies published in French or German to which I have found reference. In even more precise ways, the fluctuating levels of production of autobiographical texts, as well as the proportions written by men and women and by people in different jobs and regions, mirror the political and organizational history of working people (figs. 1 and 2). Political organizations could provide both skills and access to publishers. But even more essentially, political activity provided working people with a level of self-awareness and a sense of purpose that could both structure a life and motivate writing a life story.

For skilled workingmen, artisanal organizations and the established stages of artisanal formation — especially apprenticeship and journeyman status — provided a normative and institutional structure for the life

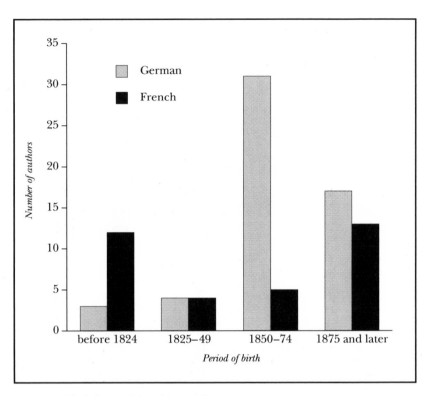

Figure 1. Birthdates of Autobiographers

course and shaped the memoirs as well. Framed by a network of stopover points, varied workplaces, journeyman hostels, and evening schools, travel fed a subculture that encouraged intellectual exchange, storytelling, political organization, and eventually memoirs. The journeyman's tramp — called the *tour de France* or, in German, *die Walze* — is the centerpiece of many artisan life tales beginning in the late eighteenth century and persisting through the first half of the twentieth. The circular journey — in principle eventually bringing the journeyman back home older and more skilled and experienced — was an institution that paralleled the picaresque literary form in some ways and probably made connections between the life and the story easier to draw. These artisanal institutions were masculine, indeed often misogynist; contemporaneous women who worked at skilled jobs and sometimes even migrated did so outside of the organizational network of the male artisans and did not produce a similar autobiographical literature.[22]

Even clearer, perhaps, is the impact of socialist organization on the production of working-class autobiography. In the French case, the early

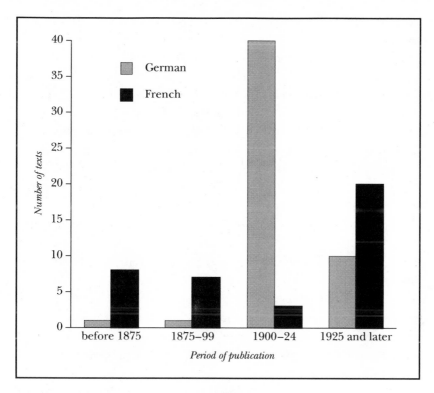

Figure 2. Publication Dates of Autobiographies

history of popular autobiography closely parallels the history of French socialism. There is the early contribution of Suzanne Voilquin, who wrote her memoirs to recount her experiences in the Saint-Simonien movement in the decades before 1848 and to record her disputes with the male leadership of it. Norbert Truquin was also involved in Utopian socialism. In the same year that Truquin published his autobiography (1888), so did the Republican socialist Sebastien Commissaire, who recounted both his personal life and his political activities. The Communards who were involved in the urban insurrections of 1870–71 produced a wave of memoirs. Some of these were fairly restricted political memoirs, but others were full-fledged autobiographies. Victorine Brocher, for example, a Communard and anarchist exile, plotted her autobiography around the chronology of rebellion that punctuated her life. She interwove her personal story into the larger political history she recounted. Activists in the late-century French socialist and syndicalist movements continued the tradition, if at lower levels of production. The anarchist tradition also produced its autobiographers, such as Henri Tricot and Louis Lecoin. Even as women fared better or worse within these movements, so women's autobiographies reflect their presence or absence in the various branches of the French workers' movement.[23]

The German chronology of the emergence of working-class autobiography is somewhat different. After a much slower start, restricted largely to journeymen's memoirs, workers' autobiography flourished under the encouragement of the Social Democratic Party only after its relegalization in 1890. The next two decades, however, witnessed an unprecedented and subsequently unequaled period of vitality in the genre. Not only did well-known socialists such as August Bebel publish their autobiographies during this era, but so did many relative unknowns who saw themselves, or were seen by their editors, as exemplary. These accounts range from those of such classic proletarians as the miner Nikolaus Osterroth to that of Franz Lüth, agricultural laborer and socialist propagandist. Bearing titles like Osterroth's *Vom Beter zum Kämpfer* (*From Prayer to Fighter*), these texts marked the passage from unwitting victimization to militancy. And even as the presence of women in the German socialist movement began to grow, the first German-language autobiography of a politically active working-class woman appeared in 1909 when Adelheid Popp published the anonymous first edition of her memoirs. Just as women were underrepresented in the movement, so were their autobiographical works but a small minority of the outpouring of socialist memoir literature. The differing temporalities of political development in France and Central Europe are reflected in the chronological patterns of publication of workers' memoirs in the two languages (figs. 1 and 2). In particular, the early nineteenth-century surge in French texts and the later development of the genre in German are noteworthy. Obviously, this difference also implies that the cohorts of workers whose experiences were most likely to end up being recorded also varied. This comparison also makes plain the stronger concentration of the German memoirs in time and their rootedness in the specifically Social Democratic version of militancy.

Political militants are strongly represented among lower-class autobiographers, but they were not the only people motivated to tell their stories. Other kinds of accounts tap into alternative life trajectories— interclass mobility (especially upward mobility, but sometimes downward), notorious criminal activity, interclass marriage or migration. All could provide the impetus for self-revelation, and these trajectories tended to bring with them different institutional connections and resources encouraging writing. The upwardly mobile could find support from patrons and self-help groups who saw their lives as exemplary but reflective of a different moral than that which militants' tales illustrated.[24] Inmates, some but not all of whom were political prisoners, had time on their hands and sometimes received pointed encouragement from their wardens or doctors to confess or to describe the origins of their predicament.[25] For some women, "marrying up" could bring both the leisure for writing and the connections needed for publishing.[26] Such alternative trajectories, which inspired workers with a wide range of institutional connections and motives to recount their lives, form the basis of life stories that provide interesting counterpoints to those of political militants. Throughout the book, I will be making comparisons among these different variations on the genre. Militants' lives account for by far the largest subset; success stories are fewer but provide enlightening contrasts, as do the narratives of "accidental autobiographers," whose stories emerged from different impulses and follow neither of the two main models.

Workers' Education and the
Peculiarities of Worker Autobiographers

Autobiographers were not average workers. While their experiences of family life or at work may have been much like those of others of their class, clearly their relationship to the written word was distinctive. Most of their texts are clearly written; many are of astounding literary quality, although some, their editors note, had to be edited for publication. As the authors rarely had formal schooling beyond the elementary grades, self-education must have contributed to the eloquence the texts exhibit. More directly, the stories themselves call attention to their authors' participation in workers' education movements and suggest caution to readers looking for insights into working-class subjectivities. The views they reveal come from a very particular location within working-class culture.

Just what kinds of educational institutions were important to the autobiographers' intellectual development, and how did they help to make these authors distinctive? The texts themselves offer many clues. It seems likely that the earliest cohort of French worker autobiographers was profoundly affected by institutions of workers' self-education, whereas this influence appears stronger in the German texts beginning in about the 1860s.[27] The Austrian painter Josef Peukert moved to France in the 1870s in part, he recalled, because so many momentous events in the history of the workers' movement had recently occurred there. The Austrian hometown he left behind seemed relatively backward to him, but he nevertheless had been able to take advantage of the many workers' organizations that had been founded there in the early 1870s. He was disappointed to find no evidence in France of either workers' educational associations or even a serious workers' press such as he knew back home.

The French workers' education movement, however, appears quite lively in accounts from several decades earlier.[28] In Martin Nadaud's memoir, adult education was crucial to both Martin's personal destiny and the implementation of his political vision. Nadaud was critical of the deficiencies of schools that he felt "offer our youth for their entire stock of knowledge only insignificant catechism lessons. This instruction is so inadequate to address the needs of our era and the need for a moral sense among the people that they find themselves in a state of complete ignorance, not to say brutishness" (144). Martin had begun to perceive further education as a requirement for his political career. He initially decided to go to evening school after making the acquaintance in Paris of working-class militants. As a rural migrant, he was determined not to appear rustic to his new acquaintances. He went first to a free *école d'adultes*, where he was soon asked to be a monitor (a kind of student-teacher); seeing that he had little to learn there, he sought an *école payante* and studied geometry and design in the evenings. "Left to myself, sustained by the thought that I had to educate myself, I kept on and eventually passed the course. . . . It seemed that I had grown in my own eyes; I had in effect discovered in myself a willpower and persistence in intellectual work that I hadn't recognized before" (152). At about the same time, under pressure to help pay off family debts, he decided to teach in order to earn extra money while pursuing his strategy of self-improvement. This entailed very long days—from 5:00 A.M. to 11:00 P.M.—a schedule he continued for ten years beginning in his late teens. These were also the heady days of the 1840s, to Nadaud's thinking the most important years in the history of the working class. "You could see then something that had never been seen in previous epochs—a group of workers joining together to start a newspaper." This landmark would be followed by electoral victories as well and eventually by the development of public schooling that was so crucial, in Nadaud's mind, to future class improvements. His account reflects the rich political life of the 1840s. Workers affiliated with "L'Atelier," members of socialist groups beginning with the Saint-Simoniens, Republicans, neo-*catholiques*, adherents of the *compagnonnage* movement of Agricol Perdiguier and of the Icarian communism of Étienne Cabet all parade through Nadaud's text. Cabet's movement, Nadaud pointed out, brought together weekly the bourgeois left and the workers—serious, well-dressed, "like well-brought-up people" (326).

Like Nadaud, Sebastien Commissaire recalled that when as a young man and a confirmed republican in the 1840s he felt the desire to improve upon his elementary education he "sought out the company of workers who liked learning." Such workers, he felt, "nearly always end up getting involved in politics. . . . In general those involved in politics were the most intelligent and consequently the most competent workers" (76–77). It was harder, he recalled, to become educated in those early days than at the time when he was writing in the 1880s. Adult courses were rare, and the working day was longer. He had had to make an arrangement with his boss to make up on Saturday the hours he missed on the three nights a week he left work early to attend classes. Only by setting up on his own as a home weaver could he arrange his work schedule to fit in time for classes. Before long, he found himself teaching; "since ignorance was rightly considered the principle obstacle to progress, communists and republicans of all stripes in Lyon formulated a project of establishing schools for adults of both sexes. . . . These schools were meant to survive without official authorization and outside of official surveillance. . . . I was designated to teach grammar" (107–8). Movements such as Icarian communism also offered important informal opportunities for learning, centering on "evening get-togethers for men, women and children . . . fables, songs, discussions about political and social issues. This was an excellent way of getting people used to speaking in public. To please the women and children, the evenings usually ended with innocent games. Since these meetings were illegal it was lucky that when the police showed up on several occasions, we were playing innocent games" (97–98). The lives of other early-century militants — Suzanne Voilquin, Vinçard — also testify to the importance of the early Utopian socialist organizations and their active encouragement of intellectual activity for all workers, including the unskilled and women. This inclusiveness distinguished them from artisans' educational activities run by the exclusively male *compagnonnages* of this era, as, for example, Perdiguier described.

The intellectual and political vitality that these early accounts recorded was suppressed during the long period of political repression of the French Second Empire (1851–70). Only with the legalization of workers' organization in the mid-1860s and the emergence of syndicalism toward the last decades of the nineteenth century does evidence appear in the French memoirs of the reemergence of organizational efforts combining intellectual self-improvement and political militancy. Even then, the often radical and violent style that dominated union organization by the end of the century tended to overshadow the strains of self-improvement. Still, the memoirs of Moïse Teyssandier, Gaston Guiraud, Louis Lecoin, and Jeanne Bouvier suggest the intellectual second chance as well as the path to political militancy that the syndicalist movement provided. Bouvier remembered an editorial in *La Voix du Peuple*, written in terms that resonated with the older French Republican tradition, that addressed itself directly to women. Its author remarked that "the admonitions, example and advice of the mother alone create firm and solid opinions." Unions were defined to this female audience as "school[s] where we learn what they forgot to teach us as children: to know our rights and to defend them" (70). In Bouvier's recollection, "In this era, union men were all feminists . . . my life from then on was intimately tied to syndicalist organizations." And even if "feminism" in this context meant support for working-class women as mothers and educators of future generations, it provided Bouvier with an intellectual and political opening even though she neither married nor had children.

Bouvier's memoirs also attest the persistence of the association between self-improvement and militance. Bouvier was careful to point to the frugality, forethought, and seriousness of purpose that she felt distinguished her from so many other workers. In 1901, when she was thirty-six, she was fired from a good job in a dress shop because of her syndicalist activities; she was then, as she put it, too old to find work and too young to retire. "My hair was turning white. In those days, that was a nearly insurmountable barrier to employment for a seamstress. 'Too old!' (73). She thus quit the world of the *atelier* for independent work at home, but she also dedicated an increasing amount of time to the movement and eventually to a laborious self-education within it on the way to becoming a historian of the female working class. Her tireless pursuit of "higher" culture was presented as a foil to the habit of wasting time she saw as all too common among workers. She thus continued within the workers' movement the self-improvement strain which argued that dedication to high-quality literature and awareness of the history of their own working conditions would brings benefits to workers. She felt that the best efforts of political intellectuals were thwarted by the reluctance of unions and workers to invest in such intellectual activities. In these sentiments, she echoed Commissaire's assertion a half-century earlier that the self-educated represented a "better class" of workers. But in her times she also felt an isolation from the political mainstream that Commissaire had not.

In Germany, the workers' education movement came later and persisted longer. The workers' clubs, evening classes, and *Bildungsvereine* that were founded in increasing numbers after the mid-nineteenth century were critical to the specialized and advanced training of the cadre of socialist and trade union leaders that began to emerge in the 1860s. Many ambitious workers engaged in programs of self-education under the auspices of one of these new organizations; Gustav Noske is one of the few autobiographers who felt he had "conducted his own further education. In fact, it is almost possible to reconstruct the spread of the Central European workers' education movement through its impact on more than a dozen of the individual autobiographers who included specific details about the role of adult education in their destiny.

Wilhelm Bock was born in the 1840s and was one of the early participants in both the workers' education and the socialist movement in Hamburg in the 1860s. He joined the General German Workers' Union and spent evenings at its headquarters reading works that "made me an enthusiastic follower of social democracy" (11). His reading in the well-stocked reading room,[29] he recalled, included the works of Lasalle and Engels. Perhaps more telling, he developed new self-discipline. When his master's wife noticed the change in him — that he no longer danced on Sundays, but read instead — he replied, "I have become a different person; I've learned to see that man is not born merely to work and fool around. Nature has given human beings reason, so that they'll use it. Man has rights to demand and duties to fill. And in order not to stray from these goals, the poor man has to study to supplement the inadequate education he got in elementary school. The power of the rich and dominant over the poor rests on their ignorance" (12).

Josef Peukert described the significance he saw in workers' education societies in his town in the Austrian Isertal region at the beginning of the 1870s in similarly moral terms.

These associations were workers' association through and through; they brought the worker an awareness of his human worth, nourished and developed his independent thinking and feeling, raised his awareness and knowledge in hitherto unimagined ways. These associations acquired whatever German literature could offer in the way of enlightening or instructive texts and made them freely available for their members' use, popularized them through lectures, discussions and technical instructions and made them digestible; the result was that in a short time a high level of mobilization was reached that shook the whole population of the Fichtelgebirges region out of its customary indifference and intellectual lethargy (4–5).

Heinrich Lange's migration to Leipzig in the mid-1880s after his years as a journeyman turner brought a "new life" for him. After his first master suggested he consider improving himself, he began to attend Sunday drawing classes (87). Through the self-improvement movement he got involved with social democracy more formally. His account of the workers' education associations emphasizes their cross-class character. In the *Arbeiterbildungsverein*, Lange met such people as Rosalie Nielsen, who had been a comrade of Mazzini and Garibaldi, had lived in Leipzig and studied there at the time of the Paris Commune, and corresponded with Nietzsche and Wagner. She took on the education of young Heinrich as a project: Nielsen took him to hear the Wagnerian opera as kind of "experiment," gave him a portrait of Nietzsche, and presented him with a German grammar book because she felt that "the mastery of language was the precondition of intellectual activity" (85). The *Bildungsverein* also brought Heinrich into contact with the German feminist pioneer Louise Otto-Peters and, eventually, the socialist feminist Clara Zetkin. Lange's story emphasizes the contacts across both class and gender boundaries that occurred in the context of the workers' education movement. It explicitly reveals how some forms of workers' education did indeed involve crossing cultural frontiers. Workers who participated, as did many of the autobiographers, knew themselves to be products of a complex cultural formation rather than simply representatives of "working-class culture."

Workers' education held different meaning for different cohorts. By the time Wilhelm Kaisen became involved in the *Bildungsvereine* movement during the first decade of the twentieth century, it was already very well organized and offered clear, if demanding, opportunities to the ambitious urban worker. New connections between the workers' movement and intellectuals from academic circles also appeared. Wilhelm worked a ten-hour day and then twice a week attended classes at the Barmbeck *Arbeiterbildungsverein*, an hour's walk from work, in the evening. "This era was marked by rapid change in many notions that had formerly been understood as immutable, but now had been called into question. It was the time of the intellectual emergence of the workers. . . . Workers came into direct contact with the great problems that were to play such a large role in the beginnings of the historical struggle between the capitalist and the socialist order. The question confronted me as well—how to find a solid and convincing system of thought? Of course—only by acquiring information and knowledge that the schools had not conveyed. We had to sit down again and study. For this, the *Arbeiter-*

bildungsvereine and their many courses offered the opportunity we sought." (32–33) This particular school was located in the basement of a tavern, and received no subsidy from the state; "on the contrary," Kaisen wrote, "state institutions were regarded with suspicion" (32–33). Still, Wilhelm also took courses in sociology and national economy taught by a university instructor who had lost his post for speaking critically of Emperor Wilhelm II's policy. Wilhelm read Owen, Sombart, and Marx (and noted that he found Marx's theories of surplus value and immiseration to be tough going). Eventually, he advanced to the famous Social Democratic Party School in Berlin, which in the first decade of the twentieth century assembled the leading cadres of the party to hear lectures by academics and independent intellectuals who sympathized with the socialist cause.[30]

This route into the workers' movement persisted into the Weimar era, but it probably did not play the same role for later generations of socialist activists. Ludwig Turek, for example, who was born in 1898, came to the socialist movement by a different organizational route when he joined a party youth group at the age of fourteen in 1912. His activities in the youth group in turn led him to antiwar activities and eventually to his arrest. For Max Hoelz, who became a socialist relatively "late" (his term) in life (at the age of thirty) in 1919, and for others of his generation, socialist organizing during World War I was the definitive experience.

Although men predominated in the various evening school classes, reading groups, and other institutions that were so critical to militants' intellectual development, some socialist women had stories to tell about similar experiences. Ottilie Baader, for example, recalled that "as a young girl I belonged for a while to the *Arbeiterinnenverein* that Lina Morgenstern had founded. Courses in reading, writing and German were offered, and, of course, all completely for free" (20). This particular association was run by middle-class women who knew of but were not sympathetic to socialism. Baader recalled that "one day some of the members of the Morgenstern *Arbeiterinnenverein* remarked: 'These women, these Social democrats Frau Stegemann, Frau Cantius... they must be real wildcats.' But others among us had the reasonable thought: 'We can at least go and listen to what they have to say. . . . When I went to a social democratic meeting for the first time, I really sat up and took notice. Here people were speaking frankly, calmly, in a straightforward manner, and it was like a revelation to me. It was still quite some time, however, before I became a social democract" (20–21).

Not all working-class autobiographers were influenced by these institutions and the visions they represented, but many were. Clearly, the educational associations, union libraries, university lectures series for workers, and other forms drew in some workers and not others. Their members were working-class intellectuals. Even when these workers identified politically with other workers and sought to use their education on behalf of class improvement through political militance, their passion for education distinguished them from many of their fellows; the autobiographers knew this and felt it keenly. Moreover, much of what they read and heard about and appreciated in these clubs, evening meetings, and lecture halls would have been drawn from what they thought of as the best or most useful of the thinking and writing of educated, upper-class intellectuals. Their efforts reflected an ambition to democratize higher learning — to bring it into the grasp of people otherwise deprived of it. But it must also have added to the cultural distance that separated them from many other workers. Their learning put them "on the margins" of their class in some respects. They were, I would argue, in a privileged position from which to observe and write about working-class life, although they could not speak for all workers.[31]

The Reading Public and Political Discourse

The last aspect of the history of the genre that needs attention is that of audience, "the public" to whom these memoirs were addressed. The nineteenth century brought important developments in the public sphere. First, the mobilization of mass-based political organizations appeared as an innovation and then a necessity. These ranged from the various national branches of the international socialist movement and its affiliated trade unions to such organizations as the patriotic German Naval League, reformist groups including the *Ligue d'enseignement*, or umbrella groups such as the League of German Women's Associations. In addition, literary genres such as the social and naturalist novel, the parliamentary *enquête*, poetry and fiction in the *Heimatskunde* tradition (which centered on local traditions and cultures) and, of course, workers' autobiography brought to the attention of the reading public pictures of life in the depths of the industrial slum or the "vanishing" peasant countryside.

Historians and political theorists have noted connections between this public of common readers and the public sphere of shared political life.[32] This reading public was from the start segmented along the lines of class, gender, region, and religion. Men and women were not often readers in common; indeed, women were in some homes forbidden to read that most public of all literary genres — the newspaper — and were criticized for their devotion to novels. Similarly, readership was also structured by class cultures. Proletarian autodidacts could point with pride to their feats of learning and to the texts they felt they shared with the educated classes. Ulrich Bräker, for example, spoke of the impact on his intellectual development of Shakespeare and Rousseau. But reading matter of a more ordinary sort often separated rather than bound classes together.

Still, none of these segments of the reading public was rigidly demarcated. Readers and writers could cross the lines that separated them, perhaps more readily than they could cross the other institutional boundaries that divided classes and genders; it could be argued that forays across the usual boundaries between audiences are characteristic of moments of political mobilization. The nineteenth century was punctuated by several such moments. Certainly the decade or so that led up to the revolutions of 1848 saw transformations in both reading and political publics, especially in France.[33] Recent historical research on political development in Europe in the last decade of the nineteenth century also emphasizes the evolution of an increasingly mobilized and organized mass political base. Geoff Eley, for example, has argued that in Germany during the 1890s *Honoratorien* politics dominated by a small group of local notables gave way to a mass politics more familiar to the twentieth century.[34] In both instances, political strategies raised the public level of interest in and worry over the "working-class condition." From the 1830s onward, fictional works with lower-class emphases were among the earliest mass sellers, and new forms of factual reporting about workers met the demand for information that bridged the chasm between classes.

How did these political developments connect with the evolution of readership for working-class autobiographies? Many workers' autobiographies, especially those published under the auspices of the socialist or trade union movement, suggest at first glance that workers were writing to their own kind. Militants such as Georges Dumoulin, Julius Bruhns, or Adelheid Popp saw themselves giving advice or hope to younger workers; some autobiographers were actually organizers or propagandists in the socialist movement. But the audience was in fact more diverse. Ironically, the most immediate and direct spur for the writing of workers' autobiography in Germany came not from a worker at all but from the theology student Paul Göhre. He had disguised himself as a worker, spent three months in a factory in Saxony, and then wrote of his adventure. His book, *Drei Monaten Fabrikarbeiter*, was a surprising success when it was published in 1892, and its reception inspired Göhre eventually to edit several "genuine" workers' life stories and so help to encourage the genre.

The audience for workers' life stories clearly extended into the bourgeois reading public.[35] Some autobiographers wrote self-consciously for a crossover audience. The success story by Bruno Bürgel is one such case. In the preface to his autobiography *Vom Arbeiter zum Astronomen* (1919), he claimed he was telling his story because "in our times, with their powerful economic and political conflicts . . . it seems appropriate to describe the ascent of a worker" (11). Bürgel wanted to show not only middle-class readers what it was like to see life from a basement window but also his "proletarian brothers" that "the man in the better coat . . . could be just as subordinate in everyday life as the worker" (12). But even the more militant accounts often had a dual audience in mind. Lucien Bourgeois berated middle-class authors for their misrepresentation of working-class experience; he, in contrast, could argue that "I know my own. . . . I also know their weariness, their capitulation under relentless physical effort. . . . I can say that I owe them everything, even if they don't always understand me" (9). Dumoulin had advice for young militants, but he also had a message for others: "I have read Jules Vallés.[36] . . . I understand the sorrows, the grief and the torments of those who have gone to school until the age of twenty or twenty-five to become members of the elite . . . but I ask myself if they know ours. Do they even have an idea of our struggles?" (11)

That the aim of reaching an audience beyond workers could influence the worker's impulse to write is also made explicit in the (probably fictional) autobiography of the German waitress "Mieze Biedenbach." Biedenbach's "memoirs" were written and published under the influence of a literary friend identified in the text as Frederic. He had given her a copy of the recently published first-person account *Tagebuch einer Verlorenen* and suggested she write the same sort of thing. "The public has a great deal of interest in this sort of reading, and rightfully so," he told her.[37] To cite another example, "Marie Wegrainer" (the pseudonym for Marie Frank) wrote her memoirs as a sort of dowry for her otherwise impoverished son. According to the autobiographical novel written by her son Leonhard Frank (who became a renowned writer and artist in his later years), she wrote her own autobiography in the hope that it could be published, sell well, and provide him a source of income.[38] The awareness of this audience is even more explicit in the forward by Paul Pflueger to Anneliese Rüegg's autobiography: "The book before you is one of the so-called workers' autobiographies, of which a number have recently appeared in Germany in particular. To the heretofore published autobiographies of factory workers, we now add the memoirs of the worker in the hotel industry" (3).

Not surprisingly, writers of working-class origins also used experiences close to home to structure fiction, and some of these writers eventually wrote autobiographies as well. Several working-class autobiographers wrote professionally for income and thus had access to channels of literary publication and to a broad reading public. Their autobiographies and autobiographical novels were part of a larger literary opus.[39] Given the market for accounts of "how the other half lived," writers of working-class origin could expect more favorable editorial response to their life stories, stamped as they were by their voice of authenticity. The editor of René Bonnet's memoirs assured the audience that Bonnet had escaped all of the traps into which working-class autobiographers so often fell. Instead of filtering his childhood memories through "the deforming prism of . . . ideology," Bonnet instead presented a text "completely simple and naked in its truth" and in so doing expressed "life's beginnings for thousands and millions of rural contemporaries in Limousin, in Auvergne, in France, throughout Europe!" (7–8) The editor of *Dulden* admitted to translating the author's dialect expressions into standard German and censoring her more shocking revelations, but he still underscored the memoir's claim to authenticity: "Her memory reproduced experiences . . . with the exactitude of a photographic plate" (4).

The emergence by the late nineteenth century of this new demand for working-class narratives not only provided writers with an additional, commercial incentive to write autobiography, but it also no doubt selected the sorts of autobiographical texts that would eventually see the light of day. Interpretation of these stories needs to be framed by an awareness of the constraints of publishing and the nature of the reading public toward whom they were addressed. The history of the genre of workers' autobiography cannot be disentangled from the history that is read out of these texts.

The illustrations grouped here show the authors and their milieux as they were originally represented in the authors' autobiographies. They are ordered chronologically by the author's date of birth. The autobiographers and their editors chose a variety of strategies of representation and poses. Many of the portraits are no more than simple sketches. It is particularly striking that there is only one woman's portrait among these illustrations (the last one, from Madeleine Henrey's book). In fact, a large proportion of the female authors wrote anonymously or under pseudonyms. The lack of portraiture is consistent with this greater hesitancy on the part of women to reveal themselves.

Ulrich Bräker as an infant, playing at home. Illustration by J. R. Schellenberg in the 1789 edition of Bräker's *Life Story,* reproduced from Derek Bowman's 1970 translation, following p. 56. (Bräker, *The Life Story and Real Adventures of the Poor Man of Toggenburg* [Edinburgh: Edinburgh University Press])

Ulrich Bräker leaving home at age nineteen. Illustration by J. R. Schellenberg in the 1789 edition of Bräker's *Life Story*, reproduced from Derek Bowman's 1970 translation, following p. 88. (Bräker, *The Life Story and Real Adventures of the Poor Man of Toggenburg* [Edinburgh: Edinburgh University Press])

Martin Nadaud in retirement. From the original 1888 edition of his memoirs, reproduced in the 1976 edition, following p. 288. (Hachette Photothèque, 79 bd Saint-Germain, 75288 Paris Cedex 08)

Carl Fischer. Frontispiece portrait from the 1904 edition of his memoirs.

Wilhelm Bock. Portrait used on the title page of the 1922 edition of his autobiography.

Otto Richter with his parents.
Drawing by Rolf Beer from
the 1919 edition of Richter's
autobiography, p. 7.

Josef Peukert in 1906.
Frontispiece photograph in
the 1913 edition of his
memoirs.

Georges Dumoulin. Frontispiece portrait in the 1938 edition of his memoirs.

E. Unger-Winkelried. Frontispiece portrait from the 1934 edition of his memoirs.

Leon Jamin. Petit Pierre
reading. From the 1912
edition of Jamin's life history,
p. 28.

Alois Lindner. This illustration
bore the caption "The burden
of misery also oppressed my
parents" as it appeared in the
1924 edition of Lindner's
memoirs, p. 9.

Fritz Pauk. Frontispiece portrait from the 1930 edition of his memoirs.

Louis Lecoin in 1962. Frontispiece portrait from the 1964 edition of his privately printed autobiography.

WAS born on 13th August 1906 in Montmartre in a steep cobbled street of leaning houses, slate-coloured and old, under the shining loftiness of the Sacré-Cœur. Matilda, my mother, describing to me later this uncommodious but picturesque corner which we left soon after my birth, stressed the curious characters from the Auvergne and from Brittany who kept modest cafés with zinc bars. Behind these they toiled, storing in dark courtyards or in windowless rooms coal, charcoal, and firewood dipped in resin, which the inhabitants of our street, who never had any money to spare, bought in the smallest quantities such as a pailful at a time. The Auvergnat traders in particular formed a clan of their own, each knowing from which village the others came, all speaking patois, and so unaccustomed to French that they mangled it when speaking and could only write their names.

Madeleine Henrey. The first page of the 1953 edition of her autobiography. (Henrey, *The Little Madeleine: The Autobiography of a Young Girl in Montmartre* [London: J. M. Dent and Sons])

I didn't think of myself as a child. (Adelheid Popp, 9–10)

THREE

THE FIRST MISSTEPS

THE WRONG SORT OF

CHILDHOOD

Adelheid Popp, who was born in 1869 into a family of village weavers in Austria, began her memoirs with a litany of what she had missed in childhood: "No bright moment, no sunbeam, no hint of a comfortable home where motherly love and care could shape my childhood was ever known to me" (1). When Popp's family moved to Vienna when she was ten it was left to her to complete the residency registration because her mother could not write. She recalled that she left the column labeled "children" blank. Popp recalled, "When I'd rush to work at six o'clock in the morning, other children of my age were still sleeping. And when I hurried home at eight o'clock at night, then the others were going to bed, fed and cared for. While I sat bent over my work, lining up stitch after stitch, they played, went walking or sat in school" (10). At the time she accepted her lot, except when she had the recurring fantasy "just once to sleep in." Only later would it strike her that her plight was unjust. "In later years I was often overcome by a feeling of boundless bitterness because I had never enjoyed childhood pleasures or youthful happiness" (11).

Two perspectives on her childhood are superimposed in Popp's memories — a reconstruction of events she had experienced *as a child* and an *adult's* interpretation of those events formulated in the context of an understanding arrived at later in life. As a child, Popp claimed, her fate seemed hard but was usually unquestioned; this sort of claim is echoed in other accounts of working-class childhood. As an adult, looking back, Popp saw injustice and made an implicit comparison between the suffering child she had been and a vision of what childhood, she now had come to see, was supposed to have been like. For the adult Popp, an activist in the Austrian socialist women's movement, recollections of her childhood crystallized a class experience and bore a political message.

Missing Out on Childhood

In most of the German memoirs that recount nineteenth-century workers' childhoods, especially but not exclusively those of socialist militants,[1] variants on Popp's themes recur. Like Popp, many authors eventually came to new understandings of what childhood was supposed to be like; they conjured up this ideal only to demonstrate how different it was from their remembered childhoods. The metaphors of "brightness" and "golden years" play against the darkness that marked the start of their lives. Anna Altmann, another member of the Austrian socialist women's movement, explicitly compared her remembered childhood of the 1850s with the imagined childhood of the class enemy: "The garlands woven by the proletariat on the path through life aren't like those of the rich and fortunate, because by the cradle of the proletarian child there stand behind the actual parents a second couple — Father Sorrow and Mother Need — who also claim their rights. Today when I recall . . . pictures of the past, the first to emerge are the dark shadows of my ruined youth. The golden days that the children of the rich enjoyed under the protection of their guardians were never granted to me" (23). Franz Lüth, who was an agricultural day laborer born in Mecklenburg in 1870, put it this way: "The happiest days of a person's life, the golden years of childhood, passed slowly, joylessly and full of despair for small and needy Franz. At home, he was so overloaded with work that not an hour of free time was left. School seemed more like a respite from the treadmill of household work . . . than intellectual stimulation" (11). Robert Köhler remembered his grandmother as "the single bright spot in the dark sky" of his youth (3).

With few exceptions, several socialists' stories, as well as most Christian trade unionists' stories, and "success stories" among these[2] autobiographical accounts of German lower-class childhood are narratives of deprivation. They brutally contrast remembered experiences with the ideals defining childhood in other milieux, models with which they were familiar enough to draw the comparison.[3] Their deprivation was drawn most forcefully in material terms, the hunger, inadequate clothing, and relentless work regimes to which poor children were subject. But stories could also turn on more symbolic dimensions of deprivation as well. To offer one example, four autobiographers referred explicitly to failed celebrations of Christmas. The folklorist Ingeborg Weber-Kellermann documented the expanding use of Christmas trees and the elaboration of gift-giving rituals in German middle-class families in the nineteenth century. Although Christmas was an intimate moment, the surrounding political economy — middle-class reliance on lower-class servants to create their domestic comforts, the use of Christmas trees in guild halls and poorhouses, the representations of Saint Nikolaus or the Christ Child as anonymous gift-givers, the increasingly elaborate "Christkindmarkt" where toys were purchased and Christmas foods and wares publicly displayed — spread awareness of the celebrations to those not privy to bourgeois drawing rooms.[4] Children from poor families caught glimpses of what they were missing. Aurelia Roth recalled her mother promising them presents at Christmas if they worked diligently. But, she recalled, "On Christmas day, I was always very unsatisfied, because I never got what I had wished for" (53). Alois Lindner claimed, "I can still see before me a picture from a blissful Christmas Eve, as we crowded around the shop windows brightly lit for us small town children. . . . There were dolls dressed in fine fabrics for fifty pfennig each. There was a wagon for 2 mark 50 pfennig — but there was nothing there for the poor, it was only to look at" (8). The author of *Im Kampf ums Dasein* recalled her father being sent off with a few carefully saved coins to purchase a tree only to return empty-handed, having drunk up the money (43). Adelheid Popp told an even starker version. Her mother had actually managed to get a tree and a few modest gifts for the family when Adelheid was not quite five. On Christmas Eve, mother and children waited for the return of the father to light the candles, as the ceremony required. They waited for hours, and still he failed to return, which meant that the children had to go to bed without lighting the candles. When he did return he was drunk and had less of his pay than was expected. He then took an axe and destroyed the tree as Adelheid watched (2–3). These stories exemplify how in workers' memoirs the contrast between what was supposed to have happened and what did had become, in the era of working-class formation in the German-speaking world, the basis for a political claim. If, even late in the nineteenth century, "normal" childhood was still denied many working-class children, its elusiveness fed an emergent critique of society and gave some workers an incentive for political activism aimed at least in part at making a proper childhood a possibility for future proletarian generations.

Not So Bad, Despite Everything

French workers' autobiographies tell somewhat different childhood tales. To be sure, there are a few French accounts of childhoods marked by cruelty, neglect, and exploitation.[5] Pierre Henri, for example, who was born in 1795, remembered a childhood of mostly benign neglect: "To my parents, I was just another mouth to feed. They wanted me to survive and not suffer; their attention didn't go beyond this — it was their way of loving. Poverty was always at the threshold; sometimes it even opened the door and came in, but I don't remember having noticed it" (17). Henri's nonchalant tone was broken by his recollection of his father's alcoholism and intermittent cruelty that on one traumatic occasion resulted in the death of Pierre's younger sister. Norbert Truquin's similarly heartless father abandoned him entirely to his fate when he was a child of six. But such tales are notably rare and invariably date from early in the nineteenth century. Stories from the second half of the century recount sentimental home lives and warm relationships with mothers and often fathers as well, even in contexts of stark material deprivation. For example, Élise Blanc, whose family were tenant farmers in a village near Moulins, recalled the warm rapport of her family life: "I really loved to tease Papa, who returned my teasing. He'd say: 'This one deserves to be loved a bit more, because she wasn't nursed long enough.' He'd tell [stories] . . . and

I'd laugh with pleasure. . . . [If I had a toothache] I'd seek refuge in my mother's apron, my head on her shoulder and that seemed to bring me comfort. We really loved our parents" (255).

Louis Lecoin, born around 1888 as the third of seven children of a day laborer, offered another example from a different milieu. The family lived from hand to mouth with each of its members contributing in various ways to its survival. Sources of income, Lecoin recalled with obvious pain, included the bread his mother earned by sleeping with the miller. Lecoin nevertheless denied that his childhood was solely a time of suffering: "Am I, despite myself, going to claim to be a child martyr and have you believe that my early years passed in gloom, without horizon, without brightness, with no joy? That would be false! In the first place, my parents never treated me badly" (17). Lecoin never blamed his parents for their poverty, he claimed, nor did the family's struggle for survival make him sad. Instead, he suggested, it created enormous solidarity among family members and a special appreciation for parents not felt by upper-class children: "In our family we didn't do much hugging, but when my mother rested her hand on my head, I appreciated her gesture as the equal of the most tender caress. I have kept from my early childhood, which was very fine despite everything and even though it took place in the blackest poverty, the impression that the poor possess one advantage over the rich, in any case a noticeable compensation — I think that the kids of poor folks feel a closer and better affection for their parents — but have I observed well?" (13)[6] Lecoin was writing in a later era than the German authors cited earlier, which no doubt shaped his tale. Still, he felt more compelled to refute the association between material and emotional deprivation than to use childhood suffering to fuel a charge of social injustice.

One could say the same for Angelina Bardin, a *nourrison* (or abandoned infant) born around 1901 who put at the center of her story the suffering caused by her mother's abandonment of her at birth. Nevertheless, her foster parents were in her account warm, loving, and supportive. Only when she went to work as a farm servant at the age of thirteen did her story turn for the worse and center on her abuse at the hands of employers.[7]

Lecoin and Bardin did not publish their accounts until the middle of the twentieth century (Bardin's, like quite a number of the French autobiographies, was written in the 1930s). However, most French autobiographies composed earlier, even those by socialist and syndicalist activists, depict childhoods that were "despite everything" not so bad. Jean-

Baptiste Dumay, half-orphaned before his birth in 1841 by his father's death in a mining accident, lived his early years in difficult conditions. His life story describes his rebellion against the Creusot industrial enterprise. Nevertheless, he wrote, he and his mother survived well, and he even enjoyed a relatively carefree childhood, supported in part by his mother's widow's pension. The life story of Jeanne Bouvier, born in the Isère in 1865 to the family of a barrel maker and railway worker, was punctuated by her struggle toward a militant syndicalist consciousness and her arduous self-education. But her economic and intellectual struggle began only when she left home at age eleven. She recounted her earliest childhood in a series of anecdotes of childish adventures; their often nostalgic tone was offset by the memories of her brother's death and her mother's sometimes abusive discipline, but she was not deprived of childhood entirely. Georges Dumoulin also faced severe material deprivation as the child of northern French laborers in the 1880s, but the story of his childhood was dominated by the central role of a loving mother, a warm family life, and success in school. Dumoulin became a militant syndicalist, but his narrative of political evolution did not open with a joyless childhood. The French stories, in short, certainly recount hardship and injustice, but *not* unrelenting suffering, as the lot of the proletarian child.

Working-Class Childhood as a Counternormative Experience

These images of childhood in French and German autobiographies provide clues to the historical connections between accounts of working-class childhood and broader historical transformations. They suggest some of the ways in which childhood memories varied over time and from one European proletarian milieu to the other. Still they all *share* something as well: in both French and German accounts proletarian childhood was clearly distinguished from the dominant norms from which it departed. Most autobiographers recalled their childhood as somehow different from how it was supposed to have been. And the accounts in both cases date the dawn of awareness of class difference to experiences that occurred in childhood and to the eventual recognition of having lived a life that defied the norms, even if the German accounts paint the imagined contrasts more starkly than the French. These stories of childhood bear relation to the development of class identity in three respects. First, they are probably connected to the varying demographic and economic regimes of working-class families in France and Central Europe in the nineteenth century. These regimes distinguished working-class families from those of the propertied classes, and they varied from one proletarian milieu to another. Second, particular kinds of childhood experiences were most frequently associated in memory with poverty. In particular, these authors saw poverty as undermining practices that presumed that children were innocents requiring protection and nurture. Third, the autobiographers' assessments about the intersection of family dynamics, class, and social justice, reveal the long-term ramifications of childhood experiences for class identity.

A Regime of Demographic Uncertainty

"The death of my father," Lucien Bourgeois recalled, "dates the end of my happiest memories and the beginning of all of our miseries" (15). In nineteenth-century Europe, the death of or abandonment by a parent was still an omnipresent threat in lower-class families. Moreover, death was clearly, as one historian has put it, "a social disease."[8] In contrast with more comfortable milieux, parental death was not only more likely but also more devastating in working-class families. The autobiographies testify to the consequences of this demographic regime for the quality of children's lives. Even though some of the authors recalled experiencing a sense of relief at the departure or death of an abusive father, for the most part the probability of a troubled childhood was far greater in a single-parent household. Often autobiographers pointed to the moment of parental death or abandonment as the moment when their childhood turned from bright or tolerable to dark and unmanageable. Norbert Truquin's mother died when he was six. Her death, which triggered his father's financial problems and Norbert's subsequent abandonment, signaled the end of his childhood and his entry into full-time work. Ottilie Baader recalled her mother's death when she was seven as the loss of the one who had taught her "all that was best" in her life (11). For Joseph Voisin, Christian Döbel, Heinrich Dikreiter, and Heinrich Holek, the loss of the mother marked the end of emotional support and happiness or even the breakup of the household. In the stories, widowed mothers struggled to keep their children, but widowed fathers rarely did.

Children who lost their fathers more commonly remembered the loss in terms of its devastation of the family economy. For such authors as Lucien Bourgeois, Karl Grünberg, and Anneliese Rüegg, a father's early death meant entry into the labor force even earlier than usual. Moreover, the German accounts make clear that temporary or permanent abandonment by a father could have the same consequences as his death. Even though mortality was declining in the nineteenth century, the possibly increasing frequency of paternal abandonment in this era of intensified migration may well have offset the decline.

Child Labor and Different Family Strategies

If parental loss darkened many working-class childhood stories, so too did the need to start early at "earning one's bread." Echoing images made familiar by fairy tales, some autobiographers depicted childhoods of incessant toil under the supervision of unfeeling parents, stepparents, or masters. In the seemingly timeless fairy tale plot, very young children are merely "mouths to feed." They are then pushed into the role of worker at a tender age.

However, the autobiographies suggest that remembered patterns of child labor and expectations about it shifted over the course of the century in both French- and German-speaking areas. A work-free childhood was apparently readily imaginable in late nineteenth-century French popular milieux. A high proportion of the earliest French authors (those born before 1870) remembered starting to work at least part time before age thirteen, but among the group born later around half recall no significant paid work at all (fig. 3). Among those exempt from serious labor demands, several lived on the margins of the petite bourgeoisie and the better-off peasantry. Victorine Brocher was the daughter of a shoemaker of bourgeois origins; Henri Tricot was raised by grandparents who were shopkeepers; Charlotte Davy was the daughter of a minor railroad employee; Eugène Courmeaux was the son of a vigneron (who grew wine grapes) and a shop clerk who had become shopkeepers; Frederic Mistral was the son of a second marriage of a wealthy peasant to a day laborer. Others who recounted childhoods free of work lived unambiguously in the world of manual labor. Philippe Valette, the son of a rural day laborer and a cook, suggested that he only began to work as a herder at the time of his First Communion. Jean-Baptiste Dumay, the son of a seamstress and a miner killed in an accident before his birth, chose to go to work just before the end of his last year of school; Angelina Bardin, who was a foundling, only began work when she left school at age thirteen. If accounts from the early part of the nineteenth century include some memories of full-time work in preteen years (Norbert Truquin was a wool comber at six; Claude Genoux was an eight-year-old chimney sweep),

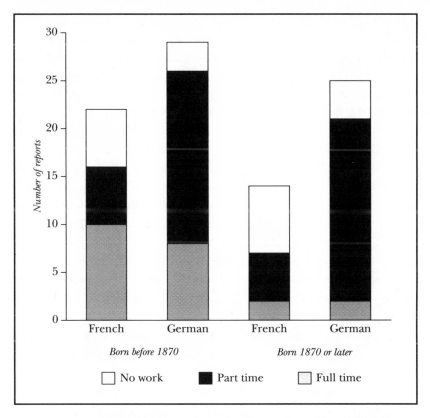

Figure 3. Authors Reporting Full- or Part-Time Work before Age Thirteen

most early French memoirists divided their childhood stories between intermittent schooling and seasonal labor. By the end of the nineteenth century, French memoirists rarely recalled major work demands before school-leaving age; their stories of childhood do not center on ceaseless toil.

In contrast, only seven of the fifty-four German autobiographers suggested complete exemption from childhood work. For example, Marie Beutelmeyer, daughter of a downwardly mobile minor official, was thrown in her teens into the ranks of manual laborers; Bruno Bürgel was an orphan raised by an artisanal foster family who made few demands on his time. However, most of the German memoirs report work as an omnipresent and engrossing childhood experience throughout the nineteenth century. The earliest stories (those of Ulrich Bräker and Christian Döbel) recall a family economy of seasonal labor and intermittent schooling such as was operating at the same time in France. But even late nineteenth-century German stories depict childhoods driven by fierce schedules that included work. Heinrich Holek recalled that he had to help his stepmother at her brick-making job before and after school. He got up at four to go to the brickyards and prepare the clay for her day's work. After school, he returned to help her make bricks and prepare the next day's work. The anonymous author of *Im Kampf ums Dasein* reported having to make a daily quota of several thousand paper bags, the quota varying more or less according to age. All of the child workers had to rise at 6 o'clock, "then we would glue until five or six minutes before eight o'clock, in order to be able to get to school by eight. . . . Breaks during school hours were our only recreation and playtime, because at home there wasn't any. In the evening we had to work until our assigned quota was finished" (31–32). Fritz Pauk also included his daily timetable as a child of ten: At 3:30 A.M. he rose to feed pigs and sheep; at 6:00 A.M. he had breakfast; at 6:30 he left for school and arrived there by 8:00 A.M.; school at 10:00 A.M. and then "at a gallop we all ran home" for the children were beaten if they got back too late" (9). These accounts describe quite different work regimes: brickworks with their factorylike discipline, sweatshop conditions in homework, wage labor on the farm. What emerges from each, however, is a grueling schedule that resulted from the combined demands of wage labor and obligatory schooling.

Marie Sans Gène recalled her childhood in Danzig in far more nostalgic terms (her autobiography is one of the success stories), but it too was filled with relentless work. Sans Gène recounted the wide range of petty entrepreneurial activities she, her mother, and her siblings engaged in to earn money: they bought wholesale and sold retail, kept geese and small animals to fatten for market, cooked for and sold food to soldiers in the Danzig garrison and also sold coffee there. "Mother would never have granted that the standing army was an unproductive state enterprise!" Sans Gène wrote (16). During the Danish War of the mid-1860s the family took over the laundry of sixty soldiers and later were commissioned to feed the same number. The children did their part to keep her bid low by getting firewood for the cooking fire and washing the dishes between each of the three seatings (18–22). Over the years, though, their biggest job was turning the mangle (the ironing machine used in her mother's laundry business). "Turning a mangle looks very easy but when continued for hours it really tortures the body. But we had the turn before and after school, often until late at night, and especially Saturday evening . . . so I learned very early to rely on my own devices, and since then the fear of poverty has never horrified me" (24). Sans Gène gave necessity a rare positive twist, but her account is strikingly consistent with the other German stories: child labor continued to dominate tales of working-class childhood even if forms of work changed over the course of the nineteenth century. Most late-century memoirists reported part-time rather than full-time labor before leaving school, which marked a transition to the lesser reliance on child labor in the first half of the twentieth century. Ironically, however, the increased schooling that accompanied the part-time child labor typical of late nineteenth-century stories may have at least temporarily increased the overall pressures on children, especially in those families where sweated labor or family production persisted as the basis of the family economy.

These stories call to mind the two contrasting family strategies historians have deduced from other sources: one hinged on having many children who were then expected to help support themselves at a young age; newer norms suggested smaller families and more care of and investment in each child. Historians have argued that the first pattern was typical of European working-class families before the decline of fertility, while the second came to dominate among properted classes beginning in the seventeenth or eighteenth century. The autobiographers' memories can thus perhaps be read as a cultural by-product of changes in both family size and attitudes towards children. They also reflect the regional contrast (between French- and German-speaking Europe) and class differences in the timing of fertility decline and the adoption of new family strategies (table 1).[9] These accounts amplify what demographic sources reveal by adding a sense of how people perceived and made sense of these competing regimes and how their awareness of alternatives fed into a sense of class identity.

Some authors explicitly recalled associations between family survival or prosperity and the presence of children to put to work. Georges Dumoulin recalled his father complaining that he did not have enough daughters. He dreamed of a owning a small farm in a region where daughters might find work, but because he had sons the family instead moved to a mining region. The same calculus was evident at the turn of the century to the carpenter Joseph Voisin. He recalled the 1890s as hard years as he raised five young children. But by the next decade conditions shifted for the better: "The children began to grow up. The house prospered — we then had a small business selling food and drinks. The mother and daughters took care of that. In 1907, my two sons began to work with me. . . . From this time on, we emerged little by little from our former poverty" (18–19).

But other accounts suggest that even if using the work of children to

Table 1. Average Number of Children* in Autobiographers' Families

	French	German
Authors born before 1870	2.84 (n=19)	6.30 (n=20)
Authors born after 1870	3.45 (n=11)	4.84 (n=19)

*Based on siblings mentioned, excluding half-siblings.

assure family prosperity had been taken for granted in France in the early nineteenth century, this expectation was being called into question by the century's end. Vinçard, born in 1796 and one of the earliest French autobiographers of popular origins, noted in describing his childhood work patterns, "They say that it's good to start children working at an early age, that they become more skilled; I'm not a very good example of this . . . despite all my good intentions, I was never more than a mediocre worker. Be that as it may, I did acquire the habit, better yet — the love of work, which is certainly worth something" (10). Prosper Delafutry, on the other hand, born more than a half-century later, saw logic like Vinçard's as characteristic of the bad old days. He knew that his mother, who had been orphaned at age five, already worked in a factory at age nine, which was unacceptable to him: "In those days, they didn't recognize the protection that was children's due. Scarcely able to walk, little children in the big industrial centers were condemned to a long and injurious work-day" (15). To a certain extent, of course, the difference is simply one of age: the first two authors were discussing their older children, a strong expectation persisted that contributions of adolescents would flow back to the parents. It was the work of the very young that was now judged intolerable.

The German autobiographers of the late nineteenth century, in contrast, tended to describe reliance on the labor of young children as persistent, if deplorable, even in their own epoch. They remembered knowing that not *all* children worked; many alluded to the contrast between their own family's demands and a world of play glimpsed longingly out the window or occasionally experienced in free moments in the streets. Julius Bruhns, for example, who was born in 1860 in the Hamburg suburb of Altona, described the oppressive conditions of children engaged in *Heim-arbeit* — sweated labor at home — in his case in the cigar rolling he began at age five: "My mother's heart bled when she saw her dear little one so tormented, but what was she to do? So I had to spend the largest part of my 'golden youth' in the dusty, smoky room of the cigar manufactory, always living and working among adults, while my more fortunate age mates ran around in the bright sunshine in the streets" (9). Anna Maier's mother was less sympathetic, but her experience was similar: "When all the other children ran around the streets with youthful high spirits and I directed my gaze out of the window, I was reminded by a slap from my mother that I had to work. . . . When you think about it, that a six-year-old child had to put all the joys of childhood behind her! What a tough order that is!" (107) Even as adult autobiographers, the German writers did not presume that such demands had disappeared. Instead, they argued for a deliverance for their own children and the possibility of a better proletarian childhood in the future. Clearly, as the comments by Bruhns and Maier suggest, there was a strong emotional as well as material cost associated with a family economy centered on child labor. Both saw their mothers as implicated in the economic disciplinary regime out of necessity. Whether they suffered along with their children or were unfeeling, they were remembered as supervisors more than as nurturers.[10]

Innocence at Risk

Beyond work, there was another particularly powerful motif available to authors who wanted to demonstrate how unlike the norm their childhood had been — the motif of sexual innocence endangered. In this case, in contrast to discussions of child labor, the discourse operates in a roughly similar fashion in both the French and German texts even if it is again more commonly deployed in German ones. Discussions of childhood sexual peril were set in the context of the nineteenth-century reorganization of sexuality. The sexual innocence of children — and the requirement that they be protected from precocious sexual experience — was a firm tenet of post-Enlightenment notions of childhood development.[11] Arguments that contemporary working-class conditions brought moral peril resonated with middle-class perceptions of and anxieties about life in the slums. There are hints in a couple of the earliest autobiographies of a different, perhaps older, perspective. Eugene Courmeaux (b. 1816) could delight in scandalizing his audience with the "funny and rabelaisienne adventure" he had at age four while playing hide-and-seek in his nursery school: "Here! hide here [my teacher] told me . . . guess where? — You cannot guess? — All right. I'll whisper in your ear. Shh! Don't repeat it, *Risum teneatis!* She shoved me under her skirts!!

. . . I stayed enclosed in this tabernacle, holding my breath, for I don't know how long, when my venerable matron was seized by an outburst of sneezes . . . [which] suddenly provoked . . . what? A shrill *trumpet blast*! My stoicism gave out and I escaped the hide-out; but oh! how my family and the neighbors laughed about this!" (29–30) Courmeaux went on to remark that he could probably find other memories of his early years if he thought about it but that some of his readers "would no doubt wish that I hadn't even said this much. . . . The manners of the times I'm sketching gave children access to scenes which, thank God!, have been refused them for a long time now" (30). Norbert Truquin (b. 1833) saw fit to recount how he, as a ten-year-old, was employed as a servant by two prostitutes. Indeed, in the context of his miserable childhood, this indenture emerges as a bright spot. Echoing fictional accounts of warmhearted prostitutes, Truquin's story allows for the possibility of a young child living in this milieu without long-term moral damage, although this episode can certainly also be read as testimony about the extremes to which Norbert was driven by his father's abandonment.

In contrast to these two stories, however, most accounts of nineteenth-century working-class childhoods that raise the question of precocious sexual experience do so to condemn it unambiguously. Several include accounts of sexual victimization stemming directly from the particular vulnerability of poor children and adolescents, especially in the workplace. For women authors who had grown up in the second half of the nineteenth century and worked outside the home from the time they left school at age thirteen or fourteen, tales of sexual harassment and sexual assault at the hands of male employers and supervisors became something of a commonplace in the context of public discussions of the vulnerability of working women and the dangers they faced outside the home.[12] Marie Sans Gène and Angelina Bardin reported attempted sexual assaults by their masters when they were employed as household or farm servants; Adelheid Popp, Marie Sponer, and the author of *Im Kampf ums Dasein* all told of sexual harassment by factory foremen and managers; Charlotte Davy recounted her rape by her boss in the office in which she worked.

Perhaps more surprising, male autobiographers also talked of sexual peril. Sebastien Commissaire warned parents of the dangers involved in sending children to work "for certain bachelors." His insight was based on a memory of a sexual assault by a male employer for whom he worked at age eleven (40–42). More commonly in men's stories, older coworkers were culpable. Ulrich Bräker recalled that fellow goatherds whose

"wicked passions" had been aroused led him out of his state of innocence. For other male autobiographers, apprenticeship or factory labor
as children and adolescents led to early sexual initiation. Alois Lindner,
apprenticed as a butcher in Regensburg in the 1890s, complained of the
bad influence of older apprentices on younger ones. Visits to brothels on
Sundays were the subject of boasts at work on Monday. Ludwig Turek,
apprenticed in a bakery in Hamburg, helped to sculpt images of sexual
organs out of pastry dough at age fourteen and was nearly seduced by a
seventeen-year-old female coworker. Heinrich Holek recalled being seduced by a female coworker in the brickyards when he was eleven. The
implication that sexual temptation surrounded lower-class children and
adolescents at every turn may well have confirmed middle-class suspicions about working-class immorality, but authors used these stories to
valorize sexual innocence and to condemn the poverty that forced children and adolescents unsupervised into the workplace. For them, their
sexual vulnerability was another dimension of the difference that poverty
produced, another measure of the failure of their childhood to approximate what it should have been.

Whom Do They Blame?: Parents as Agents and Victims

Along this dimension as along others, the failure of childhood to measure up to the ideal usually became fully apparent to the autobiographers
only in retrospect. It was only when, later in life, the authors had discovered other notions of what childhood was supposed to be like that
they came to know the full extent of their own deprivation. This uneasy
awareness of other possibilities, of other ways of thinking about children,
colored their interpretations of their own past and raised troublesome
and not easily resolved questions about blame.

In some respects, this growing awareness of different experiences of
childhood flowed easily into (or indeed originated in) a broader social
critique. Insofar as these failures were seen as a result of a subordinate
class position, they reinforced agendas aimed either at "making it" or
making a better childhood a possibility for all workers. But the narratives
are not unambiguous in attributing blame or responsibility for childhood misery. Interwoven with demonstrations of social inequity are condemnations of the most visible and direct agents of misfortune — namely,
parents. Even if in retrospect adult autobiographers saw the larger social
dynamics that lay behind their personal sufferings, they were never quite
able to forget those impressions of early childhood in which their parents

loom as most powerful. However much they had come to see their parents as victims too, they could not forget the power their parents held over them as children.

This question of whom they blamed leads into that most sensitive and elusive component of the memories of childhood in the popular classes — the depiction of relationships between parents and children and the degree to which parents are held accountable for the quality of a particular childhood. This accountability cannot be read directly from the family's economic situation. The economic interdependence of family members could either feed into mutual appreciation between parents and children, as was the case for Lecoin and Sans Gène, or to chronic tension over the contributions of various family members, exemplified by the slap from Anna Maier's mother that kept the child at work or Charlotte Davy's feud with her stepmother over the level of her contribution to the family.

In both French and German accounts, children were more attached to mothers than fathers, although sympathetic portraits of fathers in the French stories are not hard to find. In texts in both languages, portraits of heroic mothers who held families together against the odds were common. The mother's centrality to depictions of family dynamics contradicted cultural norms assigning that role to fathers.[13] Her lead role, especially marked in the German accounts, was in no small part a result of the default of the father. He was, in one way or another, often written out of the story. Among the memoirists' fathers, thirteen had died early (before the end of the author's elementary school years) or suffered from a severe chronic illness; one had committed suicide; nine had either deserted the mother or not acknowledged their paternity; two were blacklisted or exiled for political activities. At least a dozen authors indicated that their fathers had been at best unreliable providers who could not be counted on to turn over their pay envelope; most of these improvident fathers were "made tigers" by drink or, true to the Victorian melodramatic stereotype, had to be fetched from taverns on payday by their children. All told, nearly a half of the fathers were recalled as having failed to fulfill their paternal responsibilities, which were, ironically, still generally understood by the autobiographers in a normative fashion. Only a minority of the stories reveal lovable and responsible fathers. As Aurelia Roth put it, "In truth I couldn't forgive him for this even after his death, that he had never taken care of us *like a father*" (emphasis added). In other words, the authors thought that their fathers should have behaved differently even in the face of evidence that many fathers of their class could not or did not.

In most accounts, again in particular those in German, the mother is the dominant figure because, for the most part, she stays with her children. Only a fifth of the autobiographers lost their mothers early, mostly through death, although a few had been abandoned or put into foster care by them.[14] A few mothers are recalled as gratuitously cruel, even abusive. But most are tragically heroic figures. The mother was cast this way because she managed to "take care of everything and through her tireless hands support husband and children until even she couldn't do anymore" (Sans Gène, 15), or because she "was proud because we could make it without the help of strangers" (Rüegg, 23), or because, despite her delicacy, it was she "who with her needle and agile fingers built a wall against misery" (Henrey, 27).

The tragedy was twofold. First, the task was often too big for any mother. According to Aurelia Roth, "Even with the greatest effort, the greatest frugality, it wasn't possible for her to pay for everything that was necessary for the family" (53). Second, perhaps more tragic, was the psychic cost attached to the mothers' survival strategies. Alwin Ger recalled that mothers in the mining milieux in which he grew up had been "hardened to the point of cruelty" by the grim poverty they lived in; "never having known happiness in youth, they in turn withheld all enjoyment from their own children" (61). The slap that Anna Maier's mother gave her was in her mother's view simply a survival technique. But to the child, it was the mother, not the poverty, acting. Fritz Pauk's mother went to work on distant estates every summer, leaving him in the care of his aunt in exchange for thirty pfennig a day. He remembered that every spring "I would run after the wagon [she left in], until my little legs couldn't run anymore. Then I'd return, crying, to the village" (7). For Jean Guehenno, his memories of his mother were shaped by her constant activity and seemingly obsessive fear of waste: "I see her always working, always running. . . . She ran to 'turn in' her work at the factory, because if she got there too late, she wouldn't get more piecework to do: the forewoman would put it off till the next morning and that would mean a night wasted. She would run back home because the chestnuts would be overcooked and that would be wasted gas. She was always running. 'Wasted!' She never seemed to have any other word in her mouth. Everything was always at risk of being wasted — food, clothes, money, time" (78–79).

The tragedy was complicated by the fact that Guehenno and other authors who recalled long-suffering mothers could understand only in retrospect why they acted as they did. "Unfortunately," wrote Franz Rehbein, "we children had at the time too little comprehension of the value of the self-sacrificing wife and of our good mother's . . . devotion to her children. . . . We took it for granted" (12). Guehenno recalled his mother's anger at him for his inability to understand their poverty, for his refusal to "enter into her suffering," for his (and his father's) optimism in the face of her despair (88–89).

Obviously, all of the autobiographers *were* survivors, and they attributed to their mothers a large role in their ability to surmount the worst assaults of poverty. But their stories reveal that the emotional costs of survival under the circumstance of poverty were very high indeed. In many accounts, the injustices of the social system merged inextricably with the particular paternal shortcomings these injustices reinforced. And even the mothers' portraits — sketched more often with sympathy — are marred by their role as immediate enforcer of the rules. Parents appear simultaneously as powerful and not powerful enough.

Family relationships emerge as more troubled in the German accounts than in the French, and political motivations certainly impelled German authors to emphasize the negative aspects of their childhoods. Louis Lecoin, who described one of the most impoverished of the French childhoods, nevertheless pointedly rejected the title of "child martyr." For many of the German autobiographers from similar circumstances, especially those writing in the era around the First World War, it was precisely to claim this title that they recounted their lives. The accounts, in other words, were a product of presumptions about what audiences needed to hear and might find persuasive as much as they were relations of the authors' experiences.

The stories do suggest, however, that some of the attitudes about children and family practices usually associated with normative (that is, bourgeois) childhood also showed up in childhood stories emerging from proletarian milieux in France in the second half of the nineteenth century.[15] These family practices suggest that, to a certain extent, working-class families in France had developed a culture of elaborated and sentimental family life which may well have contributed to the construction of a realm of private satisfactions possible even in bleak economic circumstances. Moreover, although the French authors saw their childhoods as different from those of the upper classes, they apparently did not have as much at stake in emphasizing the extent to which their experiences were uniformly inferior to those of bourgeois children. They seem to have been freer to search their memories (as Lecoin, Blanc, and Dumoulin did) for consolations in the family life of the poor. Both political culture and family economy fed into the emotional balance the French stories suggest.

The German accounts of this same era, on the other hand, suggest that what had come to be seen as a proper childhood still eluded their authors. Compared with the French accounts, they suggest that German authors saw a larger gulf between working-class childhood and an idealized childhood of middle-class imagery. This contrast was intrinsic to the formulation of a social critique and to political activism aimed at improving childhood. Thus, according to Anna Altmann, "Our whole struggle is aimed only towards this—to create a better future for our children. . . . The only legacy that the proletariat can leave behind for his children is to work for better living conditions" (60–61). Anna Maier mentioned her dedication to winning mothers over to socialism "so that the children of the proletariat will in the future experience more joy in childhood than I had" (109). Ideal childhood still eluded late nineteenth-century Central European workers and their children, especially according to socialist accounts, but it was familiar enough to serve as a model and even as a justifiable motive for political action. Ironically, what activist workers found easiest to lay claim to was the childhood they felt they had missed out on — in other words, the ideal fashioned by their class antagonists, which they yearned for rather uncritically. These accounts thus perhaps reveal the psychological rooting of certain reformist leanings, family policies and staid aspects of the personal lives of many German Social Democrats. Although critics have often pointed to the reformism and family conservatism of the socialists as proof of their cooptation, it seems only fair to recognize the degree to which such aspirations were also compensatory and perhaps a response to personal experience of the more damaging side of working-class family life.

But the differences among accounts of childhood are not reducible either to divergent family economic strategies or distinctive political agendas, even though there is strong evidence that both sorts of factors did shape the stories. In the process of remembering childhood, long-held grievances against parents also frequently intruded upon narratives intended to denounce the social system. That parents mediated the impact of poverty often came through in the form of their despair, cruelty, hopelessness, or alcoholism. Occasionally, an author offered a general dispensation for parental behavior on the grounds that it was believed to be unavoidable. Max Hoelz, for example, recalled being locked in a room all day as a toddler, even sometimes beaten or tied to a chair, while his parents worked as farm laborers in northern Germany. He claimed not to carry resentments: "I did not have the feeling then, when I was a child, nor have I the feeling now that I am grown up, that our parents served out these hard punishments through any special cruelty or lack of affection. These were just the educational methods of the day, particularly in the rural districts" (14). Hoelz recalled his parents as conscientious. That the family lived in misery only became apparent to him in retrospect. But few autobiographers were so forgiving or so willing to absolve their parents so completely from blame. However much the memoirs of childhood were intended to serve as a condemnation of a social system that left so many families in poverty, they often can be read as accusations of a more personal sort as well. They contain implicit condemnations of the parents who could not manage to find ways to make poverty less emotionally devastating than it was or who even seemed to have brought that poverty on themselves. This undercurrent, although never absent, is more subdued in the French cases, where the emotional costs of poverty were more subtly presented — Louis Lecoin's pain at his mother's adultery for bread, Jean Guehenno's or Madeleine Henrey's impatience with their mother's inability to be happy, Georges Dumoulin's suppressed anger at his father's denying him the opportunity to advance through schooling. In the German stories, such accusations — especially against fathers, who often appear as alcoholic and brutal — are more forthright. Even the portraits of mothers held relatively blameless rarely paint them as overtly loving even as they were characterized as heroic.[16] German autobiographers, especially those who wrote as part of the great outpouring of life stories that flowed from the years of socialist growth in the early decades of the twentieth century, had a distinct political motivation for emphasizing the inescapable misery of childhood for working-class children. One could argue that their portraits of their childhoods only reflected this necessity. Still, the presence in some accounts of an undercurrent of bitterness and blame suggests that the authors were not entirely convinced that their parents were nothing more than victims of circumstance. Parents appear simultaneously as victims and as petty tyrants; glimpses outside reveal other families where treatment was not so bad in contrast with the harshness of their own lives. The pain caused by abuse, overwork, and abandonment by or even death of parents left these children with a psychic burden that later, less personal explanations would not completely eradicate.

Even more pointed, if rare, were accusations in a few German texts that it was indeed within the reach of proletarian parents to reduce their children's sufferings by adopting a family limitation strategy (already common among the French). Marie Sans Gène, who eventually married a literary critic and so had left the working classes by the time she wrote her autobiography, saw the nonchalance of her brother-in-law as characteristic of the class culture she left behind: "They were like the majority of all workers' families — they and their children lived from hand to mouth. When times were good and work was available they did fine and they starved when there was no work. It was never a question of savings. . . . When we would try to encourage him to try a little harder and improve himself he'd say: 'What am I missing? Don't I have a beautiful wife and pretty children? Shouldn't I thank the good Lord? . . . What do you want, sister-in-law? If I drink a schnapps, that's my business, and if my wife has a kid, that's hers" (120).

Sans Gène wrote from the perspective of success — she had married up. But even socialists shared her critique. The socialist Alwin Ger retrospectively condemned what he saw as the prevalent irrationality in the mining Saxon families among whom he had grown up during the 1860s and whose religiosity, manners, and ignorance he came to deplore as fatalistic: "When the women would get together in groups and talk, I'd often hear some among them raise the question of whether it wouldn't be smarter if the poor had fewer children. But this opinion always brought an angry response. The great majority of the women strongly held the opinion, 'This little pleasure is the only one we've got left; we're never gonna let them take it from us.' That they make their own lives bleak through their behavior, as well as the lives of their many children, by insisting on their little bit of pleasure — the women never think about this" (61).

The ambivalence about who was to blame brings to the fore the intertwining of the personal and the political. It was never simply one's particular family but never incontestably a bad system that was at fault for the damages inflicted on children. These stories, whatever their author's intent, provide evidence that both social arrangements in general and parents in particular were seen as responsible for the unfair burdens borne by working-class children. The anger is more intense, the ambivalence more painful, in the German accounts than in the French. Ironically, this contradiction is starkest in the German socialist accounts, for their authors were most intent on emphasizing the deprivation produced by class inequality, a deprivation which in turn was most compelling when there were no consolations even in the realm of the emotions. If miserable childhoods bred class consciousness and offered evidence that socialists could use to argue for class-based politics, such childhoods also hinted at the psychological inadequacy of the workers who were the products of these families.[17] It was a fine line to walk. Autobiographers portrayed parents as simultaneously agents and victims in these tales of their earliest age. The only unambiguous victims were the child selves their memories resurrected.

Whether I was clever or not, I never knew. I only knew that the richer and better-dressed

children sat in the front rows, and were the focus of most of the teacher's attention. . . .

Because I knew that I was going to work in the factory later in life I thought — Why bother?

You can clean machines and tie loose threads without knowing spelling and geography.

And the factory owner will calculate my wages without my help" (Anneliese Rüegg, 17)

FOUR

DIRECTIONS LEARNED IN SCHOOL

Anneliese Rüegg's first teacher in the *Kleinkinderschule* of Ulster in Switzerland was the kindly Sister Babette, who told the children stories and taught them how to make pretty things out of paper. But the harsher elementary schoolteacher who followed Sister Babette came as something of a surprise to six-year-old Anneliese. Of course, she started off on the wrong foot. On the very first day of class, Anneliese noticed that her teacher had a red nose and remarked to a school friend that he must be "a souse" because at home that was what they called people with red noses. The teacher heard her and gave her a slap with his ruler; thus their relations were stormy from the start, and there was never a basis for improvement. Still, Anneliese wanted to simplify her life by turning in better work, so she copied answers from her neighbor. When the teacher saw her doing so, he pulled her hair. This occurred with such frequency that her mother soon noticed a bald spot and told Anneliese to tell the teacher that her mother did not want to have to buy a wig for her. Neither of them realized at the time that the teacher himself wore a wig, but the allusion was enough to embarrass the teacher into ceasing his torments. Thereafter, Anneliese was free to "enjoy the pretty stories and poems that they read in their schoolbooks" (17).

The Boot Camp

In stories of early childhood, inequities of social destiny were interwoven with pain of a private sort. First encounters with the world outside the home were, by the middle of the nineteenth century, usually set in the classroom. Memories of schooling recorded in the autobiographies again are marked by contrasts between French and German texts; the different political cultures shaping schooling echo in the stories adults told about their schooldays. But school stories also introduce a new dimension of systematic variation — namely, gender. Not only do French and German accounts of schooling look different; girls told different stories than boys did.

Once again I'll begin my analysis with several exemplary stories, starting with Karl Grünberg's. More than sixty years after his elementary school days were over, Grünberg (called August in the autobiography) still remembered one particular teacher and even continued to have bad dreams about him. "I see the horribly distorted face of 'Kittneese' before me," he wrote, "and hear the screechy voice: 'August with the lunchpail, how much is twenty-seven plus thirty-four minus twelve?' And I never get the answer right" (29). As an eight-year-old schoolboy, Grünberg had gotten caught in a clash between his mother and his teacher. This "battle of the lunchpail" appears in Grünberg's autobiography as the opening foray in a life of struggle that repeatedly pitted Grünberg against figures of authority. Kittner, Grünberg's first teacher in the Berlin suburb where he was born in 1891, had had an earlier run-in with the boy's father, a socialist shoemaker. Then the family had moved away.

Soon half-orphaned and impoverished by his father's death, August found himself back in Kittner's class. One day Kittner tripped over the boy's large metal lunchbox and in his fury banned the box from his classroom. August's mother insisted that he continue to use it. It was, she declared, his right. It was without a doubt true, Grünberg recalled, that "right was on our side in this case. But [my mother] forgot in the process that the one she challenged pulled more weight and that the conflict that was about to start would literally be fought out on the back of a small eight-year-old boy who was fully in the power of this teacher" (23).

It would have been different, Grünberg later admitted, if he had stuck the box under his bench; he did not recall why he failed to. "Maybe it was because I had in my blood a good deal of the Michael-Kohlhaas[1] character of my mother, to which my father had also contributed? In later years I learned repeatedly that to be in the right and to fight for the right are two different things and that sometimes it's 'wiser' in cases like this not to bang your head against the wall. But nobody can deny his nature, which is why in this case (self-critically it should be noted) I was not wiser" (23).

The teacher expressed fury at August's defiance: "I'll show you who's in charge here — I or your mother!" In the thrashing that followed the teacher put "all the fury that swelled inside him, including the residue of that reprimand from my father years before" (24). August and his mother agreed that this abuse was unjust, but despite his mother's direct complaint, or perhaps because of it, the boy became the victim of his teacher's constant harassment. August would long bear the scars of this encounter. He began to stutter, and his life was a torment at the hands of Kittner until his mother found a sympathetic church official who had him transferred to another school. Throughout his life Grünberg held the image of Kittner's "boot camp" in his mind as a symbol of the abuse of authority.

Grünberg's school account is more vivid than most, but elements of it exist in many other narratives. Franz Lüth, the son of agricultural day laborers who was left orphaned in the late 1870s at age seven, recalled that he had no one in his Mecklenburg village to stick up for him "including his teacher, whose anger hailed down on him; the orphaned child stood defenseless against him" (9). For Alwin Ger, who was born into a Saxon mining family in 1857, the memory of schooling was "the most miserable" of all his childhood recollections. He was taught by "an old embittered bachelor who mistrusted everyone and everything in the world, including the female sex" (59). Ger's criticism of the teacher extended to the inadequacy of teaching materials and curriculum as well. There was, he recalled, only one map on the wall — of the Kingdom of

Saxony. "No map of Germany, none of Europe, no globe . . . the creation story in the Bible was taught to us as the highest divine truth. . . . We were well equipped only in Bible history, especially the Old Testament. If our purpose in life after school had been to join a nomadic tribe of the ancient Hebraic sort, only then would the school taxes been reasonably well spent" (63–65).

The rural schools of central Europe appear as the most materially and intellectually impoverished. Robert Köhler, who attended school in Bohemia in the late 1840s and early 1850s, recalled that his school, like Ger's, "lacked everything. It wasn't the primary aim to produce an enlightened population — they aren't easily ruled." In his school as in most others, there were a hundred pupils to a classsroom. There were no pictures on the wall and no teaching supplies. Practical instruction was limited to the three Rs.

The authoritarian, conservative, and vindictive schoolteacher who kept order in the classroom through resort to the cane appears as a villainous character in the majority of the German men's accounts — again most emphatically, if not exclusively, among the socialists. The limited and conservative character of what he taught only made the suffering more unbearable.

To be sure, there were a few who told different stories. Heinrich Lange, the child of Hanoverian shepherds, fondly recalled his young teacher as learned and diplomatic — traits that served him well in the late 1860s during the tense era when Prussia absorbed the state of Hanover. And Julius Bruhns recalled the teacher at the half-day school he attended in the Hamburg suburb of Altona in the early 1870s with admiration and affection. Thede, this teacher of peasant origins, cared about his impoverished pupils, taught them all he could, and even provided them with occasional much-needed amusement in the classroom. He used punishment only sparingly, and then in consultation with the pupils themselves: "Thede was brilliant at developing and strengthening our self-esteem, to the extent that a large number of the pupils would have seen it as the greatest shame to be corporally punished by him" (17). Wilhelm Kaisen, who was also born in a suburb of Hamburg, contrasted his "genuine teacher" with the harsh and hated schoolmaster of the type he knew was common: "What distinguished him was his great art or gift of pushing and teaching his pupils to do independent intellectual work. . . . Every pupil had open access to him and he took pains to create a humane atmosphere in the school, for which he was ridiculed by the schoolmasters. But I loved my teacher and remained bound to him into his old age"

(18). Urban schools like Hamburg's were often described as better equipped than their rural counterparts as well, but they too suffered from overcrowding. Julius Bruhns's admiration for his half-day teacher was enhanced by his awareness that this man taught more than a hundred pupils in each of his two half-day sessions. If the accounts of Lange, Bruhns, and Kaisen reveal glimpses of a more benign pedagogy (at least in those German states on the periphery of Prussia), such positive recollections of schooling are rare among the accounts of German working-class boyhoods of the nineteenth century.[2]

The stereotypical drillmaster was a figure far more prominent in boys' lives than in girls'. Central European accounts of working-class girlhood (most of which are not drawn from Prussia) tend to present teachers in a softer light. In some, to be sure, such as Anneliese Rüegg's, the classroom tyrant does make his appearance. Rüegg's account, despite its devastating portrait of the schoolmaster, nonetheless has a comic tone that distinguishes it from the unmitigated bitterness of most of the men's recollections. And even with this limitation, Rüegg's account is far more negative than those of other German-speaking women. Aurelia Roth, for example, echoed a recurrent theme when she recalled her school in the Austrian Isergebirg as preferable to home: "I often had to miss school to work. That was for me the biggest sacrifice I ever had to make. I had very little time for studying, even less for play, but what sickened me the most was when I had to miss school. . . . I didn't want to stay at home; I liked it better at school. The teacher always liked me because I was so attentive" (52–53).

Even more poignant was Lena Christ's account of her teacher as her defender, however ineffective, against the abuse she suffered at her mother's hands. Christ, who was the illegitimate child of a servant, had moved to her mother's home in Munich in the late 1880s after spending her early childhood with her grandparents in rural Bavaria. She found cruel treatment awaiting her there. School was a retreat:

My teachers took my part and once when I came to school in the morning barefoot, my mistress sent me home with a note in which she reproached my mother. But this only brought a new beating with a walking stick that belonged to my father. . . . My mother never loved me; she never kissed me nor showed me any other tenderness; now though, since the birth of her first legitimate child, she treated me with open hatred. . . . Because I wore a dress with short sleeves, when I returned to school my teacher noticed the black-and-blue marks on my arms as well as on my neck and face, and despite my fear of further punishment, I had to report the whole truth to the principal who was called in. A letter to my mother brought the result that I got nothing to eat for the whole day and had to spend the night in the corridor of our building, kneeling on a log (52–53).

Girls contrasted the relative leisure of school with the continual demands at home. They were required both to contribute to the family income and to help with such domestic chores as cooking, cleaning, and caring for siblings. Anna Perthen, for example, recalled, "As the oldest, instead of playing or studying after school, I had to take care of children, sew buttons or gather wood in the forest. . . . When I was twelve years old, I had to go into a textile factory where the workday lasted from 5 in the morning until 7 in the evening. In the afternoon from 4 to 6 we went to the factory school. . . . There wasn't much learning going on, of course, we thought of these two hours more as rest" (113). In these recollections, there is little allusion to the relative freedom of home, street life, or work life that might have served to counter the confinement and restrictions of the schoolroom. The negative portrait of the home was most exaggerated in the case of Christ, whose mother grew obsessively concerned with a propriety that demanded submissiveness, self-discipline, and modesty on her daughter's part.[3]

The relatively greater appeal of school to girls was reinforced by the more gentle treatment they apparently received there — from male teachers but especially from the growing number of female teachers who toward the end of the nineteenth century were deemed particularly suitable for instructing girl pupils. Women teachers in religious orders had long been common in Catholic areas of Europe, but lay women teachers recruited from among the daughters of the middle classes (in contrast with the more modest social origins of their male colleagues) appeared throughout Germany by the closing decades of the nineteenth century as a cheaper solution to the mushrooming demand for elementary teachers that accompanied population growth and increasing schooling.[4] In the context of different experiences at home and different pupil-teacher relations in the classroom, school could easily appear to girls as a tolerable or even pleasant release from more intense demands of family life.

If German girls' schooling was recalled as less brutal than that of the boys, it was certainly no more ambitious intellectually. Girls did not dispute the claim that their learning was minimal. Ottilie Baader learned to read and write and calculate from her father. Then she went to a cloister school that was supposed to be good, which meant that "good manners" were taught there above all (14). Anneliese Rüegg and the author of *Im Kampf ums Dasein* mentioned learning geography, but such references are unusual; most remembered learning little beyond religion, reading, and writing. The most common intellectual result these women reported was, not insignificantly, their love of reading.

Years of Conquest

The contrast between German and French school accounts mirrors and amplifies the distinctive autobiographical treatments of childhood at home. To be sure, there are stereotypically negative portraits to be found in the French autobiographies, but, like the accounts of bad childhoods, they tend to date from early in the nineteenth century. For example, Agricol Perdiguier provided such a portrait in his recollections of a schoolmaster in his Provençal village: "The very word 'school' made me shiver. . . . I didn't ever want to go to school . . . if my father hadn't forced my will, if he hadn't made me learn despite myself . . . I would never have been able to learn how to read. . . . Did the pupil read badly? A slap. Did he look to the right or the left? A lash with the belt. The cane at the teacher's side rarely rested" (5). The families were not pleased, Perdiguier remembered, but they had little choice. "We were beaten and remained ignorant by necessity," Perdiguier wrote, until a younger teacher arrived who practiced better methods. At most, he recalled, "I spent scarcely two or three years in school; I knew how to read, write and calculate, but in a very minimal fashion" (8).

But there are alternative narratives even from this early period. The memoirs of Sebastien Commissaire, who was born in 1822 and spent much of his early childhood in Lyon with his silk-weaving family, provide an early example of a different kind of school story. Commissaire recalled his parents' commitment to sacrifice for the education of their children despite the family's poverty. Sebastien's parents allowed their children, sons and daughters both, to take turns going to school so that each would get a minimum of schooling but one would always be available to work at home as a bobbin winder.

Sebastien attended a school run by the Brothers of the Christian Schools. There free tuition was offered to poor pupils. He learned the rudiments of literacy and left with generally good impressions despite his eventual conviction that schooling should be secular. Although the brothers were noted for their strict classroom discipline (as illustrated, for example, in Philippe Valette's account of his persecution), Commissaire's story prevents drawing a conclusion on the basis of pedagogic theory alone. His favorite teacher was transferred to a different school because of his sexual relationship with a woman who came to delouse the pupils. So attached were the pupils to their teacher that after his forced transfer they went off in search of him and conducted a three-week "mutiny" in protest. The mutiny eventually ended "amid a volley of blows with the cane," but Commissaire's account attests to the very strong and positive attachment between pupils and teacher that even a disciplinarian regime could foster (37–40).[5]

Whatever the mix in these early school accounts, the French public schoolteachers — *instituteurs* and *institutrices* who play an increasingly important role in memoirs dating from the Third Republic — were typically recalled with respect and affection. Georges Dumoulin, the son of day laborers in a small town in northern France, recalled his schooling in the 1880s in the most glowing terms: "What beautiful years of my life! How sweet it is to recall them even now, these years of conquest, of reward, in the course of which all the satisfactions of self-esteem were bestowed upon my sensitive nature! I consecrated a veritable cult to my teacher Charles Latour. He ran the school like a father, and he loved me like one of his children. It was he who gave me the books, the school supplies that my parents couldn't afford to buy and above all the good advice that was aimed at helping me to avoid suffering because of my situation" (18).

The teacher's personality was important; so was the physical world of the classroom, so different from the intellectual impoverishment Dumoulin experienced at home: "His three classrooms with their sparse furnishings, the posters attached to the walls, the collections of insects, the curious stones and rocks, the globe resting on the teacher's desk, commanded my respect and instilled in me a feeling of pride" (18). René Bonnet lived on the eve of World War I with his grandparents in a small village in the Limousin while his parents worked in Paris. He didn't start school until he was almost eight years old because his grandparents knew he felt some anxiety about it; yet his parents insisted, and so he went. His fear was countered by the sympathy and sensitivity of his teacher: "From the first lessons, Mr. Chalard realized that I was timid and he contrived to build my self-confidence. He avoided asking me troublesome questions to which I might not know how to reply" (17). Bonnet recalled that later he would pass the time while tending cows during the school break making plans for the improvement of his grandparents' farm on the basis of lessons in agricultural economy taught in his school.

For French working-class girls, *institutrices* could be equally significant figures. As in Germany, lay women teachers were recruited in increasing numbers in the closing decades of the nineteenth century to teach the growing number of female elementary pupils, and in France they were often recruited from among the ranks of the middle class. Their elevated social status seems often to have been an element in the girls' admiration of them. Several Parisian teachers were particularly memorable. Madeleine Henrey recalled her schoolmistress as a powerful influence during her girlhood in a working-class district of Paris before and during the First World War: "My mother decided to send me to the state schools. I was twelve and terribly backward, and the drastic change was at first very upsetting, but I was so very conscious of my apparent ignorance, so determined to do better than the other girls, that I began to climb higher in the class by sheer hard work . . . Mlle Foucher encouraged me. Of Alsatian descent, she was ardently patriotic, of rare intelligence and humanity. Her lessons acquired polish and extreme simplicity. Young, pretty, elegant, always beautifully shod, she seemed to dress for us. This combination of beauty and intelligence has ever seemed to me the most desirable thing on earth. . . . She was ours. We loved her" (206–8).

Charlotte Davy moved to Paris to begin schooling after having spent her early childhood with her grandparents near Melun. Between the public schools of Paris and her father's educational program, the young Charlotte had quite an extensive education despite the family's poverty and her mother's chronic illness. She established a good rapport with her *institutrice*, who apparently allowed her leeway to push herself beyond the rudiments of elementary instruction: "Then came the time of the school-leaving exam, which I passed rather brilliantly. My father decided to let me pursue my studies as far as possible. I followed the graduates' course in the same class, but, accustomed to my teacher, who liked me a lot, I became insupportable and all sorts of ideas came into my head" (17). Charlotte founded a society for the defense of a pupil who had been punished; she started a school newspaper and even began to write a novel entitled *Amours de la jeunesse*.[6]

Even the more humble village *institutrice* could get results. If Elise Blanc's schooling in Moulins in the 1860s was limited to "church history, the New Testament, catechism and a little grammar," the state-trained teachers of the later century were more ambitious for their pupils. The foundling Angelina Bardin, who was raised *en nourrice* (by foster-parents) in the Department of the Sarthe on the eve of World War I, recalled the combination of emotional involvement and intellectual gravity that characterized her teachers in the village schools. When she first entered school, she recalled, she was extremely frightened. "I clung next to a wall, so as not to see anyone. My young teacher leaned over to me and stroked my hair. . . . Hidden by her white shawl, I didn't move. . . . The fringes of the wool shawl rubbed against my face; I counted them. I knew how to count to ten. . . . It was a great effort, one that left you a bit short of breath. Mademoiselle said to me then: Why are you afraid if you know how to count to ten? The justice of this remark made me raise my head. She repeated to me that when you knew how to count to ten, you didn't have to be afraid of anyone" (27–28). Certainly the teachers could be tough when the school-leaving certificate was at stake. In contrast with the gentility of the first encounter, Bardin recalled that in the days of the *certificat* exam "the mistress was terrible. She made us come to the blackboard for our problems, and while one sought the solution amid hiccups and sobs — because for every mistake she received a volley of smacks — the others wiggled like worms. We all had stomachaches. When my turn came, I was sick all over" (84). Bardin did extremely well on the exam, however, and was one of only two pupils who successfully interpreted a subtle turn of phrase on the dictation. The teacher was ecstatic at her success and showed her approval in demonstrative terms: "Mademoiselle came toward me. You would have thought that she had a lamp in each eye. You came in second in the *canton*! You do me credit. And she kissed me again" (88).

Schooling and the New Discipline

From a "boot camp" in the working-class suburbs of Berlin to the "beauty and intelligence" of a classroom in the working-class suburb of Paris, schools left a remarkable range of impressions upon their working-class pupils in the late nineteenth century. Far from being random, the variation in school accounts follows the contours of gender and political geography. Memoirs by Central European authors, especially male authors, show that the classroom tyrant was a fixture of popular culture. Beloved teachers appear only occasionally in German tales, but they play prominent roles in autobiographies from throughout France (map 2). In their patterned variety, these school stories provide a privileged inroad into the intellectual and political meaning of schooling for Europe's popular classes.

Historians of education have argued that the schools were a terrain in which new styles of discipline could be taught and learned. The order of

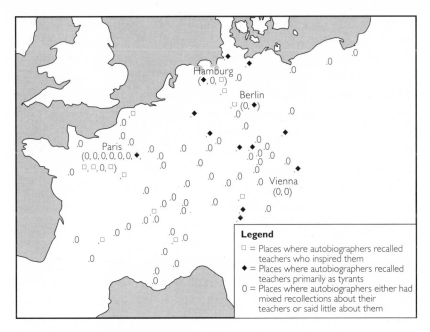

Map 2. Portraits of Schoolteachers

the modern classroom, in contrast with the order of the peasant or proletarian home or preindustrial community, rested on a hierarchy based on merit, self-discipline, coordinated and regimented group activity, and calculated reward and punishment. To adapt to the requirements of factory labor and a market ethos, workers had to internalize new incentives to work to replace the orientation toward subsistence and the reliance upon physical coercion that had characterized productive relations under the precapitalist order.

It is easy to find historical evidence for a new rationality in the school systems that resulted from the ambitious educational reforms undertaken throughout Western Europe during the late eighteenth and early nineteenth centuries. It is more difficult, however, to assess the *consequences* of school reform and expansion for the lives of the children of the popular classes, who were most directly affected by the changes. The autobiographies allow the examination of not only recollections of actual classroom interactions during the generations of school reform but also subjective assessments of the long-term consequences of classroom learning and discipline in the lives of the children who sat on the benches.

The autobiographies substantiate the claim that the expansion of schooling did indeed expose children from the popular classes to a rigorous form of discipline. They also point out, however, that styles of classroom discipline varied widely at least into the twentieth century and, moreover, that the consequences of this discipline were not always predictable. The most prominent characteristic of classroom relations as depicted in the German boys' accounts was the authoritarian order reinforced by corporal punishment. The emphasis on corporal punishment left its sting on children's bodies and its imprint on their memories. Even in the last decades of the nineteenth century—the era of intense industrialization in Germany—many German teachers relied not upon the internalized discipline of the psyche but a rather more old-fashioned control through physical pain. In the more positive of the German accounts and in the French accounts, in contrast, the emphasis was upon the power of the teacher as a model who, through judicious reward and punishment and seriousness of purpose tempered by affection, could achieve classroom order and high levels of accomplishment without resorting to physical discipline. There was no single style of pedagogy required or determined by the demands of the European industrial capitalist order; the variations can be understood when the schools are set in the context of Europe's political history as well.

By the late nineteenth century, the schoolroom had become a defining institution of childhood and the character of its social relations a telling feature in the socialization of working-class children. The contrasts between the German and French accounts, and no doubt between men's and women's accounts as well, originate *both* in the conduct of teachers in the classroom and in differences in the political discourse about schooling that influenced the autobiographers' later lives. Both are pertinent because both contribute to mythologies about education, its character, and its impact upon and meaning for the individual life course.

Memories of Schooling

The images of school in the autobiographies does seem to reflect the contrasting political contexts in which school policies were determined, at least as far as men's memoirs are concerned. French *instituteurs*, in the spirit of solidarism, reasoned with their pupils; German teachers relied on the cane, as befits authoritarians. But it would be a mistake to leap too quickly to conclusions about the ultimate *impact* of these contrasting styles of school discipline. For this discipline could produce unanticipated consequences of which the autobiographers themselves provided ironic evidence. Experiences that children had in school did not occur in a social and political vacuum. They were interpreted with reference to available ideological frameworks.

Working-class children and adults living in late nineteenth-century Germany did not have to look far to find such a framework. Pronouncements on the subject of popular education made in a speech by the socialist leader Wilhelm Liebknecht in 1872 were the opening tirade of a critique of state education that would shape socialist thought on the subject throughout the Second Empire. Liebknecht proclaimed that the schools of the German state existed to inculcate in their pupils the blind acceptance of authority and blind obedience they would later have to display in the barracks.[7] The emergent socialist analysis of the schools in turn shaped the perceptions and recollections of pupils who were familiar with the socialist commonplaces. Several of the autobiographies suggest that a critical framing of the school experience may well have subverted the disciplinary intent of the pedagogic practice. In Karl Grünberg's case, for example, the autobiographical interpretation of his torment at school was placed in the context of an evolving narrative of critique of the authoritarian state. The memory of his own personal battle in the classroom was explicitly linked with political satires he encountered as an adult: "From what I have said it is clear that this teacher was a typical 'elementary school bully' of the sort that I'd get to know in the excellent school comedy *Flachsmann als Erzieher*" (22).[8] The memory of his persecution would be an important element of Grünberg's definition of himself as rebel.

Similarly, Ger, Lüth, and other German socialists told the story of their pedagogic drillmasters in terms that both fed into and reflected their socialist interpretation of the repressive function of schooling. Alwin Ger, for example, included in his memoirs a diatribe against the school and church that "designed everything in the education of these poor people to suppress the training of the reason" (17), an account that echoes Liebknecht's charge against the German schools. Certainly not all of the German boyhood accounts marked by oppressive teaching culminated in socialist careers, nor were all socialists badly taught. But a strong connection between the depiction of boyhood encounters with state authority in the schools and the critique of state education inherent in the Social Democratic Party line is certainly suggested.

In this context, the differing emphasis of the accounts of schooling found in German women's autobiographies takes on an interesting additional dimension. As "good" pupils who appreciated and were appreciated by their teachers, the girls may well have been less subject to harsh discipline than boys were (although many male autobiographers were self-reported star pupils as well). Even more to the point, girls were more marginal to the heroic socialist narrative of rebellion that informed many of the working-class male texts. The school's emphasis on submissiveness, considered as the emblem of political and economic oppression when forced upon schoolboys in the classroom and adult men in the barracks and the factory, may have appeared more "natural" when forced upon women and girls. And girls, no doubt socialized at home into more submissive behavior, typically required less coercive discipline.

Implications for recruitment into the socialist movement begin to suggest themselves. Parallel to the more obvious gender discrimination that informed socialist practice and affected the participation of women in the socialist movement ran a deeper construction of the process of coming-to-socialist-consciousness that rested on contradictions between masculinity and submission to political authority (often first encountered in the school) that did not pertain to women.[9] Women did portray instances of rebellion, but their rebellions typically occurred as adults and centered around unjust practices in the workplace, assaults on their sexual inviolability, or contradictory practices of working-class motherhood. Harassment in the classroom was rarely part of the German women's narrative of growing up rebellious. Most women, even socialist women, did not allude to the socialist line in interpreting their experiences at school. They had to look elsewhere for the origins of their insubordination.

The political history of schooling in France provided autobiographers with a substantially different national mythology. A more humane form of discipline — one more rooted in Enlightenment critiques of authoritarianism and the political culture of republicanism — prevailed in French classrooms. The success of this educational strategy is clear in the relatively positive popular imagery of the schoolteacher in these memoirs. Nevertheless, men who praised their teachers still ended up as working-class militants. And accounts by the women who attended the schools of the Third Republic suggest that female teachers may well have resisted constraints upon them and encouraged their best pupils to defy some of the limits imposed by gender norms — to aspire to become writers, nurses, even feminist agitators.

The writers of autobiographies recounted their childhoods in or after the lingering heat of political discussion about the nature and aims of schooling. It is therefore hardly surprising to find accounts that substantiate, at least on the surface, the claims that the Prussian drillmaster was the creator of abject "subjects" rather than thinking citizens, while the French *instituteur* was the bearer of enlightenment, opportunity, and interclass cooperation. The accounts, in other words, reflected and contributed to evolving political culture, especially attitudes toward state authority in the abstract and in the concrete form students encountered in the classroom. But the ultimate impact of these encounters is less clear. Many of these Prussian "subjects" later rebelled, even if, we are told, their rebellion was eventually institutionalized in a reformist socialist counterculture. And even the more benign and rational pedagogy of the French *instituteurs* could produce well-schooled anarchists and syndicalists who apparently saw no contradiction between their glorification of the Third Republican *instituteur* and their opposition as adults to the French state. The testimony of the autobiographies suggests that the schools could serve quite different strategies of political discipline. French elementary schoolteachers may well have embodied a program of internalized self-control and rationality presumed to prepare pupils for the requirements of industrial capitalism, but their pupils nonetheless appreciated the skills and support their teachers had offered regardless of their later politics. The greater German reliance upon coercive models was less functional, apparently, since teachers alienated so many of their pupils. Nevertheless, the rebellion of former pupils was hardly automatic. Memories of schooling served as landmarks on the road to rebellion possibly only because of their susceptibility to reinterpretation in the context of an oppositional political culture such as the one the social democratic movement provided.

And the schools, whatever their disciplinary regime, provided the talented poor with a place where they could sometimes, despite everything, see potential for themselves that they might not have seen at home. The intellectual triumphs of Georges Dumoulin or Angelina Bardin were merely the most extreme versions of boosts to self-esteem that could occur more subtly as well. Even the miserable Franz Lüth recalled being "always the best pupil" whose only problem subject was math and that only because his foster mother refused to buy him a math book (9–10). And Alwin Ger, so bitter in his recollections of his irredeemably bad teacher, was nevertheless obviously proud of his role as class leader — "first place in the highest grade . . . and therefore responsible for the good conduct of my fellow pupils" (55). Moreover, the range of eventual destinies of the autobiographers, and the various uses to which they put their educational skills, make clear that the consequences of any pedagogic regime were more open-ended than they perhaps were intended to be.

These had been my experiences, more or less, when as a twelve-year-old youth I took to the streets armed with my school-leaving certificate, walking out the exit from childhood into a new phase of my life. (Franz Bergg, 29)

FIVE

LEAVING CHILDHOOD BEHIND

Like Franz Bergg, most autobiographers recalled a cluster of events — leaving school, getting their first full-time job, and sometimes a religious rite of passage — that signaled the end of childhood. Not all remembered this point of transition in the same way; changes over time, regional, and gender differences mark the coming-of-age stories workers' autobiographies tell. Yet virtually all of the authors gave some narrative emphasis to changes at the time of life now called early adolescence. And they converted their class-typical ways of experiencing the end of childhood into further episodes in the ongoing saga of their evolving self and class identity. In contrast with accounts of childhood and elementary schooling, in which their parents or teachers played dominant roles, accounts of the end of childhood mark the moment in most narratives where the authors began to become the "heroes of their own life stories."[1] They continued to measure their experiences against norms they could not reach. The events that marked their transition were generally flawed: confirmation ceremonies came too late and their clothes weren't right; leaving school (whether with relief or regret) seemed to come too early; the job was not the one they had hoped to have. But in marked contrast with the passivity and fatalism that usually characterized their portraits of themselves at earlier ages, at this moment many authors remembered themselves beginning to take charge. Their anger and frustration often led to a new kind of resolve. All but the most despairing self-portraits tell of expressing and acting on disagreements with, and resentments toward, family members, school authorities, and bosses.

Transitional Moments

Three kinds of transitional events dominated coming-of-age episodes in working-class memoirs — confirmation or First Communion, leaving school, and entering full-time work. (Sexual initiation, which many also described, was a different kind of transition; see chapter 6.) Not all children went through the religious initiation ceremony, for many of Europe's working-class families lived on the margins of organized religion, but it was nevertheless a common episode in autobiographies. Moreover, by the last decades of the nineteenth century, workers' autobiographies typically linked these three kinds of events closely together in time. Of course, "earning their own bread" had begun for many children of poor families long before they left school; at least part-time child labor continued to be critical to the working-class family economy, especially in Central Europe, until the end of the nineteenth century. But throughout the elementary years school attendance laws placed limits upon the number of hours a day, or days in a year, that children could work. These limits vanished when children left school; at that moment the family's economic needs and expectations, both for its children's immediate contributions and its future, took priority.

It is not surprising, then, that this moment was remembered as an increasingly significant point in working-class life course, more clearly defined in memoirs of the end of the nineteenth century than it had been at the beginning. The triple ritualization (religious, educational, and economic) that occurred between the ages of twelve and fourteen gave enhanced social meaning to biological development and marked in a definitive way the passage out of childhood. The institutionalization of this phase of the life course affected how life stories were told. This moment had, by the end of the nineteenth century, become a key element in its plot.

These transitional events had not always clustered together, nor had they occurred at roughly the same predictable age for everyone. Moving between school and work had once been more fluid, seasonal, and reversible; the age of entry into full-time work varied more widely among the earlier than the later memoirs. As Figure 4 indicates, far less variance occurs in reports about the age of entry into full-time work in the second half of the nineteenth century than in the first. It appears from memoirs in both languages that full-time employment had by the last decades of the nineteenth century come to be strongly associated with leaving elementary school.

Religious rites became more predictable as well. In earlier memoirs, religious initiation could come as early as eight or as late as the mid-teens. Stories varied: several of the earlier French memoirists — Valentin Jamerey-Duval, Norbert Truquin, and Claude Genoux — were living on their own by the time they reached the age of thirteen. Their formal schooling was brief and haphazard. The only one of these to mention a *première communion* ceremony was Truquin. After his mother died, Norbert's father put him into service as a wool comber. Norbert heard news of his father five years later and rediscovered many relatives, but they were shocked by his complete lack of religious education. He eventually received instruction and First Communion several years later and only because a factory boss let him off work for catechism and arranged for a free suit (48–50).

Earlier French women memoirists including Élise Blanc, Suzanne Voilquin and Jeanne Bouvier alluded to preparing for First Communion, but their age at the time is unclear; Bouvier was perhaps as young as eight years old, but Blanc and Voilquin were apparently older. Voilquin had spent some time as an apprentice seamstress several years prior to the event; for Bouvier, full-time work began at age eleven, some time after First Communion. For all three, schooling was minimal and interrupted.

For German writers, the early emphasis on surveillance of school attendance by the state school and church authorities meant that norms about

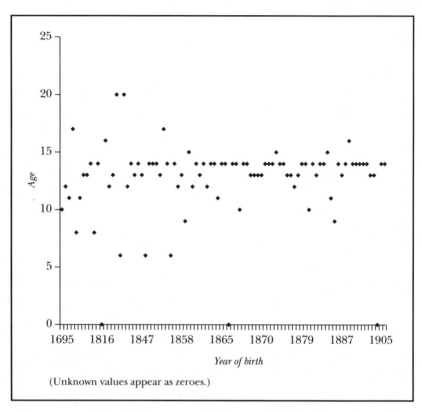

Figure 4. Age at First Full-Time Job (ordered by autobiographer's year of birth)

transitional events were clearer. Still, the earliest autobiographies show a range of possibilities: Ulrich Bräker finished his regular schooling at age eleven but was not confirmed until after he had been working for about three years. Josef Peukert quit school to work at age eleven. Anna Alt-mann, the earliest-born of the German-speaking women autobiographers, remembered starting to work at a factory when she was six and attending school at the factory only a couple of hours a day.

Practices derived from this older pattern of transition from child-hood — a process that began very early and often took many years to complete — were preserved in a few memoirs even at the end of the nineteenth century. In some areas, parents could receive dispensations from the school laws for their children if they pled poverty and could put their children to work at a young age. This was especially true in rural areas. Heinrich Lange, Georges Dumoulin, and Franz Rehbein all re-membered being excused from school attendance during the agricul-tural season to work at herding or in the fields at age eleven or even earlier. Julius Bruhns attended a "half-day school" (three hours a day) in Hamburg designed for older pupils whose parents needed them to begin work before school-leaving age; Karl Grünberg got a half-year dispensation from the Berlin school authorities so he could start work at thirteen and a half instead of fourteen.

But despite such exemptions, the enforcement of increased school attendance had the general effect of pushing school-age children out of full-time labor and of concentrating the events of transition from childhood into a relatively brief period. The ritualized character of the moment of leaving school was further enhanced by the granting of an official certificate (the *Schulentlassungsschein* or *certificat des études primaires*). The later autobiographies attest to the wide implantation of a new pattern of transition: confirmation or communion would typically come around Easter; school leaving and entry into apprenticeship or full-time labor would follow, often within a month at the end of the school year. In the stories, these events often crowd together.

In contrast with many of the experiences that were recalled as hallmarks of childhood, the unfolding of these later events was not understood to be inevitable. These moments often brought the insults and frustrations of poverty once again to the fore, whether in the form of the ragged clothes that now seemed humiliating or the awareness that a hoped-for occupational future was impossible. But typically, in contrast with their naïveté in childhood, autobiographers remembered themselves on the threshhold of adolescence as sensitive beings who felt the sting of restrictions imposed by poverty. They were still, as they had been as young children, forced into situations against their will. Decisions about education, jobs, and expenditures on clothing were still usually made by their parents. But in many autobiographies, coming-of-age events represented an important first occasion for grappling with questions of destiny; what happened was not simply the result of "the way things were" anymore. Autobiographers recalled being more aware at this age of how human actions and institutions affected their destiny. Even if they still lacked the resources to change things, by the time they set out on life's road young people had begun to imagine more than one destination.

Religious Coming-of-Age: The Last Insult of Childhood?

The transition out of childhood had long been enacted religiously in the ceremonies around confirmation (the predominant ritual in Protestant areas) or First Communion (in Catholic ones). Traditionally, at this moment boys adopted long pants and girls took on the coifs and costumes of their mothers. In the rural villages of preindustrial Europe, the religious ceremony had been the point entry into "youth" — the pool of those who were no longer children, if not yet fully adult. This status of semiadulthood would last until marriage, which took place for most people of Western and Central Europe between their early twenties and their early thirties.[2]

Certainly a few of the autobiographers' experiences reflect these traditional expectations. For Frederic Mistral and Agricol Perdiguier, both of whom came of age in southern France in the early nineteenth century, First Communion was remembered as a solemn and important occasion. Moreover, Mistral coupled the recollection of his communion preparation class in the local church with his memory of "first love" there; his narrative thus introduced a leitmotif that would recur in later memoirs. Heinrich Lange recalled the special Sunday classes in his village in central Germany in the early 1870s, classes that assembled all the village children to prepare them for confirmation. The children, he recalled, wrote verses for each other to celebrate the occasion. In his village "we [children] didn't recognize the differences between peasants with full-size holdings, smaller farmers, the marginal ones and the cottagers" (34–35). René Bonnet recalled as a memorable occasion the turn-of-the-century First Communion that he shared with his sisters in the village where he lived with his grandparents. Despite his anticlericalism his father had agreed to the ceremony in order to please the pious grandmother. René recalled that he was never so well dressed as for communion. "My mother had sent me a new blue suit, a fine armband with long fringes and a missal. All this had a special value and I was more than a bit proud to wear all of these things that came from Paris" (68). Like his predecessor Mistral, Bonnet also remembered a special girlfriend — Angèle de Javaux — who looked "so beautiful in her white veil" (69). Other village girls whose parents forbade them to attend catechism were filled with jealousy toward these lovely communicants.

Even autobiographers who had known dire poverty as children could sometimes recall this moment with appreciation. Max Hoelz had had a very difficult childhood, despite his father's frugality. The boy never had any new clothes until he was fourteen. "Thus it was a tremendous event for me, when, at my confirmation, I wore a brand new suit for the first time in my life — a suit made by a tailor. It impressed me much more than the whole confirmation, although I took that very seriously, for, being a child, I had no religious doubts" (18).

But these exemplary celebrations—all of which transpired more or less "as they were supposed to"—represented only a small minority of the thirty or so ritual stories the memoirs tell. Some authors had to adapt their ceremonies to the irregular circumstances of their childhood. Adelheid Popp couldn't be confirmed at the usual age because her mother "was too proud to ask anyone to be my sponsor. She herself couldn't buy the necessary white dress and everything that went with it, as much as she would have liked to." Only when, at age seventeen, Adelheid was earning enough on her own to support herself and her mother did she manage to buy the outfit and get confirmed. "It was splendid! The ride in the open coach, the ceremony in the church with the bishop's slap on the cheek, then an outing, a prayerbook and some practical gifts. Now for the first time I felt myself to be completely grown up" (51).

Angelina Bardin was prepared for communion by the priest in the village where she lived *en nourrice*. But like the other Paris foundlings, she had to get baptised before the ceremony. That meant finding her own godparents and worrying about who would pay for the *dragées*, the sweets that the occasion still requires (69–70).

Experiences like these underscore the marginality of many poor families to the organizational life on which the rituals of transition depended. But they also demonstrate how this marginality often turned on symbolically important aspects of simple material deprivation. Significantly, it is the *costume* that the confirmation or communion ceremony required that turns up at the center of many recollections. Because everyone seemed to know about the long-established expectation that new clothes—adult clothes—be worn on this day, the inability of a family to acquire them was often felt as a public humiliation, a statement of the family's failure to provide what the community saw as a prerequisite for entry into adulthood.

Sebastien Commissaire offered one of the earliest examples of what would become a frequently told story: "Among Catholics the day of the First Communion is generally a day of celebration; it was not so for me. . . . All of the other children wore coats of more or less fine cloth while I had only a short jacket; their candles were tall and thick, mine was short and thin. . . . Despite myself, I felt humiliated, I would rather not have been there. I was angry, envious, unhappy. Since then I have often thought about the feelings I experienced on this occasion, and once my power of reason was shaped, my intelligence developed, I recognized that I was wrong. Envy is an emotion that shouldn't exist in the heart of an honest man" (36–37).

Some autobiographers recalled pulling together a costume only with great difficulty and often with mixed results. Georges Dumoulin made his First ("and last") Communion in the same year as his *certificat* exam. "We arrived at an understanding with the curé that since I knew my catechism very well, despite the indigence which prevented me from offering a fat candle to the Holy Mother Church, I was worthy of appearing at the holy altar. And then, communion provided the occasion for little advantages, a chance to finally get a suit and shoes. I had all of that. The coat and vest were cut by my mother from an overcoat that the notary Senlecq gave her. . . . I had pants of merino wool that were too tight and scratched my thighs. . . . I was marvelous and grotesque at the same time" (23). In Franz Bergg's case, his relatives "had come up with all that was essential: hat, gloves, shoes, linens, songbook with nameplate. Mother got the coat cheap from an old acquaintance — the pawnbroker. This remarkably diverse assembling of my holiday persona undermined my sense of worth somewhat. But the others didn't need to know where all the new things came from. I had to put up an appearance — that was the main thing" (34).

For the author of *Im Kampf ums Dasein*, this necessary appearance brought nothing but pain. She had to go to church alone because her mother was sick. "Other than a cripple, I was the smallest and thinnest of the girls being confirmed, which meant I had to take a lot of teasing from the boys." She had been clothed for the occasion by charity, a distinction that further humiliated her: "We looked like outcasts in our shabby dresses, and many tears fell on them" (46–47). Louis Lecoin was also humiliated by charity; the priest mentioned out loud in catechism class that his mother had begged his communion suit. He recalled that he was "excessively sensitive to [such] wounds to my self-pride" (15). In one story after another, the element of public humiliation centering around inadequate clothing feeds the narrative of discontent. Whatever Commissaire may have come to think about his feelings later on, such emotions — humiliation mixed with self-pride, resentment, anger — were the stuff of developing class consciousness.

There was also another element. Confirmation and communion preparation classes usually included socially mixed groups of boys and girls — often more mixed by class and sex than elementary school classes had been. Moreover, because the confirmands or communicants were at a point of maturity where they noticed and even experienced particular sensitivity to social slights and could now see and compare themselves by standards outside those of their own family, the whole process was rife with occasions for insult or humiliation. Inadequate clothing was at the center of most of the recollections of failure, but it was not the only dimension. In addition to his embarrassment about his shabby clothes, Sebastien Commissaire had also noticed that at catechism the rich and poor were treated differently: "The pupils of the boarding schools knew neither their catechism nor the New Testament. [The priest] barely quizzed them so that they wouldn't be humiliated in our presence, while we had to know both under pain of punishment" (36). Philippe Valette sat quietly in discomfort in his rags, an outcast, while all the girls in his catechism class were thrilled by the antics of the rich boy who misbehaved. This injustice left him, he remembered, with doubts — perhaps "there was nothing in heaven . . . religion was invented by the rich for the usage of the poor . . . there was neither justice nor order in nature." He knew his catechism but couldn't speak because of his timidity and self-consciousness. Luckily he managed to befriend one of the girls — Madeleine Pialu — which changed his humor and his whole attitude toward life (124–30).

Still, if quite a number of memoirists recalled the ceremonies around religious initiation as times of humiliation and anger, only rarely was this sense of shame accepted fatalistically. Instead, such experiences seemed often to crystallize into the ambition to avoid such embarrassment in the future. Marie Sans Gène recalled being "not the youngest, but the smallest and least developed" in her confirmation class. Three years earlier, when her sister was confirmed, the family had given three marks to the pastor. Now they could no longer afford to. When Marie pressed her mother to give her at least something, her mother gave her a folded piece of paper containing "all she had." It was a note that read, "I have nothing" (51). This jolting reminder of the family's poverty made Marie vow to help out her parents even more by increasing her earnings as soon as she could.

Franz Lüth recalled the confirmation as the moment when he stopped behaving like the poor charity orphan he was. He did very well during confirmation lessons, impressing both the pastor and his foster mother, who previously had always accused him of stupidity. His abilities fed his ambition to become a pastor himself, but when he confessed his ambition both his foster mother and the pastor laughed at him. "Just look at the dumb squirt, stupid Franz! Hasn't even got a shirt that he can call his own and he wants to be a Herr Pastor! . . . Your parents raised you right and honorably to be a laborer . . . are you trying to elevate yourself above your station in life? . . . With this awakening from his dreamworld to the unbidden pitiless misery of life, the remainder of his religious delusion melted like snow in the hot sun; on the day of his confirmation, Franz parted with all of the illusions which had up until then attached him to his faith." To add insult to injury, they dressed him up for his confirmation in a charity "clown suit." With this bitter experience fresh in mind, Franz left for a job as a farm servant with a new and simpler ambition — to use his first season's wages "to have a suit made in which he could be seen in public on Sundays without becoming a laughingstock" (24–25).

Stories of Leaving School

Memories of leaving school also served as occasions to raise questions about justice and class injury. Narrative strategies varied considerably; among the most subtle and powerful is that of Angelina Bardin. A Parisian foundling by origin, Bardin had been a star pupil. Her account of school-leaving is a dramatic representation of how much, and how little, this success meant in her life. After the public posting of the results of the *certificat* exam, when she received her teacher's warm congratulations for taking second place in the canton, she turned to her friends and made a troubling discovery:

> They were jealous of me. However, Monette said suddenly: "We should go buy our flags" . . . we ran to the shop. There were two slightly larger flags reserved for the two who came in first.
> — "Who's the second place winner?" the shopwoman asked. She looked at each of us and each remained quiet.
> — "How can this be?" she added, "They told me that the second place winner came from your village."
> — "Well," I replied, "they pulled one over on you." And I bought a little flag, no larger than those of my friends.
> We paraded around the town, flags flying. We were crazy. But a secret vow sealed our lips about the second place. We didn't need this title.
> Only when, that evening, I burst across the immense field in which I had recited so many of my lessons, and when I saw mama and papa who were watching for me, did I let forth a huge cry of triumph. I waved my flag furiously and I shouted as loud as I could:
> — "Passed, second in the canton" (89–90).

Bardin left her readers no time to dwell on her moment of triumph. On the next page, her narrative shifts: "A week later, I had to leave. I had been hired out, for ten francs a month, to a farm in the commune of Evaillé. . . . It was over. The little girl was dead; she would never again take these paths, gather huge bouquets of flowers. I was thirteen years old and I was going 'into service' as they used to say. And I was very happy because I was going to earn my keep and be able to buy a corset that would give me a wasp waist" (91).

Bardin's transition from triumph at the exam to a future as a laborer came unusually abruptly, but her story was a common one. Bardin described her fate without direct comment; the juxtaposition is so rapid as to be shocking, and it is left to carry its own meanings. But in many other autobiographies the school-leaving story provides a moment for explicit analysis: children quit school, and the future it might have meant, because they had to. Whatever their talent, there was simply no other choice.

The connections between schooling and opportunity in the nineteenth century have been the focus of various kinds of social-historical inquiry. Mobility studies, analyses of textbooks, and examinations of school systems and the opportunities they included have all contributed to our understanding of the changing role of schooling in the determination of occupational destinies. While many historians have argued that schools became increasingly segregated by class over the course of the nineteenth century and point to the essentially conservative character of the pedagogy and texts, others have pointed out that certain types of higher educational institutions were indeed opening possibilities for some lower-class pupils.[3]

The testimony of autobiographers cannot help determine how likely mobility through education was in general or how much access to it was changing, but it can shed light on how educational opportunities were recalled, interpreted, and subsequently reconstructed in the context of recounting a life story. Autobiographers offered a look into particular trajectories. As they ostensibly gave a full account of the processes that led them to the sort of work they did and described what seemed to them to be the effects of education on their lives, they also occasionally revealed ways in which, at various moments throughout their lives, education may have affected the course of their life more subtly.

The overwhelming majority of autobiographers reported leaving school for full-time work right around the official school-leaving age (fig. 4). A few recalled the departure as a liberation, which should come as no surprise given how they described their experiences in school. Christian Döbel had been an indifferent pupil who had little time for studies given the demands he met at home: "Whether or not I learned anything in school was of no importance. . . . The main thing was that I rocked the cradle with energy and could sing and whistle at the same time. No one would be surprised that my hind quarters were always black and blue, because often a double portion was measured out to me: at home when I didn't rock and whistle according to my stepmother's wishes, in school when I couldn't recite my lessons without error. Finally, at least one freedom beckoned — I was let out of school" (8). Karl Grünberg, whose early school years had been such a torment, was on a grueling schedule as he approached school-leaving age. He delivered papers in the morning before school and worked as a delivery boy afterward. Sometimes he did not return home until eleven o'clock, and schoolwork thus became nothing more than a burden. "My whole ambition," he remembered, "turned toward one thing — to be 'free' as soon as possible, as I comprehended that with my thirteen-year-old understanding" (38–40).

Gaston Guiraud recalled having been "too drawn by the attractions of the streets" of Belle Epoque Paris to be a devoted pupil. His illiterate grandmother could hardly supervise his homework. He had never gotten along well with his teacher, and the day of the *certificat* exam was for him "one of the worst days of his youth" (24). His failure at the exam blocked the future for which his grandmother had prepared him, "but I had to tell her that I wanted never to return to school, and with a very sincere enthusiasm expressed my will to go to work" (27–28).

But the majority of the autobiographers, by their own accounts better than average pupils, left school with mixed feelings, regrets, a sense of opportunity lost. Dozens of accounts reveal that the authors loved reading or learning. Some had been encouraged by their parents; a number of them (including Bruno Bürgel, Lena Christ, Verena Conzett, Adelheid Popp, Wilhelm Kaisen, Georges Dumoulin, Otto Richter, Fritz Rehbein, Charlotte Davy, Madeleine Henrey, and Jean Guehenno) were encouraged by their teachers when parents could not imagine or support intellectual ambition. Madeleine Henrey loved her teacher and was inspired to great scholastic success by her. But she noted that despite her success in the *certificat* exam, there was no talk at home of higher education. And when Verena Conzett started the *Ergänzungsschule* she was required to attend part-time as a twelve-year-old factory worker, the teacher asked why she was not in secondary school and even volunteered to try to get her a scholarship and free materials. But Verena's father refused to consider "charity."

Many authors recalled early hopes that involved study and abandonment of such ambitions soon afterward. Heinrich Lange had wanted to be a teacher, but he was "reasonable enough to know that that was impossible because of the lack of means" (36). Similarly, the author of *Erinnerungen eines Waisenknaben* recalled that as the moment of school-leaving neared, "I would have loved to study! That would have been my highest goal. It was completely impossible, though, and so I quickly buried this desire inside myself" (115). Adelheid Popp, instead of heading to the factory, wanted to continue learning — "my ideal was to become a teacher, but for all my ten years I saw finally that it was a fantasy even to discuss it" (10).

For others, the erosion of scholarly ambition was more gradual — more the result of lack of aptitude, or so it seemed, than a denial of opportunity. René Michaud, who had been a very promising pupil, had attended special classes and worked very hard to prepare for the *certificat* exam. To his chagrin, he failed the mathematics part. He never could understand why, because math had always been his best subject. So he went off to work at age thirteen; his first job application was denied because he lacked the *certificat*, but then he got a job making boxes at twenty *sous* a day. He claimed to have reconciled himself quickly to his scholastic defeat: beginning work soon seemed, he wrote, "a sort of liberation" (60). Heinrich Holek described a similar experience. Instead of staying in the *Volksschule*, as most working-class children did, Heinrich had managed to attend the intellectually superior *Bürgerschule* through a tuition exemption. The experience was not always a happy one. His situation at home was very bad (he had an abusive stepmother), and he was constantly at odds with the school authorities over his tuition exemption and his legal residence. Finally, he moved back to the *Volksschule* because he had to help his parents at the brickworks where they worked. He didn't recall the transfer as a great disappointment. All the trials and moves had "destroyed his love of learning" anyway (150–51). Now he had new things to look forward to. He was in his last year of school. "Next October, I would be turning fourteen . . . how I longed for this moment. Then I was free" (165).

Indeed, while more than a dozen autobiographers attended some sort of school that offered more than basic elementary instruction, most of the more than a dozen who did so still quit school at the official school-leaving age to work. Only Frederic Mistral, whose father was a wealthy peasant, and Eugene Courmeaux, whose parents were comfortable shop-keepers and whose uncle helped to finance his schooling, followed the more middle-class route of continuing in school past age fourteen. Among the others who eventually went on to some sort of classical secondary or university education (Madeleine Henrey, Otto Richter, Bruno Bürgel, and Jean Guehenno) all were at work by age fourteen or fifteen. Even for these "success stories," the road to success through education was interrupted by many detours. Advanced education was delayed until the late teens or twenties. Guehenno, for example, was forced to leave school against his will because of his father's illness. Otto Richter sought "to become somebody" through apprentice in a law office, as formal schooling was ruled out and his family had access to the patronage networks that such an apprenticeship required (97).

Because most of the autobiographers thought of themselves as talented academically, the detours and deadends they faced in their pursuit of education were rarely easy to accept. Despite occasional disclaimers, their stories suggest that the abandonment or postponement of intellectual ambitions left a significant stamp on their lives. Some were explicit in this assertion. Bruno Bürgel had at first been an indifferent pupil because he could not see the point of study. He wanted to be a juggler. But when he tried out his juggling skills one day in his foster mother's kitchen, he made such a mess that he figured he had better learn what they taught in school after all! He soon caught up and became one of the best pupils—one "for whom a scholarship would be sought" (24–25). As he approached school-leaving, however, and was encouraged by one of his teachers to consider higher education, his foster father warned him that there was no future in it for "a poor devil" like him. He would never get a paying post even if he managed to complete his studies. Moreover, Bürgel remembered, "Not only was [his foster father] unable to give me a penny for clothes and support; he and Mother had, on the contrary, figured that I on my part would now begin to support them. He was old and no longer able to earn what was necessary and if any sort of illness forced him out of work at his age, that would mean the deepest misery. . . . The adult can seldom grasp the pain of a child. Mine was deep and bitter . . . [but] I did what I had to. I gave in" (36–39).

Georges Dumoulin, as the prize pupil of his *instituteur*, drew closer to a possibility. On his teacher's advice, he went so far as to take a special advanced class and then the exam for admission to the *école primaire supérieure* in the nearby town. His mother "did wonders to come up with a suit and to pay for the train fare." He passed the entrance exam and won a half scholarship; all of the full scholarships went to the sons of families of means. The problem was that his parents couldn't afford the rest or the clothes and supplies he would need. He received the news "with great sadness, bitterness, and something else clearer still—the sensation of injustice" (25).

Jean Guehenno told a similar tale. His father was ambitious for him, and when the small family became relatively comfortable on his parents' earnings in the shoe industry, they sent him to the local *collège* even though it was expensive. Jean was awkward and uncomfortable there "among the sons of factory owners, merchants, and bureaucrats." Still, he did well—he had to, he recalled, to prove to his mother that "the tuition money wasn't wasted." The prize ceremony each year was "a day of triumph" for him. His father became sick, however, meaning that his continued attendance would depend on his winning a scholarship. He failed the exam and so had to enter the factory. The experience marked him for life:

> I was certainly too young to know clearly what I wanted and what I was losing, but not too young to feel what seemed to me an injustice. Why was everything I loved being denied me? . . . I had been excluded, to all appearance, according to the rules and for lack of merit. I was condemned by my stupidity and left to it. I was not made for knowledge. . . . But all the others, my classmates, who, all of them, were no less unworthy than me and would have failed like me, why could they continue to get what was refused me? . . .
>
> This crisis of my childhood, I see it clearly, determined my whole life and doubtless led my judgment astray. The proscription under which I endured inflamed my desire into a passion. I knew practically nothing yet, and I was already an intellectual (129–30).

Guehenno's was not the only case where frustrated success in school seems to have had this indirect, but very significant, impact of instilling intellectual ambitions that were realized only later in life. It seems very likely that such experiences contributed to the creation of a cadre of working-class intellectuals who applied the skills and lessons of school days in a variety of later endeavors. For some, the denial of advancement despite their obvious talent was a decisive moment on the course toward political critique or determined self-improvement. More subtly, they drew upon their early relative success in the educational arena to fashion themselves as distinctive from their less successful classmates. It seems to have given them a basis for deciding that they had a potential to stand out, whatever the immediate pressures were. This distinction would continue to express itself in many forms — in political leadership, in extraordinary ambition, in artistry, and ultimately in autobiography.

Off to Work

Ulrich Bräker remembered how the decision was made in the 1740s about putting a child to work: "Everyone was saying: 'Get the boy into the traces, put the yoke on him — he's big enough!' " (75) In the traditional family economy of preindustrial Europe, youth either contributed full-time work at home or were sent off as apprentices or servants to other households. A family business or farm provided a built-in place into which to move in early adolescence. Jacques-Louis Ménétra's story, emerging from the artisan milieu of late eighteenth-century Paris, illustrates this process. He had been raised primarily by his maternal grandmother since the age of three, when his mother died. When he reached the age of eleven, however, his father (who had subsequently remarried and had several children by a second wife) reclaimed him to begin work alongside him as a window maker. He and his father did not get along well, and the tale of his adolescence between the ages of eleven and nineteen, when he finally left Paris for his *tour de France*, is marked by his back-and-forth moves between his father's household, his grandmother's, and the streets.

Agricol Perdiguier and his siblings worked both on his father's farm and in his woodworking shop during his childhood in southern France just after the Napoleonic era. At adolescence the children's contributions became more differentiated and specialized. Perdiguier recalled that his parents were easier on his two younger sisters because by the time they reached their teens the family already had several earners. The girls had learned how to weave and, while still living at home, were nevertheless allowed to weave "for their own profit." The older sons were under more pressure. Their father wanted one of his three sons to take over the carpentry business. Agricol and his brother Simon both wanted to farm, but his father forced Agricol to apprentice at the age of thirteen or fourteen. He left home at sixteen to continue his apprenticeship in Avignon; his *tour de France* would follow three years later.

As part of a family that made its livelihood from work on a small plot and hiring themselves out as farmhands, Élise Blanc found her occupational fate established as a matter of course by family strategies. At the age of seventeen, she was hired as chambermaid by the marquise on whose lands her family lived. She recalled that giving her up to this position "was a great sacrifice, given the amount of work we had to do at home, that my parents made so as not to disoblige the master." She wasn't well paid and had to spend part of the year with her mistress in Paris, but her parents could hardly object: they depended on these same employers for their modest salary (in addition to their cottage and plot), and they had to worry about their good relations with their employers.

All of these stories were shaped by a framework in which the household was still the effective productive unit. The reorganization of the family economy in the face of the changes brought by industrialization had important consequences for the nature of adolescent employment. Apprenticeship evolved into what was often no more than a system of cheap labor for employers who had neither the intention nor the power to set up young people for a solid future as artisans. The family itself was less likely to be the source of the shop or business or farm that would represent their children's economic future. But one thing remained true: parents relied on the economic contribution of adolescent children, especially those who came of age first and especially in the poorest families. This often translated into occupational choices in the early teen years that hinged more on immediate earnings than on the promise of some particular future occupation. From the point of view of adolescent workers, this choice seemed to betray their ambitions and talents for the sake of the family. And the depiction of occupational choice is, in the vast majority of memoirs, seen more as the result of family pressure than of individual volition or preference.

Occasionally, stories depict negotiated arrangements that took the adolescent's aptitudes and desires into account. August Batard's father went to the schoolteacher and asked him for advice about his son's aptitudes. The teacher "advised my father to have me learn the printing trade, or that of the mechanic. I could be placed immediately since requests for apprentices had already come through to him. My father agreed." He interviewed for two positions, but before he heard the results of his application, a saddle maker in his father's cafe raised the possibility of a future in that craft. The man was persuasive, and August "agreed to apprentice in this trade and dropped the idea of printing and mechanics" (12–13).

August's apprenticeship was to last three years. His father paid the master three hundred francs. Batard remarked, "In those bygone days, parents paid for the apprenticeship of their children." He completed his

apprenticeship on schedule at age sixteen and left for his *tour de France.*
He had a suitcase and a case for his tools; his mother provided everything
else he needed, and he left with fond good-byes from his parents and his
sisters (12–17).

Batard offered an account from the 1880s of an ideal apprenticeship — "the way it was supposed to be" in the popular milieux of respectable artisans in the nineteenth century. But few of the autobiographers
followed this model of entering the workforce. First of all, despite what
Batard recalled as normative, what was called "apprenticeship" could
cover a wide range of adolescent employment situations. Joseph Voisin's
experience was quite different. He was born about ten years before
Batard, in 1858, and was put to work in the fields full-time at age nine. On
his own volition, because he had "bigger ideas," he apprenticed himself
at age twelve to a manufacturer of cognac cases. His apprenticeship
lasted two months, after which period he began to earn sixteen *centimes* a
day for each box (which meant, he figured, that he needed to make
fifteen a day to earn acceptable pay.) That would have been a good
arrangement for someone of his age, but just at this moment his mother
died, the household broke up, and he had to live on his own. He had
trouble making ends meet under the new circumstances. Eventually, he
followed the advice of some coworkers who told him to learn a real trade;
an uncle helped him to arrange a free six-month apprenticeship, at age
fourteen, with a carpenter. He did not get what he was expecting: "After
having had two years of complete freedom," he wrote, "I entered hell."
He was exploited by the master and tormented by the journeymen at his
new shop. After six months, he "knew nothing more than on the first day,
not even the names of the tools." At age fifteen, he took off on his *tour de
France* (3–5).

This more informal situation, where adolescents exchanged their labor without an enforceable contract and generally without the payment
of an apprenticeship fee, was far more typical of accounts than Batard's
story. Heinrich Lange, who knew he could not become a teacher, would
have settled for continuing as a shepherd, but his father wanted him "to
be able to eat his bread indoors" and thought he should learn a trade.
They found a turner in Wittingen who would take him on for four years
without any payment as "apprenticeship fees could not be paid" (36).
Similarly, when the author of *Erinnerungen eines Waisenknaben* came of
age, he would have liked to continue with his studies, but his mother's
main concern was to find a master who would take full charge of him and
not require any fees or living costs; the trade was irrelevant. He was

apprenticed to an engraver who took over his meal costs; he only had to sleep at home, an arrangement to which his mother agreed.

Few autobiographers recalled parents leaving them much discretion in their choice of work. Carl Fischer remembered that he would have liked to have been a gardener — really anything but a baker like his father, but no one asked what he wanted. After his confirmation, he was sent off to be an errand boy in a factory owned by an uncle. He was badly treated there and, despite his rocky relation with his father, ended up coming back to apprentice with him until age eighteen. Apparently even as an apprentice for his father he served primarily as unskilled labor, because when he was given the traditional journeyman's test before being allowed to depart on his journeyman's tour in 1859 he did not even know how to tell when bread was done (120). The guild gave him a certificate anyway, he reported, out of deference to his father.

In later stories of boys' entry into the workforce, even informal apprenticeship disappears, for some because the crafts no longer offered the best jobs for workers. Once his taste for higher learning was dampened by his experience in the *Selekta* class, might Wilhelm Kaisen might have expected to follow in his father's footsteps and become a mason. But his father had recently made the move from that craft into a nearby soap factory. Even though wages were lower than what he had made as a skilled worker, they were secure, and he had less worry about seasonal unemployment. So when he was let out of school, Wilhelm entered the same factory as his father, as an unskilled worker.

For boys in the poorest families — where parents were poor farm laborers, or where there was no father — apprenticeship was simply out of the question: earnings were needed immediately. Families of such rural laborers as Max Hoelz and Georges Dumoulin lived in a poverty that seemed to preclude planning for the future. Max Hoelz wanted to be a locksmith, but, with no money for apprenticeship or clothes, he went to work as a farmhand at age fourteen. Despite his success in school, Georges Dumoulin entered a beet sugar factory at the age of age twelve by lying and saying he was thirteen.

Autobiographers who had mothers who were single, widowed, or married to men who were ill, unemployed, or unreliable providers recalled them as desperate for their children to become independent earners. Fritz Rehbein accompanied his mother to a summer job on a rye plantation and just stayed on, even beyond the beginning of the school year. He finally had to return home to finish out his obligatory time, but he began full-time work on the large farms of northern Germany immediately after his confirmation (59). Lucien Bourgeois dated the end of his happiness to the moment of his father's death. A failed effort to solve the family's problems through remarriage left no other choice to Lucien's mother but to put him to work at fourteen; he and his mother both went to work in the lamp factory (15). Nikolaus Osterroth's pious mother had intended him for the priesthood, but fate intervened: "All the big plans they had for me all fell apart as the day of school-leaving approached. Father got sick again and often we didn't even have enough bread in the house." So two days after leaving school, his father took him to a nearby village to start work in the brickworks there alongside sixty adult and four hundred other child workers. Because he was only thirteen, he remembered, he could only be hired to work for six hours a day at fifty pfennigs. Finally, Karl Grünberg, whose father had died when he was a schoolboy, saw his older sisters condemned to two and a half years of the "household slavery" of domestic service before they were old enough to get factory jobs at age sixteen. He himself took the various "boy's jobs" that the city of Berlin offered the poor and desperate — errand boy, delivery boy, office boy, what he termed "white-collar proletarian" positions (40). He would have loved to improve himself, to learn a handicraft, but his mother couldn't afford it. The free apprenticeships he tried turned out to be simple exploitation, and so he drifted, in his teen years, from one job to another.

Karl Grünberg's sisters' experiences were typical of the even harder time faced by adolescent girls confronting the job market. If men recalled themselves having been detoured from a preferred vocational path because of family needs, women recalled their paths to occupation to have been completely unmarked. Charlotte Davy had it better than most of the women autobiographers. Her widowed father had a reasonably secure job, and she was an only child, so she was not under tremendous pressure to start to work. But just what to do troubled her. "My aunt would often say to me: 'Well, you're grown-up now. What are you planning to do?' . . . In truth, I had no idea. No work appealed to me. What I would have wanted was to be able to live as I liked, to run in the meadows, gather flowers, read in the shade of large trees" (21). She attended an additional year of school, after completing the elementary curriculum; then, with no other ideas for her future, she went to live with the aunt she didn't like very well to apprentice as a seamstress. Davy was one of the few female autobiographers to describe a period of formal apprenticeship. The others who also did — Suzanne Voilquin, Amalie Poelzer, and Betti Huber — all worked, like Davy, as seamstresses.

Otherwise, the women autobiographers recalled drifting or being pushed toward one of only two other choices seemingly open to working-class adolescent girls at school-leaving — domestic service or the factory. Marie Wegrainer went into service at age fourteen in Munich. Her mother wouldn't allow her foster mother to apprentice her: "She's cost me a black dress for the confirmation already and that's enough. I cannot afford to have her not working" (12). Marie Sans Gène kept her position as a milk delivery girl for a year after her confirmation. Then she took up the first of many positions she would hold as a housemaid. The only interruption of this career in domestic service came when she found work as a porter in the grain port of Danzig, work that she liked and for which she was relatively well paid, but it was ultimately too taxing on her health.

Both the author of *Dulden* and Marie Beutelmeyer took their first factory jobs at age thirteen or fourteen. The career of the author of *Im Kampf ums Dasein* spanned the limited range of girls' jobs available. Once she had had her fill of gluing bags at home, it was "out into the world" after her confirmation (48). Her first jobs were in service, but conditions were very hard, so she looked for factory work. She held a series of these positions — in a hat factory, a cigar factory, a paper factory, a fish-smoking house — but they all struck her as too difficult or else exposed her to harassment (75). She went then to a middlewoman, a kind of employment agent, who found her her first place in the relatively new and not fully respectable occupation: she became a waitress.

These authors reported their work as adolescent girls as what they drifted into through necessity and as a matter of course. For many other women autobiographers, however, the accounts of work at this point are framed by a context of family emergency — not something predictable, in other words, but a momentary expedient. Finding an occupation does not appear as a patterned or planned aspect of the female life course. In particular, decisions to go to work were often connected with allusions to the absence or disability of a male wage earner. Women remembered going to work, or to work at jobs they might not have otherwise considered, or to work that under other circumstances would not have been quite respectable, because of extraordinary circumstance.

Aurelia Roth related her father's anger at his reliance on his children's earnings, but his alcoholism and eventual early death left Aurelia's mother with no other choice. Aurelia herself was at work full time from age fourteen on. Anneliese Rüegg's mother was proud to be able to make it on her own after her husband's death. She anticipated hopefully the time when she could send two of her children into the factory. But Anneliese didn't look forward to arriving at her "machine age. On the contrary, I had a vague fear of it. I was also proud and didn't want to become a factory girl. Because I knew that factory workers weren't worth much and were suspect in many people's minds. When I asked my mother if I couldn't rather learn a trade, she answered that it cost too much money and took too long before I would be able to earn anything. So on my fourteenth birthday, I stood behind two big spinning machines" (23).

Marie Sponer's father's illness had forced his daughter into the factory at age thirteen. He always insisted that she would "never work at a carding machine; I would never have any peace then." He was unaware, Sponer added, that the machine she worked at was really "a man's machine" and just as dangerous. Had he known, she felt that "despite our misery, he wouldn't have let me stay there" (140). Verena Conzett's trajectory as an adolescent illustrates how much a fate could be tied to the very particular circumstances of the family during these critical years. The family was relatively comfortable when her father was promoted to a position as a factory foreman. Verena's older sisters were also working and the family even moved to a large sunny dwelling. But when Verena was twelve her father went blind. The family moved to a cheaper house, and Verena took a job in a wool factory (51–54). She was soon laid off and had to lie about her age to get a job in the nearby silk spinnery in which, her father had once vowed, "as long as I live no child of mine will ever work." She would have loved to become a seamstress, but the two-year apprenticeship was too long when the family needed her wages.

These stories all suggest a certain contingency that governed occupational choice in early adolescence. For boys, fate often intervened in plans. For girls especially, there seems to have been little conscious planning, little ability to imagine occupational futures. (Indeed, Madeleine Henrey's story offers one of the rare examples of a recreated female adolescent's thought about her future—she recalled imagining herself as a writer.) Even if accustomed paths were changing for boys, there seemed to have been no well-worn female paths to occupational futures. Most available forms of employment seemed suspect, despite the fact that in the overwhelming majority of these families mothers earned money upon which their families relied. The family's situation would have mattered in terms of the kinds of employment that were considered—girls went into factory jobs, or at least *certain kinds* of factory jobs, at the risk of becoming "suspect." Certainly apprenticeship was a preferable route, but it was available only to those who could spare the years and costs it entailed. Domestic service lay somewhere in between; the girl was respectably employed and taken care of, however minimally, but her wages would hardly approach what factory labor would bring. All of the women did work, but they drifted into it without much consideration, on their part or on the part of their parents, of options for the long term.[4]

For the male autobiographers, the rules were not always clear or possible to follow. Certainly, more options were imaginable, and the stories were informed by a sense that planning was appropriate. But here again, the particular circumstances of the family during a son's early adolescence were often determinant. If his father was already dead, or disabled, there was pressure to opt for immediate earnings rather than the longer-run strategy of apprenticeship. Sons' occupational futures were supposedly the subject of planning, but in practice such planning appeared as a luxury that many working-class families could ill afford. As they appear in the memoirs, boys at least had an image of their occupational future against which to measure what actually happened to them, although this model became muddier as the century progressed. But for girls even the model was elusive. And in all cases, the aptitudes and desires of the children figured little into the calculations surrounding job placement.

Taking Charge?

Despite their recollections that family situation and parental decisions largely determined their occupational choices, the autobiographers nevertheless saw themselves as increasingly powerful negotiators within the family once they were full-time wage earners. They moved from, as they saw it, "unearning eaters" to contributors. It is also frequently at this moment in the stories that workers took a decisive turn toward more active self-determination. The authors typically remembered being proud of their substantial contributions to the family, aware of their right to claim some of their earnings for personal expenses, and conscious of their power both with respect to their parents and, to a limited extent, their life courses.

Sebastien Commissaire documented this transformation in his own adolescence. When he was about twelve, he began to care full time for his two younger siblings while his parents wove in their home shop. A year later his parents set him up at his own loom. From his earnings, about five francs a day, they returned two *sous* each Sunday so he could enjoy himself with friends who lived across town. He found out, though, that his older half-siblings worked on a quota arrangement. Once they had exceeded their daily quota, they could keep anything earned in excess. He calculated that if he switched to such an arrangement, his father would owe him seventeen francs. When confronted with Sebastien's calculations, his father replied that he should add up how much he had cost his father at fifty *centimes* a day for thirteen years. "Once you have paid me back, I'll pay you your amount above quota," he told Sebastien (65).

Within a year, however, the family had broken up. Sebastien's father left and sold the looms. The older half-siblings left as well, leaving only Sebastien, his mother, and two younger children in the household. Commissaire recalled being tremendously affected by the whole event: "I cried a lot when I was alone. I did my best not to aggravate my mother's sorrow; nevertheless, I became very serious, I lost a part of my gaiety. . . . A revolution transpired within me in a very short space of time. I stopped playing like other children or young people of this age; I became a man. . . . I exercised a lot of influence over [my mother]. She didn't do anything without consulting me. . . . Thanks to our hard work, my mother's and mine, we were soon able to repay the debts my father left . . . my mother happily gave me a franc every Sunday instead of the two *sous* my father used to let me have" (65–69).

After Verena Conzett was forced to go to work full time, she remembered mainly her pride at helping the family in its distress: "How happy I was, as I came home with my first pay packet! Proudly I laid in my mother's hands the first money I earned on my own" (54). Adelheid Popp recalled her pride at earning enough to dress so as not to be recognized as a factory worker and also to make it possible for her mother "no longer to go out to work; she earned a bit at home and also took care of the household. We now lived in a room with two windows and my youngest brother had moved back in with us" (43).

Madeleine Henrey reconstructed the bittersweet quality of the role reversal that began at the point when an adolescent child took a more active role in the family:

> I was in my fifteenth year. . . . At the end of the month, I brought home one hundred francs, and I once again witnessed my father in his more touching moments. He cried with happiness, saying that we were as lucky as millionaires. A few days later in the tombola, I won a very large coffee-pot . . .
>
> To celebrate the event we shuffled the cards for bezique. . . . My

mother played cards indifferently, and she and I nearly always lost, but later in the evening I improved so much that I beat my father, and he said:

"It's funny the way one's children always catch up with one, and then seem to do better; but what good does it do them? In the end they come back to where their parents left off."

"You're not where *your* parents left off!" cut in my mother bitterly. "At least *they* had a house of their own, whilst we are still in this miserable lodging!"

My father, the joy driven out of him, shook his head and went off to undress. Our evening ended sadly, and the disenchantment that never left my mother enveloped us like a damp fog (220–21).

At this age, the position of these writers in the family clearly shifted. It was not exactly a matter of independence or autonomy; for girls, certainly, either would have been difficult to imagine if not precisely unthinkable.[5] (Among the women autobiographers, only Charlotte Davy attempted to leave home and support herself independently of her father and stepmother, an attempt that ultimately failed.) Some girls did leave home but usually to go into domestic service, and they maintained economic and emotional connections with home. In her passing use of the term "independence," Amalie Poelzer put it in a different context. She used it to refer to her employment situation — she was able to set herself up to work as an "independent" seamstress rather than in a shop or factory.[6]

For boys, if there was less attachment out of necessity to the family, there was also little talk of independence from it. Male authors, especially in Central Europe, often recalled leaving home in early adolescence for work or apprenticeship. This literal distancing from their families was important for the development of gender-specific notions of political identity and family responsibility. It also of course fed into changing but continually gender-specific patterns of youth sociability.[7] But in the men's memoirs as in the women's, there is little rhetorical association between economic *independence* and dawning adulthood, even if an increasing capacity to contribute was central to adolescent self-image and to the negotiation of a stronger position within the family. In these memoirs there is little reference to the "male breadwinner" model that came to dominate the rhetoric of working-class masculinity by the late nineteenth century in England. These mens' stories are, instead, populated by wage-earning mothers, sisters, and wives.

These accounts of coming-of-age also suggest the significance of the early teen years for the paths that workers ultimately followed. Over and over again, they tell of how fleeting moments of opportunity could be, how quickly family needs or changing circumstances could intervene in a promising but distant future, how easy it was to become discouraged or sidetracked from even well-laid plans, and how easy it was just to drift into a future. From these stories, in fact, it appears that hypothetical opportunities were indeed visible to many of these talented working-class children as adolescents. Both men and women reported sensing educational possibilities nevertheless out of their reach. Men also could remember imagining alternative occupational futures. But rarely were they immediately actualized. In accounting for missed opportunities, authors laid blame as much outside the schools as in them — in the demands of the family economy, in the absence of the material and psychological support that was needed to keep on. The stories of this moment in life record opportunities close enough to be seen but in the end ungraspable. Those who did manage to follow a different path than the one laid out by fate, or parents, did so later in life and as a result of extraordinary means — self-education, workers' evening schools, or the unexpected intervention of a better-off relative.

Moreover, despite the stark national differences in pedagogic practice and in the political culture surrounding elementary education, the stories about after-school trajectories revealed in the autobiographies are not that different. In neither French nor German autobiographical plots did schools have a direct impact upon opportunities available at school-leaving. In both regions, the demands of the family economy and the contingencies of parental longevity or birth order were in the end compelling.

Gender differences did, however, become more emphatic. If in early childhood memories the narratives of men and women are hard to differentiate, distinctions did emerge by the time the school stories were told, especially in the German accounts. In episodes of coming-of-age, important gender distinctions appear across the national divide. If memories of male and female adolescence shared a new concern for appearance to the "outside" world and new sensitivity to the slights of poverty, other aspects of memories of this phase of life are strikingly different. Both boys and girls recalled having been talented pupils, but women's memories of having to leave school because of poverty rarely reveal the level of anger recalled by men such as Bürgel, Dumoulin, or Guehenno. However much they had been encouraged in school, scholarly encouragement did not seem to hold for girls clear promises about the future against which to measure their eventual destiny. Gender differences in accounts of entering the full-time workforce only reinforce this impression. Because the "rules" of getting set up seemed clearer to boys, they knew more certainly when their fate failed to measure up. Girls seem to have been deprived not only of a fair chance of entering a good occupation but even of ways of imagining what that future might look like.

Men and women seem to have held similar expectations for childhood; at least they described their deprivations in relatively similar terms. But accounts of adolescence do not show this similarity. Men at least knew what had gone wrong; women had a hard time articulating an alternative to what had happened to them. Still, this moment of school-leaving and entry into the workforce, even with the disappointments it often brought, was portrayed as a moment around which thoughts about one's fate crystallized. Few autobiographers let it pass without comment. Many, especially boys, remembered this time of coming-of-age as the moment in life when questioning destiny consciously began.

I told myself that they pulled me from the wilds of the forest and sent me to Pont à Mousson

to study there and acquire science and enlightenment, and not at all to fall in love and

become a fop. (Valentin Jamerey-Duval, 397)

SIX

SEX AND DESTINY

Jamerey-Duval chose to renounce sexual involvement with women in a determined strategy to make something of himself. He fell madly in love with a bourgeois woman during his teens but renounced her, and love; he declared, "The least inclination to passion such as that gripping me was certain to be absolutely useless to me and indeed harmful and prejudicial" (397). According to notes accompanying his life story, Jamerey-

Duval whipped and finally poisoned his body into submission by using a hemlock formula he read of in Descartes.

Sexuality, whatever else it is and does, marks social boundaries and helps to comprise class identity. Sexual comportment, especially for women, serves as a key mark of distinction between respectable individuals and the "others." That the realm of human sexuality was of particular concern to the European middle classes in the nineteenth century is not news. Norms about the relationship between love and marriage were changing. The emergence in bourgeois milieux in the eighteenth century of companionate marriages and the romanticization of love within marriage, along with new codes of sexual propriety, made older sexual practices such as premarital intercourse or the blatant presence of prostitutes in particular urban districts increasingly problematic in respectable circles.

More deeply, historians have argued, new notions of sexuality were essential to formulations of bourgeois individualism. They also formed the basis of middle-class challenges to aristocratic decadence, on the one hand, and to lower-class profligacy, on the other.[1] Medical professionals, sexual hygienists, psychologists, and sex reformers often addressed the sexual problems of adolescence in particular. Studies of the newly discovered male adolescent personality often emphasized the frustration of "normal" sexual development in the conditions of late nineteenth-century life.[2] Medical and psychological concern often centered on the educated classes, for it was their sons who populated the schools and universities and often waited until their early thirties to establish themselves, their daughters whose innocence, health, and capacity for motherhood needed protection. The presumption in the writings of the new group of experts on human sexuality was that among the lower classes such problems were nonexistent because early marriage or the various forms of illicit union typical among the proletariat permitted the "natural" expression of sexual urges.

Class Relations and the Naturalization
of Lower-Class Sexuality

Ironically, subsequent historical examinations of the subject have reiterated this tendency to naturalize proletarian sexuality. In their efforts to unmask the bourgeois prejudices at work in contemporary condemnations of lower-class mores, historians of the working class have sometimes implied that workers' sexual attitudes and practices were simply more natural or emancipated than those of the neurotic middle classes.[3] Carolyn Steedman has suggested further that such naturalization too often has resulted, in analyses of working-class life and history, in a complete denial of the psychological.[4]

The autobiographical accounts of sexual coming-of-age tell a different story. They make clear that workers, too, were constructing their sexual identities in the face of particular economic, psychological, cultural, and political constraints. Most of their accounts indeed report the earlier proletarian initiation into heterosexual activity that other sources suggest. But autobiographical accounts of sexual adventures are embedded in narratives in which sexual personae are intertwined with other components of social identity. The links between sex and social identity were not generally the same for workers as they were for their class superiors, but they were equally problematic.

Discussion of sexual activity was far less taboo in workers' autobiographies than it was in contemporaneous literary or upper-class memoirs. The majority, though not all, of French and German workers who wrote their memoirs saw fit to include allusions to or accounts of sexual experience, some quite explicit. The inclusion or exclusion of such episodes served a variety of specifiable ends in a life story and followed era- and milieu-specific norms about the propriety of open discussion of sexual matters. The few workers' autobiographies dating from the eighteenth century do suggest the possibility at that time of fairly open discussion of sexual matters in personal narrative forms that included jokes and picaresque fiction as well as autobiographies. In the late nineteenth and early twentieth centuries, when many accounts of nineteenth-century lives were published, sexuality was once again an appropriate subject for discussion. In the interim, however, especially in artisan memoirs, allusions to sexual activity were more likely to be indirect or discreet. Moreover, region and milieu shaped the stories told: peasants, artisans, and both protoindustrial and factory proletarians faced different sets of constraints and followed different norms about disclosure. Not surprisingly, men and women also told different kinds of stories about themselves; men's stories, moreover, display a great deal more variation. Men seemingly could imagine or describe themselves in a greater variety of sexual roles than could women, and their poses showed a more distinct variation over time. Finally, not only the social origins but also the social trajectories of individual autobiographers shaped the telling of their sexual experiences. Norms about sexual propriety were an important component of the process of becoming a particular type of adult, and stories that recounted different trajectories (success stories and militants' memoirs in particular) also varied both in their authors' willingness to talk about sexual experiences and in the content of the stories told.

Autobiographical testimony cannot, of course, be taken as proof of lower-class sexual behavior, but the various contours of sexual identity and perceived linkages between sexual and other dimensions of identity can be inferred from it. In these narratives, descriptions of sexual encounter and identity clustered into several typologies — self-portraits as rakes, reminiscent of picaresque portrayals of sexual encounters; subjective accounts of proletarian concubinage (or extramarital sexual unions); and images of sexual restraint in militants' or in success stories. The ability to categorize these accounts reveals patterned variations in stories of sexual awakening and initiation into sexual practice. These types also reflect chronological, regional, socioeconomic, and gender variation. The stories, in other words, help place lower-class sexual attitudes and practices more squarely in their historical context.

The Bad Conscience of the Picaresque Hero

Two eighteenth-century autobiographies, those of Jacques-Louis Ménétra and Ulrich Bräker, invoke the world of male sexual development in popular preindustrial milieux. Ménétra was a product of the Parisian plebeian culture that was, according to Robert Darnton, still "essentially Rabelaisian."[5] His life story reads like a picaresque novel; sexual exploits fill many of its pages. Still, through his narrative, Ménétra documented the tension between love and pragmatism characteristic of a popular culture in which men at least were free to pursue love intrigues but where marriages had to reflect practical considerations emerging from the nature of the family economy. Ménétra claimed many, and indeed many casual, sexual involvements, alongside a few more enduring relationships. His first encounter was a vague memory sandwiched between other more momentous markers of youth. He was vague about the timing of his sexual initiation, but it must have occurred between the time he received his First Communion, around the age of twelve, and the time he left Paris at age eighteen. In that interim, a maid who worked for his female employer, apparently with the encouragement of this employer, "received his first blushes." This encounter led to other relationships, including one with a prostitute who, he wrote, "became one of my closest friends" (26). Ménétra went on to claim more than fifty seductions before the practical marriage he negotiated at age twenty-six, in addition to liaisons with prostitutes. Even if an unspecifiable number of these conquests were, following storytelling conventions of this era, meant to be understood as sheer yarns, Ménétra's stories were a far cry from the young adulthoods portrayed in memoirs of the early nineteenth century.

Ulrich Bräker told a somewhat different story, but he lived in a world recognizable to Ménétra. Bräker emerged from the milieu of rural industry. His family made their living through a combination of weaving, farming, and herding. His Pietist orientation and deep concern for religious questions even as a youth invested his narrative with a sense of scruples that only occasionally surfaced in Ménétra's.

Ulrich's youthful innocence was undermined by his association as a goatherd with older goatboys whose "wicked passions" had already been aroused. "Their whole talk consisted of dirty jokes, and their songs were all filthy. . . . They had a job of persuading me to bathe in the nude like themselves . . . I no longer enjoyed my former gaiety and peace of mind. The ruffians had aroused passions in me which I hadn't known before in myself—and yet I realized there was something wrong somewhere" (73–74).

Like Jacques-Louis Ménétra, Ulrich faced the frustration of having to repress love in favor of practicality in choosing a wife. Like Ménétra, too, he recognized and maintained a distinction between sexual love and marital relations. Bräker traveled widely in his youth, having left his village at age twenty in the hopes of making his fortune. He recalled telling his sweetheart Annie that "marriage is at the moment quite out of the question. I'm still too young; you're even younger, and neither of us has a bean . . . we'd end up a right pair of tramps" (100). Subsequent romantic encounters punctuate his travel narrative, although he claimed to have maintained his technical "innocence" into his early twenties. When he eventually married at age twenty-six, he confessed, "It was really political motives which drew me to my wife . . . I've never felt that tender inclination towards her, generally termed love" even if she was "by far the most suitable" match for him (156).

Thus even men who led active premarital sexual lives linked the narration of a sexual persona with contradictory moral and economic choices particular to their culture. If Ménétra resolved this tension by becoming an unrepentant rake, he nevertheless suggested that he paid in many ways (physically and emotionally) for his sensuality; for Bräker, control over this sensuality before and even after a loveless marriage was a source of considerable anxiety and anguish (here his literary debt to Rousseau is evident). For both, the struggle between passion and practicality was a leitmotif in the story of adolescence as it was experienced under the constraints of the lower-class family economy of the preindustrial era.

The constraints Ménétra and Bräker faced were not peculiar to them. Certainly, sexual norms had long been bound up with peasant and artisanal regulation of marriage. Tight patriarchal controls over marriage and female sexuality characterized most popular milieux in the early modern era, especially when the intergenerational transmission of property was involved. Guild customs throughout Europe rested upon notions of honor that had important sexual dimensions. Most guilds, for example, banned illegitimate children from membership and even restricted the choice of spouses for members and their children, although male sexual activity outside of marriage was not necessarily subject to control. Indeed, connections with prostitutes seem to have been taken for granted during the apprentice and journeymen phases, both carrying implicit proscriptions against marriage. Among peasants, even where premarital intercourse was common practice, sexual encounters occurred within the confines of community controls. Normally, sanctioned intercourse was confined to couples who were appropriate matches and were presumed to be engaged. Bräker's testimony suggests that such restrictions could even pertain in more modest circles, where very little property indeed was brought into the marriage, although he hinted as well of less confining practices that would come to be associated with protoindustrial and later urban proletarian sexuality.[6]

Although both of these early male autobiographies are peopled with compliant women, no contemporaneous woman's narrative with a corresponding heroine is known to exist. Such women may indeed have existed outside of masculine memory, but, if they did, they evidently did not write autobiographies. The earliest account I know from a woman "of the people" — that of Suzanne Voilquin (b. 1801) — dates somewhat later — and tells a markedly different story. Voilquin, the daughter of a Parisian hatmaker, described her first intercourse as rape by her fiancé when she was twenty-one. The rape traumatized her at the time — "in the days that followed, [my fiancé] dried my tears with his kisses and calmed my conscience with the promise to marry me as soon as possible" (84) — a promise he failed to keep. It also resurfaced later as a key moment in her evolving sensitivity to male injustice. She feared to tell her eventual husband (whom she later married "*freely* but without love") about the rape. However, when both joined the Saint-Simonien movement, she decided to make a clean slate of it. After she "confessed" to the Père, he saw fit to comfort her husband (who had in the interim given her venereal disease) instead of her, leaving Suzanne with a bitter experience of "the iniquitous dispensing of male justice" (114–15).

Early nineteenth-century accounts testify to the persistence of arranged, pragmatic unions in the propertied sectors of the lower classes, both artisanal and peasant. In contrast with these three early accounts, however, later ones generally maintained a silence or discretion about personal sexual experiences or described them in terms that suggest an abandonment of the picaresque braggadocio now relegated to the realm of "tradition." Martin Nadaud, who migrated seasonally between the small peasant farm of the Creuse in southeastern France and the building trades of Paris, recounted a world quite unlike Ménétra's. He confined discussion of sexual experience to the account of his marriage. Nadaud reported his family's negotiations with three prospective brides before a satisfactory arrangement was made. His shyness in the encounter with his prospective bride and her silence marked their first meeting as future spouses; still, "having asked to kiss her, this authorization was nevertheless granted" (210). Some historians attribute such sexual reticence to supposedly "traditional" practices of propertied peasants, but Nadaud saw it differently—as something relatively new.[7] Nadaud's account of his wedding marked explicitly the chronological and cultural distance he felt his society had traveled from an earlier sexual world: "A custom which is nearly lost and scarcely to be regretted is the strange ceremony of the chicken. Two hours after the married couple is in bed, their room is invaded by a crowd of young lads and girls who start out by offering a chicken thigh and a salad bowl filled with cold wine. You exchange handshakes, and, one after another, the young girls kiss the bride who stays seated in bed; the whole crowd sings the song of the newlyweds. Its wording is so singularly improper that you'd think you were still in the era of Rabelais, when they'd call a spade a spade" (215).

Other autobiographers of peasant and artisanal origins who were born in the early nineteenth century shared this delicacy. Victorine Brocher, the daughter of a shoemaker of bourgeois origins, recalled her arranged marriage without comment. "They married me off at Orleans on May 13, 1861" (61). She revealed nothing of her own sexual experience. After conflicts with his mother and stepfather, Jean-Baptiste Dumay left home on a sort of *tour de France* during which he had "amorous adventures like those of all youth of this age, but which [didn't] have anything to do with my story" (91). The male autobiographers of artisan or peasant origins born in the early nineteenth century—Agricol Perdiguier, Eugene Courmeaux, Sebastien Commissaire, Frederic Mistral, Christian Döbel, Karl

Fischer — were reticent about their personal sexual development, although Commissaire and Courmeaux used sexual motifs as devices in their narratives of childhood "innocence."

Proletarian Insouciance

Other sexual mores may well have predominated in the culture of propertyless popular milieux. Recent studies of different propertyless groups, ranging from northern French putting-out workers to servant maids in Austria and cottagers in Bavaria, document the apparent frequency of extramarital heterosexual liaisons and the flouting of norms of respectability that predominated among the propertied.[8] But rare are the sources that allow historians to examine these purportedly insouciant proletarian unions from the inside — that is, from the perspective of the individuals involved. I have found no autobiographical accounts from these milieux until the great wave of proletarian autobiographies that began to appear in increasing numbers toward the end of the nineteenth century. In autobiographies emerging from the fully formed rural and urban proletarian subcultures of the later nineteenth century, the character of sexual episodes indeed departed from both contemporaneous middle-class practices and from those rooted in the artisanal petite bourgeoisie and propertied peasantry.

These accounts describe as typical the early entry of proletarian adolescents into nonmarital unions. Some of these unions culminated in marriage, but many did not. Quite a few lower-class autobiographers, particularly among those born after the middle of the nineteenth century, described themselves entering into or having been conceived in such unions. Robert Köhler, Marie Wegrainer, the anonymous author of *Im Kampf ums Dasein*, Lena Christ, Fritz Pauk, and Angelina Bardin were the children of mothers who never married their fathers. Marie Wegrainer, Franz Bergg, Moritz Bromme, and Georges Dumoulin told of common-law relationships. With the exception of Dumoulin's narrative, however, the accounts of these unions reveal anything but a casual attitude toward sex.

In the women's stories, illicit relationships were always viewed as problematic.[9] For Angelina Bardin, the anguish brought on by her unknown mother's abandonment of her at birth punctuates her story. Marie Wegrainer's relationships with her mother, stepfather, husband, and children were by her account soured in negotiations over sexual respectability. Her mother did not marry until Marie was fifteen, and she did not marry Marie's father. She and her mother battled constantly over Marie's developing relationships with men, liaisons Wegrainer recounted as quite proper. Her situation at home became less and less tolerable to her until she left at age fifteen in the aftermath of an attempted sexual assault by her stepfather. Marie herself entered into a common-law relationship and bore a son at age twenty, five years before her marriage. In her autobiographical account, Wegrainer falsely claimed that this son died, presumably in the hopes of sparing him embarrassment.[10]

Lena Christ's mother was a rural Bavarian servant maid who left her illegitimate daughter with her parents and went to Munich to work. Her mother eventually did marry, though not Lena's father, and relations between Christ and her mother (who, Christ claimed, "had never loved her") deteriorated after the marriage and especially after the birth of a legitimate half-brother. Once again, tensions came to a head around Lena's sexual awakening: during her early adolescence her mother's mistreatment turned to downright abuse. When a confessor's inquiries and subsequent discussions among Lena's schoolmates brought to light the children's sexual explorations, the principal informed her mother. As a punishment, Christ recalled, her mother commanded her to undress and kneel down while she hit and kicked Lena in the breast and in "the parts of her body with which she had sinned. I screamed loud for help but she stopped my mouth with a cloth and continued to beat me." The stepfather was also called in to beat her. Finally, she was rescued by her neighbors and sent back to live with her grandfather in the country.

The anonymous author of *Im Kampf ums Dasein* provided another complex narrative of illicit sexuality. She, too, was the child of a common-law union. Her mother bore three children and was initially prevented from marrying her sweetheart by her parents, who opposed the union. The eventual marriage occurred in anger, for the father had already taken up another mistress. The autobiographer herself revealed many unresolved anxieties about sexual propriety in her own life. She seems to have drawn a line between respectable and promiscuous sexual encounters, but, once again, the effort to discover that line and place her life on the right side of it structured much of her narrative of coming-of-age.

These women authors did not all treat their sexual identity in the same way, but none viewed proletarian concubinage casually or as unproblematic for young women. Christ and Wegrainer both portrayed women and their illegitimate children as victims of these types of unions and described their own period of sexual awakening as troubled by conflicts over appropriate sexual behavior. If the author of *Im Kampf ums Dasein* took a more pragmatic view of her sexual powers, she was nevertheless concerned to defend her own virtue and distinguish her limited promiscuity from the easier virtue of the prostitutes with whom she mingled. She developed a refined system of gradations of social and sexual propriety. All of these women placed great narrative emphasis on the sexual decisions (their own and those of their parents) that they saw as having had a profound effect on their life course.

Three male autobiographers who described entering nonmarital sexual unions did so in somewhat different terms. Georges Dumoulin's narrative provides some confirmation of the casual concubinage some historians argue was at the center of proletarian sexual behavior. He briefly mentioned moving in with a woman when he was in his late twenties and fathering a child when he was twenty-seven. He considered and then rejected the idea of marriage. The other two male accounts tell more ambiguous and complicated stories. Moritz Bromme described how he "got himself a 'bride'" when he was about twenty. Moritz had met an "honorable *Bürgerstochter*" at a dance; when she refused to go home with him because he played cards, he went home with a poor girl and before long "was going with her." Up to this point in his life (around age eighteen or nineteen), Bromme recalled, his relations with women had always been "harmless and completely virtuous." Eventually, relations between his new girlfriend and himself grew "quite naturally more intimate" (216).

One incident that occurred when Moritz "was going" with his girlfriend Emma suggests the variety of categories of sexual respectability that Bromme, like the author of *Im Kampf ums Dasein*, employed. When he returned home from evening visits with his "bride" (a term he applied to Emma, following common practice, although they were not legally married) the servant girl who lived across the hall from him often attempted to seduce him. Bromme recalled that "she'd never close the door . . . her shirt was open in the front so that her fully developed chest was abandoned to my view . . . the frivolous abandonment of her bodily charms put me off and I thought of my bride whom I visited almost every evening. She was much more appealing to me because she wouldn't even change her jacket in front of me, but always went behind the door" (218). Only when Emma got pregnant did Moritz decide to marry her, an outcome that in retrospect (if not at the time) struck Bromme as a trap.

Franz Bergg described his evolving friendship with a young woman in similar terms. Their courtship followed its course until one evening at his apartment "Marie became mine. . . . When she had recovered from her first embarrassment she said 'I knew that it would come to this. You took me today as a maid. Now keep me as your wife!'" (155) The relationship grew difficult when Marie's parents opposed the match and when Bergg discovered that his intended did not share his love of education, the theater, and books. Eventually, Marie also got pregnant, pushing the couple toward a marriage that Franz no longer wanted.

Clearly, proletarian men and women were sexually active before or outside of marriage, but these narratives offer no evidence that sex was somehow more "natural" or casual in these milieux or that concerns of propriety and status were irrelevant in sexual encounters. There are in fact strong suggestions to the contrary. The stories offer narrative connections between early sexual activity and entrapment in unwanted relationships. They reveal moral ambivalence: women authors described these relationships defensively, and both men and women placed the women involved in nonmarital liaisons in tenuous positions in a moral hierarchy structured primarily by sexual virtue. The stories also suggest the important ways in which decisions about sexual activity affected these heroes' and heroines' sense of destiny. The impact of sexual decisions on life course becomes even clearer when these stories are compared with other kinds of stories — tales of sexual restraint amid surrounding promiscuity.

Sex, Ambition, Mobility, and Respectability

Surviving or evading sexual perils through adolescence also played a narrative role for many autobiographers; it served these writers as a predictor of upward journeys. If sexual victimization or seduction was a constant danger, resistance to the threat and the allure of sex often differentiated the autobiographical hero from those who remained behind. As was true for the middle classes, for nineteenth-century workers sexual self-definition appears as a key element in identity and life trajectory. And, as for the middle classes, the route to social or political accomplishment often lay in self-control or abstinence. The early stages of a life story with a happy ending often entailed a sex-free adolescence, most clearly in men's "success stories," autobiographies that recount the steps of transformation from worker to intellectual, writer, or professional.

Valentin Jamerey-Duval, who wrote what is arguably the first such "success story" in the middle of the eighteenth century, offered the example that began this chapter. His life overlapped those of Ménétra and Bräker, but his trajectory ruled out sexual involvement.[11] Otto Richter, the son of a factory worker who became a professor, ended his story of success with his entry at age seventeen into the *Realschule*—an institution of higher education that was less prestigious than the classical *Gymnasium* but nevertheless a triumph for a worker's son. In the course of his account, Richter told of an adolescent crush on his employer's daughter, the first of many he would endure. But he kept quiet about his feelings, and certainly he did not act on them. His "move up" began when he managed to get himself apprenticed as a legal copyist in a lawyer's office. There, at age sixteen, he had to take testimony in a paternity suit from a peasant girl, "a delicate matter for a sixteen-year-old boy" (111). She won her suit, and he emerged "without appreciable damage" from the incident, which was the closest encounter with the dangers of sex his narrative mentioned. This studied distancing was surely a signal of Richter's seriousness of purpose and a significant signpost on his road to self-improvement.

Jamerey-Duval's explicit abstention and Richter's subtle distancing from sex are consonant with the even more discreet approach of other men who told "success stories." Bruno Bürgel mentioned having to battle drink to make something of himself, but he was silent on the subject of sex. Silent, too, was Prosper Delafutry, a poor peasant who became an *instituteur*. Jean Guehenno, who made the trajectory from a shoe factory to the *Académie française*, knew love only in the form of a hopeless crush on the daughter of a wealthy merchant. His sexual innocence caused him pain and alienation from his fellow workers. They teased him when they knew of his plans to pass the baccalaureate exam; particularly painful was the badgering of one who "tended to suggest that the true science of males was love and that at that I was no expert. My coworkers split their sides laughing" (148). These accounts of adolescence empty of sex are filled instead with tales of prodigious feats of self-education.

Women autobiographers who made successes of themselves related trajectories in which adolescent sexual abstention played a different but equally marked role. Three women's "success stories" involved marrying up: Madeleine Henrey, Marie Sans Gène, and Verena Conzett were manual workers who married educated professional men. Henrey eventually became a professional writer of some renown.[12] They all discussed adolescent sexual experiences, but all intimated that they, unlike their less fortunate and less successful proletarian sisters, preserved their virginity.

Verena Conzett was exposed to inappropriate talk at the factory where she worked, but it seems not to have imperiled her. She was still a sexual innocent at age twenty when her family discussed her marital prospects with her and advised her that she shouldn't wait for a rich man. The occasion of her later pregnancy (after her successful marriage) reminded her of some of her less fortunate childhood friends—since become unwed mothers—whom she then visited.

Marie Sans Gène made a more explicit link between her sexual caution and her successful marriage. She noted the relative freedom of working-class girls compared with the more supervised upper-class girls. Her mother's warning, "Don't let me down, my daughter!" was really not necessary.

> I had too much maidenly pride, to let even the thought enter my mind to enter lightly into a love relationship; moreover, I didn't have much respect for those girls who thought they couldn't live without a "bridegroom." . . . It was distasteful to me to see them in the evenings standing in front of the door or in the corridors with their sweethearts. I was too taken with myself, and too conscious of my good reputation to have ever been able to do that. Finally, I actually felt no need to tie myself down so young or to throw myself away. I knew only too well the pressures of poverty to want to jump thoughtlessly into the first possible marriage that presented itself; I rather hoped silently that I would be able to achieve a better situation for myself through marriage and to that end I sought to preserve my good reputation" (106–8).

Madeleine Henrey was not so deliberate about it, but she too resisted the danger or allure of casual adolescent sexual activity around her on her road to success as a writer and bourgeois wife. Probably more than any other autobiographer, Henrey openly admired several women acquaintances who had used their sexuality in an instrumental fashion and in defiance of prevailing norms. She presented a favorable recollection of two women who were important influences during her formative years —her neighbors Madame Maurer and Didine, a prostitute. Madame Maurer "had traveled from Paris to Chartres in a stage-coach; she had kept rendezvous with famous men in closed carriages . . . had lived and loved in Paris when people said of it: Paris . . . the paradise for women" (178). Similarly, Didine's success inspired Madeleine with ambition: "Oh, how I envied her! With what ambition she filled my breast!" (201) However much the success of these women impressed Madeleine, it is clear that Henrey's own happy ending—her marriage to a proper Englishman and a career as a writer—depended on an adolescence that featured self-improvement rather than sex.

The only other women's "success story"[13] is that of Angelina Bardin, who went from being a foundling and farm worker to a nurse. Bardin suggested that she might have used a sexual ploy to create an alternative future for herself, but she refrained from doing so. Angelina fell in love with a rich peasant boy in whose village she worked when she was sixteen. The boy's mother opposed the match as unsuitable, whereupon Angelina's friend counseled her to sleep with him and get pregnant in order to force the match as was, she argued, the common practice. Angelina refused and eventually lost the boy, whose mother sent him away. Her rise out of the fields was facilitated not through sex but through the intervention of the foundling bureau.

You Don't Like Women; You Only Like Books: Sex among Socialist Militants

If workers who found success in the form of social mobility saw sexual restraint as intrinsic to the story of their success, so too did many political militants. This association is perhaps more surprising in view of the fact that the dominant culture often coupled socialism with sexual license. Early experiments with Utopian socialism offered notorious examples of both communal living arrangements and ideological attacks on marriage. The reputation was hard to live down even long after the Utopian movement had dissolved. Mid- to late-century socialists found themselves charged with advocating sexual license, usually depicted as "common property in women."[14]

A few accounts reinforce this image — in particular by coupling socialist affiliation with a rejection of paternal responsibilities — but they did not emerge from the socialist mainstream. The female author of *Im Kampf ums Dasein*, far from being a socialist herself, portrayed her socialist father as brutal and negligent. Franz Bergg's account illustrates even more baldly the mix of radical politics and paternal irresponsibility. Franz had planned, however reluctantly, to marry his pregnant girlfriend, but before the wedding he was arrested for participating in a socialist demonstration. By the time he was released from prison, the baby had been born and taken away from (or sent away by) his wife to a foster home. Franz found and retrieved the child. Later, when the three moved into a room together, the girlfriend, Marie, went home for four hours and left the crying baby in Franz's care. He refused to forgive his wife for this lapse and ejected her from the house; if she had loved her child, he argued, she would never have let it go hungry. Franz then left the child with a wet nurse and forbade his wife to visit her daughter. Bergg claimed that his daughter became the focus of his existence, but she had clearly been left in poor care: she soon died of diphtheria. When Franz announced the death to the child's mother (whom he never had married), he then dismissed her. "Good luck, Marie," he said. "Forgive me and be thanked. Be happy if you can." When Marie cried out to him and tried to hold onto him he tore himself loose and left to grieve alone. His period of grief only ended, according to his account, when a colleague convinced him that he had to put the tragedy behind him. "Though I had lost everything, enough remained to build a life worth living. Despite everything! . . . My family was taken from me, but out there there awaited me a larger family" (170–72). Bergg left his readers to ponder his cruelty and denial of his own guilt as a motivation for embracing "the movement." However accurate a rendition of Bergg's history, his was not the usual socialist narrative. Bergg wrote it in prison at the command of the prison director, who hoped that the activity and self-reflection would bring about Bergg's reformation. This fact makes it less surprising, perhaps, that the memoir seems to reinforce the popular perception that the socialist movement was home to licentious opponents of family life.

In contrast with these rather sensationalist accounts, however, many militants insisted on their sexual restraint. This tradition of self-control had a long history in socialist workers' culture. The class-conscious male worker often distinguished himself from peers by some sacrifice of alcohol consumption or sexual expression in favor of disciplined self-improvement. The models for self-denial date from early in the nineteenth century, in the workers' education movements that succeeded or accompanied the early experiments with Utopian socialism.

The Republican socialist Sebastien Commissaire offered an early example of such restraint in his anecdote of a female coworker's attempted seduction of him one night when both were lodging at their boss's house. She appeared at his bedside, and when Sebastien, rather than accepting the obvious invitation, asked her coldly why she was there, she answered, "You don't like women; you, you only like books." He answered, "Pardon, I like women, but I don't like those who affront me the way you do." Commissaire then went on to claim that he could take no credit for his willpower, that it was really his love for another woman that saved him from seduction. But clearly a strong note of moral condemnation fed into his response. His disapproval was amplified in his subsequent claim that men and women should not be allowed to work alone together (71–76). Love and political activities competed for Sebastien's attentions as a young man, a leitmotif in later socialist autobiography as well.

Few went as far as Max Hoelz, the very title of whose autobiography described the path he took "from white cross to red flag." The White Cross was a Lutheran young men's chastity league to which Hoelz belonged in his early twenties. He recalled considering "any relations with women outside marriage as immoral and wicked. My erotic desires, on the other hand — I was only twenty-one — were very strong, so I joined the 'White Cross,' a Lutheran 'Chastity League.' During my six months' probation period . . . I was obliged to confess my sexual thoughts and actions daily to the head of the League. After six months of 'purification' I was accepted as a member of the League in a very solemn meeting" (30–31).

Hoelz's move into socialism apparently involved a rejection of the extremity of his adolescent views, bound up as they were with his religiosity. But the strains he felt were shared, if less intensely, by other German socialists. In some cases, the articulation of "enlightened" views about sexual relations served as a basis for an alternative understanding of relations between men and women and for a critique of existing proletarian sexual practices.[15] Among the autobiographers, Alwin Ger, a socialist propagandist from a Saxon mining community, developed these views most explicitly. Ger used his memoirs to attack religious teachings about sexuality, which he felt poisoned children's minds about "the natural facts of the sexual life"; these teachings, he claimed, triggered a lifelong devaluation of sexual activity. "So it happens, that adults speak of the highest and most holy act of human existence, on which not only the preservation but also the ennoblement of the human race depends, only in terms of dirty jokes. There were always a considerable number of such stories and jokes in circulation, and since the grown-ups of the male sex always offered them on every possible occasion unbothered by the presence of the little ones, soon they were current among the kids as well." Ger also condemned such popular customs as *Ausjagen* — a form of night courting accompanied by supervisory visits from male youth groups — because it encouraged intimacy among young people too soon after school-leaving (46–51).

Not all German socialist men shared Ger's suspicion of precocious sexual activity, and they weighed their adolescent sexual experiences differently in their personal development. Some, like Moritz Bromme, Franz Bergg and Ludwig Turek, presumed that nonmarital sexual relationships were typical for proletarian youth. Turek's account also offered explicit commentary about the formulation of male sexual identity within the socialist movement in the immediate prewar era in Germany.

Turek, whose childhood was spent mainly in Hamburg under difficult circumstances, was apprenticed as a typesetter at age fourteen. Through contacts at work, he joined a coeducational group within the Socialist Youth Movement. The group's defense of the mingling of boys and girls produced "an unavoidable discord" between the youth and the more conservative leadership, who wanted to avoid all possibility of sexual scandal, "but with the slogan 'Love is a private affair' which we hammered energetically into everybody's head, we predominated. In the face of all the excuses raised by our older comrades, I have to say among us in these groups, in which there were only young people up to the age of eighteen (until the beginning of the war), and although we were often with girls at night, absolutely no offenses against morality took place" (54).

Turek's account of his sexual initiation is separated from this story of the youth group and comes later in his narrative, in the context of a discussion of "the sexual problem." "We tortured ourselves with it almost completely without an orderly explanation. I can still remember clearly the gigantic shock I received when I experienced my first nocturnal emission. I even still know the date. I was seventeen years old, it was the 5th of January." He had gone skating with a group of young people, including a certain Fräulein Butterweins, who apparently attempted, unsuccessfully, to seduce him. A troubled night followed during which Ludwig thought of her. She had never been taken into the youth group; she seemed unworthy and lacked the qualities he "thought ideal in a girl." It therefore troubled him that she aroused him sexually. The conflict led him to renounce women completely — a vow that lasted until April, when "he made his first conquests." Soon he had had a string of five affairs, for which Turek later condemned himself (81–82). This story underlines particularly sharply the confusion of at least two diverse and contradictory formulations of male sexual identity for German proletarian youth. Turek was simultaneously enmeshed in a socialist youth culture that emphasized companionship between *Genossen* and *Genossinnen* (male and female comrades within the movement) and adolescent sexual restraint on the one hand, and the proletarian practice of extramarital coupling in the late teens years on the other. In Turek's account the women available for the latter were "unworthy" of the former. Turek simultaneously apologized for his sexual aggressiveness and, in tune with the contemporary critique of inadequate sex education, condemned of his remembered sexual ignorance. While there was apparently no single acceptable sexual stance for young men within the prewar socialist movement, there was nevertheless a clear heritage linking adolescent self-constraint with militancy and a demonstrated ambivalence about the morality of at least female extramarital intercourse. Becoming a militant, like becoming a success, was a process that involved sexual choices.

Contraceptive Rationality or Sexual Fatalism?

Another dimension of sexual behavior was interwoven with social identity — namely, attitudes towards contraception. Most of the autobiographers came of age during the period when fertility was beginning to decline in Europe. French popular classes had begun to practice family limitation relatively early, while in Central Europe lower-class families remained large until the turn of the century. Although few of the autobiographers discussed these questions directly or in detail, several accounts offer insight into subjective views of contraception and into associations between family limitation and social identity.

The account of the socialist Alwin Ger or the success story of Marie Sans Gène reproduce an explicitly Malthusian[16] argument that workers were responsible for their own poverty and that they should show sexual restraint and limit their family size for their own good. They implicitly condemned working-class parents for their refusal to offer their children a better future by having fewer of them. Both of these writers were discreet about their own (presumably different) rationality of limitation. Indeed, in accounts by autobiographers who either came from or themselves produced small families, little was said about strategy or rationales. The few autobiographers who talked explicitly about their own pregnancies or those of their mates suggested that control over fertility was either unthinkable or unmanageable. Lena Christ, for example, saw her pregnancies as the direct result of her husband's lack of control: "Already after three weeks . . . my husband once again burned with passion and he overcame with force all the reluctance that a wise nature instills in a mother in such a condition — even among the animals. It was no use to show him the little one who nursed at my breast and say: 'Go, don't take the food out of his mouth! Leave me in peace! I am ill!' Once his desire was aroused his reason was silenced. . . . So it happened that after a few months I was expecting again" (290–91).[17]

Max Bromme, who got married in 1895 after his girlfriend became pregnant, learned something of contraception after his second daughter was born two years later. "One day our foreman brought some Parisian articles along with him to work, which is how I first heard of them. Before this I had not known about contraceptives. The foreman sold me a single

Vorortsgeschäft — actually a mining term + an evocative one — working at the pit face.

pessary for 1.20 marks. I even bought a second one. After that we'd talk a lot among ourselves about such 'protections.' Then, you'd hear things that people would never admit in writing. The most sure method was supposed to be 'suburban business.' 'Coitus interruptus' is the technical name for this. . . . Even though I tried the pessaries and even the last-named technique, a year later my son Ernst was born" (224–25). Three more children would be born before Bromme brought his narrative to a close in 1905 when he was still a young man. Despite his explicit association between the augmenting misery of his family and too many and too frequent births, Bromme raised the subject of contraception only to bemoan its ineffectiveness.

The autobiographers who alluded to marriages occasioned by pregnancies suggested perhaps that insofar as pregnancies were strategic at all, they forced a marriage that might not otherwise have occurred. Although these few narratives offer an inadequate basis for understanding alternative rationalities of childbearing, they do suggest that calculating attitudes about the employment of older children could coexist with fatalism about conception. Such fatalism was explicitly condemned in several accounts, but there was a tantalizing silence about strategies among those couples who limited births, which must have been most of the autobiographers and the parents of the vast majority of the French autobiographers as well. We can conclude little more than that deliberate family limitation, and the respectability with which it was increasingly associated, was accompanied by discretion about its specific impulse and practices. If having too many children was a fit topic for comment by those who had them, having just the right number apparently was not.[18]

odd that neither I nor Linse is cited

The autobiographical evidence can only hint at this dimension of the relationship between sexual behavior and class identity. Authors were simply too circumspect to offer more. Some, however, had apparently come to articulate a connection between contraception and class identity. This association was not simply an economic argument about fewer mouths to feed; it went deeper, for to adopt "enlightened" views on sexuality and contraception was for some authors part of a larger project to reshape their lives. The few authors who discussed conception cemented the links between profligacy or restraint and class position. They argued or implied that their lives were better (or could have been better) because of sexual restraint; in this manner as well, sex and its consequences were written into the story of success or failure, of evolving identity.

Autobiography, Trajectory, and Sexual Respectability

The various ways that autobiographers used their accounts of sexual persona and experience in their life stories adds some nuance to our understanding of the construction of sexual identity and sexual choices in the popular classes. In many of these accounts, sexual choices were typically seen to have important consequences for life trajectories, and sexual self-restraint played a role in several patterns of accomplishment. Without necessarily imitating dominant norms, many workers connected sexuality and social identity, and in describing their own sexual experiences they often implicitly contrasted their own behavior with that which they believed to be characteristic of the popular milieux surrounding them. This culture is itself accessible to us, in other words, largely in the accounts of workers who separated themselves from and often condemned it. The real limitation of this autobiographical evidence, then, is that it presents sexual narratives primarily in the context of only certain kinds of personal trajectories. The testimony itself suggests that success stories and militants, who comprise the overwhelming majority of lower-class autobiographers, probably distinguished themselves from their peers in terms of their sexual attitudes and behavior. Equivalent accounts of sexual development and its role in life trajectory from other workers — the vast majority who did not write autobiographies — obviously do not exist.

The few autobiographies that related less coherent or less predictable stories do provide some suggestion of the role of sex in working-class narratives other than militants' or success stories. In particular, several of the women's autobiographies — that of Lena Christ and the two anonymous works *Im Kampf ums Dasein* and *Dulden*[19] — come closer, perhaps, to being exposés. Dr. G. Braun, the editor of *Im Kampf ums Dasein*, saw its author as "a social victim of horrifying social abuses" (8). The author herself appears to have been much more active in shaping her future and seems not to have shared her editor's moral condemnation of her life. She defended her previous occupation — serving drinks in a café — as morally superior to prostitution. In her life story she included several episodes wherein she defended her sexual virtue against threatened seductions and rapes. What apparently appeared to her editor as evidence of final degradation is interpreted by the author as her path to success — the grace of a distinguished male benefactor who set her up in her own apartment and taught her a "bourgeois" occupation. Her ownership of the apartment and her new skill allowed her to fend for herself even after her friend abandoned her. Author and editor part ways over the *specific* definition of sexual morality, but the author was as eager to circumscribe proper mores as was her editor.

Lena Christ seemed most bent on using her autobiography to expose the particular cruelty of her mother and of her first husband. She was the victim and antiheroine of her own life story; she in fact eventually committed suicide. Christ's portrait of her mother offers an example of a servant maid who bore an illegitimate child, but not without guilt. In the eventual process of acquiring respectability as an innkeeper's wife, the mother became obsessively bitter and repressive about sexual matters and made her illegitimate daughter suffer for the mother's offense.

"Kathrin," the anonymous author of *Dulden* (*Endurance*), wrote her story at the suggestion of a psychologist in the Swiss clinic where she was committed after a conviction for infanticide. The editor, who admitted to censoring the most graphic sections of Kathrin's narrative for fear of offending readers, attributed Kathrin's candor to a kind of simple-mindedness: "Reflection has changed nothing, just as little has there been the influence of that other factor which so often distorts and represses in the case of cultivated people and especially women — namely, feelings of personal shame. This is foreign to Kathrin's naïveté — just as this naïveté protects her as well from that other extreme common in these times, forced exhibitionism, that lies as often as does prudery" (5).

Her editor thus meant Kathrin to be taken as a product of nature rather than culture; her tragedy was depicted as the result of the frustration of her natural inclinations, specifically toward motherhood. Her own understanding of her motives in writing is hard to deduce. She wrote under duress, but she used the text at least in part to defend herself in the face of her criminal conviction. She dated her sexual difficulties to a liaison with a cousin that began when she was eighteen, a relationship her mother opposed because the boy was kin and Catholic. Despite her mother's vigilance, she had intercourse with her cousin: "He said he didn't want to buy a cat in a sack. At first I didn't want to, but eventually gave in. Afterwards he told me how pleased he was . . . that I was still chaste" (20–21). Kathrin agreed not to marry the boy because of her mother's deathbed request. She subsequently became involved in a series of other relationships. She claimed that the two infants she bore in her early twenties were stillborn. The father of the first child had wanted her to abort the fetus, but she refused. The second married her a month before the birth of her second child but with suspicions about his paternity that would only have been assuaged if the child had been born later than it actually was. She thus had reasons to conceal both births for a while (and she in fact kept the infants' bodies, concealed, long after the births), but in each case she was eventually found out. She presented herself as a victim of her mother's interference, of the men in her life, and of circumstances, but her remorse centered on her loss of the infants, not on her sexual activity. The account of her earlier life had indeed included mention of an attempted rape when she was ten, brutality in the hands of her father, and, eventually, attempted incest when she was sixteen. But she did not use these incidents to build a coherent narrative that directed her life in some way or made sense of her subsequent actions. Sexual activity played a central role in shaping her life, but the course of the life itself is elusive, seemingly patternless. The editor's attempt to impose order on her alienation by calling Kathrin a victim of frustrated maternal drives simply fails to convince.

These stories that in so many ways defy the usual forms of classification share with the others a close attention to the connections between sex and destiny. Their authors did not invoke common categories to describe their lives, nor did they share the view of militants or successes that their lives would have been better had they resisted their sexual impulses. They spoke, perhaps, from the margins of the genre, but for them, too, sexual coming-of-age was a critical part of the story they had to tell. Because they defy categorization, these stories speak to the existence of multiple realities, alternative life courses that risk being forgotten in that so many of the autobiographies fall into a few easily identifiable categories. These less typical stories hint at the many lives that never culminated in autobiography.

Still, despite the clear limits of autobiographical memory, this testimony serves to undermine the belief that because adolescent sexual intercourse was more frequent among the lower classes it was somehow unproblematic or that proletarians, because of their lack of property, were necessarily freer, more spontaneous, or somehow less products of their society and culture than were their propertied class superiors. Even if notions about adolescence, and in particular the trials of adolescent sexuality, were developed by experts concerned about middle-class boys, the path to sexual adulthood was hardly less circuitous and perilous for boys and girls of the working classes. For them, too, sexual choices were shaped by their position in social hierarchies, by milieu- and gender-specific notions of the links between sexuality and respectability, and by expectations about their future. Moreover, the autobiographers clearly saw sexual decisions they made as young adults as consequential in the lives they eventually led, the paths they eventually followed, their fates as heroes or heroines (or antiheroes and antiheroines) in the stories they eventually wrote.

I chose to go by way of Fleischergasse, where I had grown up, and thereby bid farewell to my

childhood and earliest youth and to all my memories of Danzig. Probably they appeared

lovely to me, illuminated as they already were by the passage of time; but over them lay like

a chill fog the constant material need that had weighed upon my family and so upon me as

well. This I hoped finally to leave behind . . . I boarded the train and with my mind

reassured, rode toward my unknown future. (Marie Sans Gène, 225)

SEVEN

SETTING A COURSE

Marie's farewell to Danzig, a transformative moment in her life, serves as the climax of Sans Gène's memoirs. Her life, readers know, is about to change forever. Her specific fate is left unclear, but she left with an image of a better future in her mind. In ending her memoirs with this climactic moment Sans Gène mimicked the novelist more closely than did most of the other autobiographers: such a promising ending—one that even approaches closure—is rare in these stories. Still, nearly all the authors included somewhere in their story an account of a moment in late adolescence or early adulthood when their life changed significantly. Their plotting of these moments varies widely; some, like San Gène, made a decision to follow an opportunity that eventually led to a better future. For others, including Jean Guehenno, a missed opportunity generated unbending resolve to succeed. In militants' accounts, the transformative moment more typically was the choice to embrace a movement. Alwin Ger vividly recalled how a Sunday afternoon immersion in a socialist tract made him forever "a completely different person." The afternoon's reading led to his commitment to socialism and so put a stamp on his whole subsequent life. His autobiography was structured to lead him (and the reader) to this denouement. Charlotte Davy's encounter with the feminist speaker Nelly Roussel worked a similar transformation in her life; through it she was drawn out of an unnamed despair and into the feminist movement. But whether the new road takes the author toward militancy or on an upward social climb, these narrative moments signal plot turns wherein the hero or heroine set off toward the destination from which the life story was retold. To put it another way, these moments signify the point when the plots of their life stories were revealed to their heroes or heroines.[1]

As they reconstructed their life stories, how and when did autobiographers signal their most significant moments? At what point, in their estimation, was the route they followed through life mapped out? In the militants' tales, key features distinguish French from German, and men's from women's, accounts of their trajectory into political life. In the relatively rarer success stories, gender appears to have been definitive in the structuring of opportunities; differences between the French and the German texts are of less apparent significance. Moreover, for all categories of autobiographers self-invention was an important stage in personal development, and for all of them it involved coming to grips with the separation from their parents and the cultural world of their childhood. Through the recollection of these transformative moments, authors reconstructed the process by which they came to imagine and pursue possibilities for themselves other than the ones to which they had seemingly been born.

The Paths to Militancy

Alwin Ger recalled a highly significant moment on his trajectory: "Actually, I had wanted to go on a long autumn hike that had been arranged by a group of young people for this Sunday. A cloudless sky and golden sunshine lured me outdoors. But, lost in reading, I forgot about the autumn and the hike, the sunshine and the blue sky. My excitement rose from column to column; never in my life had anything gripped me so deeply . . . the far too great poverty that I had had to witness in my childhood and experience myself — it wasn't an act of God or providence as the man in the long black cassock always claimed, but rather the product of bad human institutions. . . . When I had finished reading everything, I was overtaken by a joyous, truly religious mood that flowed from my awareness that on this Sunday I had become a completely different person" (147–48). Ger experienced this moment of clarity while alone on a Sunday afternoon, but there were obviously particular historical circumstances that shaped his awakening — his religious background, the development of the socialist press in Saxony, even the institution of Sunday afternoon leisure as the prerogative of male workers. Private experiences of their early lives — childhood deprivation, injustices encountered as an adolescent — might have provided many workers with a starting point down the road toward rebelliousness, but it still took specific circumstances to propel them into lives as militants. There had to be institutional and ideological support for making the connection between personal grievances and political solutions. They had to come into contact with organizations and ideas. They had to acquire the skills needed to pursue organizing activities. They had to be able to imagine themselves as participants in or even leaders of a movement whose aim was to alter the course of history. And these specific institutions, organizations, and subcultures had an impact on the kind of militant someone could imagine being and then become. Some of these institutions, especially workers' educational institutions, had a profound influence on the intellectual development of working-class militants. But certain organizations and circumstances allowed or encouraged workers to imagine and adopt a specifically militant life.

Several roads, not just one, took workers along the path to activism in the various socialist or trade union movements that were at the center of so many autobiographers' lives.[2] Time, place, and gender influenced the choice of particular routes authors later followed.

Workplace and Class Identity

The classic marxist narrative about the origins of class consciousness — that it would emerge from the relentless concentration of proletarians in factories and factory towns — does indeed resonate in some autobiographical tales. For men, especially the French, the workplace was the most often mentioned site of political initiation, and quite a few recounted an abrupt transformation from aggrieved worker to political militant. More than a dozen of the male militants' memoirs describe specific aspects of their work settings that were conducive to political discussion.

Among the French, one of the earliest such accounts is that of Norbert Truquin, who recalled that while he was working in a mill in northern France in the 1830s a friend read aloud from Etienne Cabet's Utopian communist tract *Voyage en Icarie*. Jean-Baptiste Dumay became involved in organizing activities at his job at the Creusot works just after midcentury. Quite a few turn-of-the-century French accounts also tell of workplace-centered transformations. Georges Dumoulin first encountered syndicalism in the mines at Courrières when he was still a teenager in the early 1890s. Gaston Guiraud, born just a few years later than Dumoulin, was also in his teens when he participated in his first strike at the plant he worked at in Paris. Without any organizational experience or support, Gaston joined a strike to reduce his workday from twelve hours to nine. Striking for such a demand, Guiraud recalled, was an idea that by then was "in the air": "A faith in the improvement of the condition of the working class would from that moment on be a law to me. Without any intellectual baggage, without general knowledge, I felt all the more heavily the weight of responsibilities. As for the socialist movement, I was ignorant or almost completely ignorant of it; what I knew, what I understood, was that there was a class that was suffering and that class was my own. I had no idea what a *Bourse de travail* was. Like many, I had heard tell vaguely — really vaguely — of the C.G.T."[3] (142).

Guiraud's story of becoming a militant through a strike, after little previous attention to political questions, is echoed in two later French accounts. Louis Lecoin dated the beginning of his political career to his imprisonment for refusing to break a strike when he was working as an agricultural laborer in the Parisian region on the eve of World War I. René Michaud worked as a teenager in a shoe factory during the war and through strike activity at his plant became involved in syndicalism and anarchism.

Among the German male militants, workplace political activities were also significant, but their context and the paths they led to were typically different. Julius Bruhns began working as a child in a cigar-rolling shop in Hamburg. He soon was assigned the job of reading newspapers aloud at work, mainly the socialist papers which had, he claimed, converted him to socialism by the time he was ten (11–12). "Soon I tossed aside the monsters and giants, Indians and other enemies and after them the knights and heroes of the fist and dreamt only of becoming a leader of the people, of fighting for the rights of the people against their enemies with gripping articles and flaming speeches. To become a Social Democratic Reichstag deputy and, after a successful revolution, a leader, minister, even president of a social democratic republic, this appeared to me to be the epitome of all greatness, the single worthy goal of my ambition" (15). In Bruhn's account, this moment of imagining his future in a different way is pivotal, and it underscores how porous the boundary was between fiction and self-fashioning. But, significantly, Julius abandoned role models he had found in fiction to imitate the living heroes of his political culture. By the age of seventeen Julius was himself living out this image, taking on party electoral work and writing and speaking as well. His life of commitment had begun in the cigar shops, but it took a highly specific form defined by the political leadership of the emergent German Social Democratic Party. Its chronology was shaped explicitly by the party's history, for Julius was banned from Hamburg at age seventeen and his story ends with his triumphant return when the party was relegalized in 1890.[4]

Franz Bergg also worked in the Hamburg cigar industry, where he had taken up an apprenticeship as a fifteen-year-old in the early 1880s in the shop where his brother worked. Reading socialist newspapers and books out loud at work also led him into the then-banned party (56). Franz's participation in illegal political activities was critical to his subsequent life. His story, however, written from the margins of socialist subculture, remains an outlaw tale first and foremost; deviance — political and sexual — overrides all other elements of socialist identity. It may well be that Bergg's imagined audience — the prison director at whose request he wrote and the more bourgeois public beyond — was more interested in this kind of a story than the tale of the working-class hero that Bruhns told his audience from the same starting point. To offer yet a different, and later, variation, Wilhelm Kaisen entered the socialist movement in a much more settled era through trade union activities; he became familiar with these organizations at the various construction sites he worked on in the first decade of the twentieth century in northern and western Germany. For him and other later autobiographers and their audiences, more routine channels for becoming a socialist and writing about the transformation that this move involved had been established. To choose such a path no longer required becoming an outlaw, or even a "hero."

Such a course could unwind from a fairly complacent childhood and a calm and uneventful adolescence.

Particular patterns and stories of "becoming a militant" were thus shaped both by the changing nature of social movements and political organizations as well as by the conventions of the genre of the particular tale being told. Both regional and generational factors that affected recruitment into these movements at the moment in the militant's life course when such a decision was typically made — that is, the later teens or early twenties — were crucial. Autobiographers born in France early in the nineteenth century were likely to find their way into politics through Republican electoral activities or to come to workplace militancy out of some prior exposure to a radical political philosophy. In contrast, stories from later in the century featured the workplace as a starting point. It was possible for a later French militant such as Gaston Guiraud to learn about strikes and how to join them as a very naive teenager without much political awareness, for the syndicalist movement was already "in the air" in Paris by the turn of the century. Indeed, for many of the French men writing about turn-of-the-century experiences, workplace militancy signaled the beginning of politicization, and these lives often remain centered in syndicalist activities even if a worker entered electoral politics. The institutions that surround these later French stories of "coming to militancy" are the strike, the demonstration, and the syndicate.

In contrast, few German socialists recalled having been "naive" at work. The close connections between workplace and party activities meant that in the latter decades of the nineteenth century workplace militancy easily led into the highly institutionalized Social Democratic movement and subculture. Those less organized and institutionalized manifestations of workplace militancy that German labor historians are beginning to document were not pronounced in German memoirs. Moreover, the special character of German socialism during its long-recognized "outlaw period" between 1877 and 1890 also reverberates in the plotting of turns to militancy. Illegal and heroic resistance shaped the path to militancy for the influential generation of socialist leaders who lived through this era, in marked contrast to later socialists. Interestingly, both workplace and political activities remain heroic in German militant self-fashioning at least until the 1920s. Even if strikes figure importantly in many German men's stories, so too do accounts of distributing socialist tracts and papers, writing editorials, doing electoral work — much of this activity made more heroic than it might otherwise have been by its underground character.[5]

The stories that women militants told highlight this important, but nationally different, place that workplace experience plays in men's accounts of their road to militancy. For women, the workplace was much more problematic as a political space. Many of them were uncertain whether they even belonged there. Often the conditions at work were as likely to prohibit as to encourage their political efforts. I did find one account in an Austrian woman's memoir of becoming politicized by strike activities around the turn of the century in ways that echo men's stories. The author, Amalie Seidl, was working at age sixteen in a factory employing three hundred "workers and women."[6] Amalie was a packer and therefore among the best paid workers. She was an advocate of better organization and, in 1893, argued in favor of the celebration of May Day, the recently established workers' day of protest. When a foreman heard her state as much during a break, he fired her. When she got home, she found her house surrounded by police, and all her coworkers were already there. "So," she recalled, "I gave a 'speech' on a chopping block in which I told my coworkers that it would be wonderful if they didn't take this quietly; but, if they wanted to strike they should demand more than simply my reinstatement" (344). They followed her advice, asking for her reinstatement and a shorter working day. After two weeks they had won a ten-hour day, a higher minimum wage, and May Day off.

But there are few such stories of workplace heroics among the women militants; even for Amalie, her significant moment of heroism occurred not *at* work but on the street outside her home. Many women who cherished their "respectability" were uncomfortable in the factory. Adelheid Popp had always distanced herself from the factory girls she thought of as not quite proper. It was only when she became more politically conscious through other avenues that her aloofness at work diminished. She took on the problems of women workers as her main political concern and, building on the custom of work-time gossip and storytelling, used her workplace as site for politicizing coworkers. But she was never quite at home there: "I had often told stories before, when people had asked me to. But now, instead of . . . the fate of some queen or other I told of oppression and exploitation. . . . During breaks, I read articles from social democratic newspapers out loud and explained, as nearly as I could understand it, what socialism was. . . . So it often happened that one of the office employees would walk by and, shaking his head, say to another: 'That girl speaks like a man' " (64). Switching her workplace conversation from storytelling to political exposition reversed the gender of her discourse.

Many women did not have such "public" workplaces. Significantly, several of the militants who became involved in organizing women were themselves homeworkers and found homework a more suitable basis from which to organize women even if homeworkers were supposedly notoriously hard to organize. Ottilie Baader, who became one of the leading German women socialists, was a seamstress who worked at home. Amalie Poelzer complained that her coworkers at a Viennese clothing factory in the 1880s were all antisocialist and afraid of anarchists. They played cards at work and read from conservative, sensationalist papers such as the *Weltblatt* or *Extrablatt*. She was more sympathetic than they to trade unions because of her family history. Her grandfather was a brickworker, and she knew the real misery of such occupations. Moreover, her father bought socialist publications such as *Gleichheit, Arbeiterzeitung,* and then *Volkstribune.* These Amalie "read eagerly. . . . In the shops I dared not say anything about this because you'd be suspect if you had dealings with 'such people' . . . my every effort was directed toward becoming independent" (104–6). She found herself constantly lying about her real beliefs and commitments to her coworkers and to her boss. Only when she finally saved enough to set herself up as an independent seamstress could she organize her own schedule to include political activities. For all of these women, with their varying degrees of discomfort in the workplace, the institutional framework that the socialist movement provided was critical. Even there, of course, they faced obstacles based on their male comrades' ideas about women workers, but at least they saw a space wherein they could define themselves as militants. There was a real, if small and ambivalent, place for the identity of female socialist militant to emerge.[7]

On the French side, the career of Jeanne Bouvier was similar in many ways to Baader's, but her story was not often replicated in French. She went back and forth between the small ateliers of Paris and homework, liking the former situation for its conviviality, the latter for its independence. Ironically, it was one of her middle-class clients (she was working *journées bourgeoises,* sewing dresses in the homes of middle-class women) who introduced her to syndicalism. "One of my clients, Madame Norat, was a feminist. She became a devoted reader of [Margeurite Durand's feminist journal *La Fronde*] and while I tried dresses on her she spoke to me about it, as well as about the women's demands and injustices concerning them" (64). Norat also encouraged her to join a union and help in organizing working women, which she finally did. By simple persistence at meetings, according to her account, Bouvier began to be noticed and, as one of the few working women involved in the movement, to be invited to join committees. She found a few allies within the workers' movement, which she even characterized as "feminist," but she worked most closely and easily on its intellectual and political margins.[8] She no doubt provided a model for the new role of female militant, but she was apparently pretty lonely in this role; indeed, she spent more time in the later sections of her memoirs describing days spent in isolation in the Bibliothéque nationale than on her work in political settings. The relative isolation her account discloses contrasts with the female conviviality and solidarity that emerge from the stories that German and Austrian women told.[9] Bouvier was not recounting a path that many turn-of-the-century French women workers could readily follow. In a similar fashion, earlier waves of militancy in France — the Utopian socialist era and the commune — each inspired at least one account from the pen of a female militant (Suzanne Voilquin and Victorine Brocher, respectively). But once again, each of these heroines lived her life under fairly exotic surroundings (Voilquin in travel; Brocher in the midst of the heroism and chaos of Paris under the Commune.) It must have been hard for the average French woman worker to imagine herself as the heroine of such a tale.

Militancy at Home

For women autobiographers, the more usable models may well have been those that centered on possibilities closer to home. For many militants, and especially for women, despite the ambivalence about the family that childhood stories suggest family life stimulated feelings of injustice, political ideals, and aspirations. Of the nearly sixty stories that can be characterized as militant autobiographies, about a third mentioned relatives as responsible for their political initiation. If men most often mentioned the workplace as the place that triggered their political work, women were particularly likely to recall being introduced to politics by a family member, generally a male relative. Not only were other routes (such as recruitment at work or through electoral activities) often explicitly blocked to women; it was also easier for them to take part in political activities with the encouragement of fathers, older brothers, and husbands — encouragement that was, of course, not always forthcoming.

Ottilie Baader and her father did not always agree about the kinds of political activities that were appropriate for her. Her father wrote articles for the socialist press, but he only permitted her to go to meetings when she insisted, and then only when he could accompany her. When the party was outlawed, she helped her father smuggle forbidden books, which they read together at home: "Father read aloud and we'd discuss while I sewed. We spent a whole year reading Marx' *Kapital.* Bebel's *Frau* I read alone later on" (25).[10] Her decision to attend a meeting alone was depicted as a definitive moment of rebellion against her father's restrictions and the point at which she embraced the movement as her own. "I gradually freed myself somewhat from my father. That was not very easy. I had learned through my reading to form my own opinions, but I was not permitted to go to meetings alone. Eventually, this no longer satisfied me. . . . All of a sudden I had a forceful moment and declared: 'This evening I am going to the meeting of the shaftworkers!' My determination must have completely surprised my father. He remained completely silent and let me go alone to the meeting. At this meeting I spoke for the first time" (29–30). Some of what Ottilie said was published in the newspaper the next day, which pleased her father when she told him of it. Apparently, despite her need to break loose from her father, Baader's involvement in the socialist movement would have been unthinkable without his influence.

Anna Altmann recalled that her father supported her efforts to win severance pay when she was fired. He took her to meetings, too. "My father was very proud of me when I stood so openly at the podium without the slightest trace of what's called 'stage fright' " (26). People were surprised when she asked for the floor, but they were impressed when she spoke. In those days, women were either "treated with hostility or ridiculed" at political meetings; things had changed little, Altmann felt, by the time she wrote in 1912. "People still don't look favorably on the female sex involving itself in public life" (27).

Adelheid Popp first learned about socialism through her brother's newspapers. "Every single Social Democrat I got to know through the newspaper appeared godlike to me. It never occurred to me that I could join with them in struggle. Everything I read about them seemed so high and lofty that it would have seemed like a fantasy even to think that I — ignorant, unknown and poor creature that I was — could actually one day take part in their endeavors" (60). Going out to meetings was for her, as for Baader, a challenge; Adelheid's mother reminded her, "Good girls are found at home" (62). Eventually, she persuaded her brother to take her to a meeting, where she was the only woman present. Other meetings followed, that Adelheid always attended in the company of one of her brothers and sometimes her sister-in-law until she had established a career as a socialist organizer. She was eventually able to find a role for herself in the movement based on her considerable "feminine" talents as a storyteller.

Sophie Jobst also owed her political education to her brother; in Anna Perthen's case, her husband encouraged her. Among the French women autobiographers, Victorine Brocher's father took her to witness important political events of her childhood, such as a demonstration against Louis Napoleon; she later did the same with her own children. Charlotte Davy recalled that when she was about ten years old her father "undertook to fashion my thinking. . . . He didn't fear to take me to meetings. While very young I learned that there were people who were oppressed and that I suffered from such injustice" (16).

If men more typically found their political commitments in the workplace, there were nevertheless quite a few who also saw their militancy as a product of family tradition. As a schoolboy, August Batard listened with "impassioned interest" to the political discussions in his parents' café. Philippe Valette learned a political lesson from his grandfather when he read aloud from his school history book in the 1890s. "That's not true!" his grandfather interrupted. "It's the 'White' who says that." Valette recalled his grandfather's advice: " 'Listen child.' . . . For the first time he held me close to him and hugged me for a moment. — 'Listen, little one . . . never take the side of the 'White'! We, all us others, have suffered too much at their hands, the old ones from the old days! The 'White'? that's the bourgeois full of contempt who likes his dog better than the poor and who keeps the peasant unhappy.' . . . I replied: 'Yes, grandfather,' but it was really only later that I understood" (32–33).[11] Philippe attended his first political meeting with his father when he was twelve, and he "always remembered" a peasant's speech there about building a better society. René Bonnet remembered the gatherings in Paris of the uncles and cousins who had all moved there from the countryside. They were all socialists, and political discussions peppered their family get-togethers. Indeed, such familial traditions — the transmission of historical memory through storytelling and family gatherings — seem to have been particularly important in peasant milieux and may have been a distinctive feature of the rural rootedness of socialism in France that had no parallel in central Europe.

But familial traditions also surfaced in men's memories of the more formally organized German Social Democratic milieu. Heinrich Holek remembered being taunted as a "Sozi" by his classmates almost before he knew what that meant; his father at one point managed a socialist cooperative. Later, when he was old enough to understand what it meant to be a socialist and even to be proud of the family's affiliation, he was sometimes called upon to perform at political gatherings. On one occasion, his mother took him to buy a real suit and a red tie (a color he insisted upon), and he recited a poem for a huge assembly on a dais decorated with busts of Marx and Lasalle: "It seemed as if it wasn't I who spoke, but rather another. When I was finished, the applause resounded through the park and I ran to my mother. From this day on, I thought of myself as a socialist" (68–69). These somewhat less expected stories with their emphasis on the role that ties to home played in coming to militancy illustrate patterned variations in the ways autobiographers remember imagining their militant future and finding a way to it.

Religious Identity and Militancy

French and German accounts of coming to militance also differ in the specific role religion played. With few exceptions, the French authors spent little time discussing religion at all once they had told their First Communion stories. On the other hand, for many of the German militants (with the important exception of the Christian socialists), the deliberate rejection of Christianity was often recalled as an intellectual and political milestone.

Religious institutions, of course, played a marginal role at best in the lives of many urban workers, especially in France, where popular ties with the Catholic Church were already weak in the eighteenth century and where Catholicism, at least official Catholicism, became closely associated in the Revolutionary era with political conservatism. If left-wing or militant religious movements appeared as an interesting possibility in the early nineteenth century (Victorine Brocher, for example, described the cult of *Jesus revolutionnaire*), by the latter decades of the century most socialists had ceded the terrain of religion to the forces of conservatism and were personally sympathetic to the virtually official anticlericalism of the Third Republic. Many workers would simply have casually agreed with Louis Lecoin's assertion that "the servants of Rome were agents of the bourgeoisie" (15).

In Central Europe, relations with churches were more complex. For some autobiographers, disillusionment surrounding communion or confirmation had soured them on their faith by the end of childhood. For Franz Lüth, for example, his bitterness at confirmation was a turning point in the trajectory that transformed a "superstitious boy who sought the status of a Herr Pastor" into a "thinking, ambitious man, a true priest, a fighter for the suffering subservient working people" (87).

Several of the German life stories signal an even more precise and personally important association between religious doubt and the adoption of a new political stance. The classic example is Nikolaus Osterroth, who called his autobiography *Vom Beter zum Kämpfer* (*From Prayer to Fighter*). Ironically, as a teenager he had sharpened his skills as an orator by speaking at meetings of the antisocialist Catholic Youth League in his home village. By the late 1890s, however, he was disillusioned by the Church's proemployer stance in a local dispute between miners and mine owners. His observation that the church abandoned the needs of the poor in this case caused a crisis of faith. "A horrible storm raged within me. I doubted everything that I had formerly held for noble and good. . . . In my crisis of conscience, I sat down and wrote a forceful letter to the village pastor in which I laid out the social problem we confronted, criticized his behavior, and revealed my tormenting doubts" (133). When instead of addressing his doubts the priest directed his next sermon *against* the "unsatisfied" workers, Nikolaus was ripe for rebellion. Just on this day, a Social Democratic election leaflet was tossed into his window. "Suddenly I saw the world from the other side, from a side that until now had remained dark and unilluminated. I was especially taken by the criticism of the tariff system and indirect taxes." But the pamphlet's author didn't only criticize; he offered alternative solutions: "God! How simple and clear it all was! How different this new way of thinking was that gave to the worker the weapons of self-knowledge and self-consciousness, compared with the old world of priestly and secular authority in which the worker was merely the object of domination and exploitation!" (135)

Alwin Ger described a similar moment of conversion. Like Osterroth, Ger was prepared for conversion by religious disillusionment. He emphasized how the rejection of his previous religious understanding of the world's and his own problems helped him to see causation in a new way, not as "an act of God or providence" but instead as the effect of "bad human institutions."

In a similar vein, Adelheid Popp, Robert Köhler, and Anna Maier linked their rejection of religion with their adoption of socialism. The common theme in their stories was the link between the abandonment of a religious world view and the adoption of an understanding of causality that emphasized human agency. But there were deeper and more complex connections as well. Osterroth was not alone among the militants in owing his faith in the power of the word, and his significant verbal abilities, to early religious training. Franz Lüth, Wilhelm Kaisen, and Heinrich Lange all recalled the intellectual importance of their religious background. In other words, the intellectual rejection of the specific tenets of religion did not simply undo all the effects of religious upbringing. Religious experiences, moral commitments, even turns of phrase and metaphors still helped some to make sense of their place in even so apparently secular a movement as socialism. Indeed, the common personal experiences of having "converted" from Christianity to socialism may well have contributed to the fervor of commitment and to the imitative aspects of socialist culture that historians of socialism in Germany have identified. It was an important formative experience that distinguished German militants from their French counterparts.

Certainly, antisocialist stereotypes throughout Europe branded socialists as rebels against all that was sacred—the church, the state, and the family and its constraints. There is basis in the recorded experiences of militants for this association. And the association was more than ideological. Following a path to militancy, autobiographers emphasized, was an intensely personal journey which entailed coming to grips with and reevaluating earlier relationships, experiences, and beliefs. The antireligiosity of many of the German militant autobiographers came not *after* their turn to socialism required or led to it. Rather, religious skepticism appears frequently as an important step on the way.[12]

Several of the German texts also refer to the role of Christian-Jewish relations in the definition of working-class political identity. The "orthodox" socialist texts allude to their authors' rejection of anti-Semitism, again as part of their adoption of the more rationalist socialist stance. Adelheid Popp recalled that when she was still under the influence of the conservative and Catholic Press "a certain strongly anti-Semitic current was apparent [and] I sympathized for a while with this tendency" (59). In her thinking, she was influenced by the anti-Semitic literature then commonly found in Vienna. She presented these anti-Semitic views as misguided, ones she clearly left behind her as she turned to socialism. E. Unger-Winkelreid, in contrast, writing in 1934 to justify his conversion from socialism to Nazism, made a somewhat different point. He emphasized the extent to which the Socialist Party's stand against anti-Semitism was seen by the "workers" in the party as a leadership policy. He argued that "the social democratic workers, in their hearts, were not lovers of Jews but only reconciled themselves with their Jewish leadership . . . because the party program required it" (63–64). From very different standpoints, these texts agree that the official discourse of the socialists encouraged Christian-Jewish alliance but that this discourse ran up against strains of anti-Semitism in the popular culture.[13] The very different handling of religion in French and German texts underscores how militant identities took shape in and from highly specific cultural contexts.

The institutions and the ideological frameworks—unions, parties, families, churches—that guided workers along the path to militancy at different moments in time and in different political cultures naturally had an impact on life trajectories. Most obviously, some futures were unavailable at certain times and places; more subtly, some futures were simply unimaginable. Deep-seated gender differences also came into play. If for quite a few men the classic awakening to class identity in the workplace helped them to make sense of their lives, this was not so easy a story for women to live or to tell. And the fact that women experienced the workplace differently meant that if they were to find a path to militancy at all, theirs would be different from the classic one. Women militants faced a much more difficult task of self-invention.

Paths to Success

How did the upwardly mobile find the road to success? I have fewer than a dozen clear-cut success stories to contrast with the accounts of finding a path to militancy. Generalizations about them are harder to make.

In success stories written by men, most commonly extraordinary educational endeavors made the path to the future possible. Despite the characteristic obstacles to pursuit of learning and despite the inevitability of starting work right after elementary school, some men eventually either educated themselves or made it back to school as they tried to move out of the working class. These authors usually emphasize their persistence and hard work, a leitmotif in their stories that echoes the similar prodigious efforts many of the militants recorded. But even if the story ostensibly emphasizes effort that bred success, a countercurrent of contingent events—specific institutions, individuals, encounters—also moved their plots along.

Several years after leaving home, Valentin Jamerey-Duval learned to read by trading food for reading lessons from literate shepherds with whom he worked (191–92). He learned quickly, and within a few months he was devouring fables and tales and retelling them. He developed a passion for geography and "a swelled head . . . I resolved to associate only with learned persons, and from then on I was only to be found with the schoolteacher and the sexton of the parish" (193). During the several years he spent in a hermitage in his late teens, he spent hours a day reading and learned to write when he was about sixteen. His fate — to become renowned as the self-educated shepherd-turned-scholar — was established when he had a chance encounter with Duke Leopold of Lorraine, who was impressed with his erudition. He eventually found a post, and a future quite different from herding, through aristocratic patronage. Valentin's narrative, while emphasizing his intellectual efforts — efforts that eventually brought him to the attention of people of influence — is also set in a world of providential intervention. Jamerey-Duval certainly claimed at least indirect responsibility for his success through what he portrayed as single-minded intellectual ambition. But he still felt the necessity to tell his readers, "Providence directed my steps and led me to good fortune by a road followed by those who avoid and disdain it" (219).

A chance encounter on the road also changed life for Claude Genoux.[14] It involved a wealthy fellow countryman — a former Savoyard, like Claude, who gave him "five five-franc coins" with which to make his fortune. "Man's existence here on earth means so little that the seemingly simplest incident changes his entire destiny. Our hero's life is one of a thousand examples we could cite . . . in fact, without the unanticipated encounter with his rich compatriot, Claude would have led the same style of life as his numerous cousins from Savoy" (8). Instead, with this blessing of fortune, he decided not to return to his uncle, with whom he was traveling as a chimney sweep; he took another road that, after many twists and turns, brought him to a future as a poor but learned man.

Nikolaus Riggenbach, although born less than ten years later than Genoux, had already adopted a more modern rhetoric of destiny. Half-orphaned as a child, his mother gave him two pieces of gold when as a teenager he went from Switzerland to France to pursue his destiny. Once he arrived there, however, all resemblance of his life to fairy tale ends, and the hero turns into a self-made man. He left nothing up to fate. Instead, he and three friends decided to change their destiny and thus to distinguish themselves from their fellow workers. "We all knew well that we wouldn't get very far with the work of our hands alone. We had to add theoretical to practical education. But we had neither the necessary educational preparation nor the wherewithal to throw off the title 'worker' and devote ourselves to technical studies at the *École Centrale*" (10). The four met in later years to exchange their individual success stories and congratulate themselves for their choices. "We four friends . . . were pleased that we had put our time to better use than most of our agemates, because we certainly would not have advanced if we had been satisfied with our manual labor alone and had not at the same time taken courses. We were glad that in our youth we hadn't filled our free time in the evening with the pursuit of pleasure, but rather had smoothed the way to an ascending life course through the zealous pursuit of knowledge" (12–13).

At first reading, the story line is clear and, to more modern readers, even predictable: rocky roads can be made smooth through determined individual effort. But here again, the story between the lines is less straightforward. Riggenbach attributed his success to his conscious plan of education, but the details he offered about his career pointed to other factors as well. His friendship with a French engineer was ultimately determinant; this friend was offered a railroad post in Karlsruhe but refused to go without his German-speaking friend Nikolaus. It was really here in this post in Karlsruhe, Niggenbach saw in retrospect, that his fate was made (13). And it was made by more than just hard work. For example, he and his friend knew the significance of wearing a proper coat rather than a "worker's blouse" — and because the two friends only owned one between them they took turns wearing it on important occasions (14). Fitted out culturally and sartorially, they were able "gradually to break into bourgeois circles . . . especially the young teachers at the Polytechnique Institute." Shortly after, in 1848, Nikolaus earned the trust and patronage of his superiors when he served as a mediary between management and rebellious workers and tried to explain to the latter in their own terms why, although hunger was to be deplored, "poverty was necessary to encourage industriousness" (24).

Like Riggenbach's, several later-century success stories emphasize hard work as *producing* success and de-emphasize analytically the very many contingencies their narratives nevertheless reveal. Otto Richter, as a young apprentice secretary to a lawyer, recalled that wine cellars held little attraction for him; "books" he wrote, "were my only love" (115). He used some of his wages to subscribe to a lending library and read Scott and "our poets." He bought cheap editions of the classics. "I craved the delights of knowledge. The paradise of which I dreamed was the *Fürstenschule* [the local elite secondary school]. I held the green cap of the *Fürstenschule* pupil in about the same regard that the bourgeois man held the officer's uniform."[15] Otto had a friend there because his father and sisters had worked for school staff members. It was this friendship that allowed him to imagine alternative futures for himself — as a scholar, journalist, or politician (116–17). But again, a chance encounter with a stranger was telling. While walking in the park one Sunday, he met "a cultivated-looking man who asked directions and then asked me to accompany him." It turned out that he was a *Gymnasium* professor in Dresden. This man told Otto the story of his life. "He had originally been a waiter in Leipzig and had devoted all his free time to education. A student whom he waited on every day and who knew about his thirst for knowledge gave him lessons and prepared him for the *Gymnasium* exam — that's how he'd become a scholar. That was grist for my mill! Why shouldn't I too experience such good fortune one day?" (118) The story gave Otto a concrete example of a path he too might follow. He went to his older brother, already a prosperous artisan, who agreed to subsidize his further education. Without this subsidy, Otto would not have been able to make a break. His brother agreed to help him get enough education to assure him of "a modest official post." That was good enough for Otto, even if his ambitions eventually exceeded that mark. So, at seventeen, he headed off to Dresden and higher education in the *Realschule*, at which point his story ends.

Prosper Delafutry's success story is more ambiguous. Delafutry wrote his memoirs for the proclaimed purpose of "teaching workers what can be accomplished by work, perseverance and economy adjoined with honesty," but the hero came across as achieving his modest success almost despite himself. First, the mayor proposed that Prosper go to normal school and become a teacher. His mother took it from there: "My mother, seduced by such a brilliant prospect and propelled by her maternal love, devoted several months to overcoming my resistance" (32–33). Prosper himself would have preferred to farm. But he and his mother would never have been able to own their own farm, and he would have had to be a farm servant or a day laborer all his life. So Prosper decided to acquiesce in the plan to prepare for normal school and a future as a schoolteacher. He was serious and intelligent, but his accent and handwriting presented problems. In 1874, when at age sixteen he took the test for admission to the school, he came in fourteenth of twenty-one candidates. There were only ten scholarships. He persisted, but then eyestrain forced him back into agricultural labor. At the next exam attempt, he was feverish, which ruined his handwriting; he was dismissed from the exam before it was even over "like an ass or a sluggard" (35–37). Still, farm work became increasingly intolerable to him; he had now acquired higher expectations and was "bothered by the ignorance of his coworkers." Finally, the *instituteur* took on the job of "pulling him out of his sorry state" — namely, that of a young man with a certain amount of education who continued to work as an unskilled laborer. He went along because "I wanted in this era, to give our dissolute society a new and inspiring example of success through hard work, perseverance and devotion" (69). In the end, this apparently lackluster youth managed to get his teaching certificate and, with the influence of a cousin in the Parisian school inspectorate, to win an appointment there. The story he tried to tell was clear: hard work breeds success. But his loyalty to the details of his life continually interrupted and undermined his plot. Delafutry, like Riggenbach and Richter, had a story to tell — a fairly new one about the possibilities for upward mobility despite modest origins. But the details of these plots, and especially the contingencies that brought about their success, tend to undermine the overt narrative emphasis on success as the result of determined planning and hard work. Success came about only because of the intervention of a better-placed patron — a relative, a stranger encountered on the road, a boss. The narrative of individual triumph is subverted by repeated evidence that these men really did not make it on their merits alone.

For the female success stories represented among the autobiographers the surface plot is quite different; the most common story of upward mobility followed the familiar plot of fortunate marriage, even if these stories rarely contained the happy ending. Marie Sans Gène hints in her preface that she found her upward path this way, but her text itself alludes only indirectly to this fate. Madeleine Henrey's story also only hints at the resolution; other sources document that she married a well-off Englishman and had the luxury of pursuing a writing career. Verena Conzett married a middle-class socialist journalist.

Yet this fairy-tale plot of rescue, wherein the heroine herself plays the passive role of virtuous beauty, typically conceals a more complex story. The Cinderella motif hinged to a certain extent on chance, of course, the chance encounter with the right man; each of these stories features such an encounter. But on closer examination, these narratives of success through marriage show a great deal of evidence of strategy — the heroines waited for the chance they always thought was possible, but they also readied themselves to seize it. Sexual respectability was essential for this kind of success, of course, but other ways of preparing for this anticipated destiny existed as well. Verena Conzett recalled a discussion of her marital prospects at age twenty. Her family assured her that she would never find a rich man, that she should not wait too long for him. In the context of the family discussion, her brother-in-law asked her to describe the man of her dreams. "First, he should be tall; second, he should have dark hair and shining dark eyes; third, he must be someone, certainly something special; fourth and fifth, I must love him fiercely and he me." (All three of these heroines, in fact, chose to forego earlier prospects on the way to making their fairy-tale match.) While waiting for this ideal mate, Verena seized opportunities to make herself the kind of woman who would appeal to him, including taking "lessons in superior humility" (which went against her nature), politeness, frugality, and even French, which she learned in her job as a shop girl. Her educational ambitions had been greater: "I was often overcome by a deep regret that I, who loved languages and learning so much, was denied the possibility of pursuing learning" (92–95). But her use of her modest resources and her patience paid off. Her story describes how she met her future husband, their mutual attraction, the fact that he "didn't look anything like a worker" (113). At this point — one might say in *true* fairy-tale fashion — Verena's story proper ends. Shortly after the account of the marriage that sealed Verena's fate, her autobiography turns into more of a biography of her husband (although she continued to play a featured role), and Verena's story ceases to occupy the center of the book.

Marie Sans Gène used her employment as a domestic in an upper-class house to advantage. "I soon became more careful in my manner of speaking and reflected more on what I said or refrained from saying, because good form consists primarily in not saying much of what you think and saying much that you don't think. Along the way I carefully observed my three mistresses and noticed how they behaved in various circumstances and, aided by my female sensitivity to what was proper and appropriate, I quickly acquired the necessary polish and what people call good manners" (99). This she did even though she knew that real politeness consisted in the desire not to hurt others, a quality she had "seen more often in fourth class cars than in second" (100).

The offer she had been preparing for came in the form of a housekeeper's post for an educated man she had met earlier. She sensed this to be a moment of destiny. At first she turned down the offer on her mother's advice because he was not yet old enough for the arrangement to appear respectable. But then she reconsidered; at his insistence, they met to discuss it. "I remarked that we would not suit each other since considerable differences in age and temperament divided us, along with, more significantly, a large gap in education, habits and life experiences. When I said these things he replied that they didn't matter: when he wanted to involve himself in scholarly exchange, he had his books; but when he'd had enough of them, then he would really take pleasure in conversation with a natural and unspoiled creature. Scholarly and affected women were a torture to him. Besides, I was still young and could learn" (220–

22). This was a job offer, but one with distinct overtones of possibility. Marie self-consciously decided to take this, her perceived best chance.

Although there is never a direct telling of the moment that brought actual success, both Sans Gène's account and Madeleine Henrey's feature premonitions of it throughout the narrative. These intimations often serve to attribute a kind of foresight to the heroine and a sense that her fate had been imagined or anticipated. They offer specific instances of what the authors regarded as their instrumentality in first imagining and then bringing about a better fate. Madeleine Henrey began very young to imagine "other destinies." In 1913, when she was about seven, she and her cousin Rolande had the good fortune to spend time in the country instead of remaining in Paris. In her memory, this summer stood out as the time "when I became conscious, for the briefest moment, that there were other destinies than the sort of servitude my mother bowed down to with a mixture of bitterness and submission, never able to leave our miserable flat and the burning streets" (57). She also remembered the occasion of her neighbor Madame Maurer telling her that " 'what you want in life you must ask for. It's all very well being proud and waiting for destiny to bring it along on a silver dish, but that's really romanticism. If you have read Grimm you will know that fairies always asked little girls what they wanted.' 'Oh, yes,' exclaimed my mother, putting down her needle and looking wistfully out of the window, 'I who have always blushed, always been timid. You see what has happened to me!' " (183)

Henrey recalled her own sense that a different fate lay in store for her and her preparation for it. She felt it as she watched boys flying kites in her neighborhood:

The boys used to arrive wearing their fathers' kepis. A few were nice, but most of the boys had the gestures and the words of their fathers. Anybody could see they would continue in the tradition. As soon as they were married they would drink too much and pick quarrels with their wives in one-room flats with the children looking on, not understanding, afraid. Yet some girls already ran after them, resigned after marriage to serve them, and probably get a beating when the pay was spent on drink.

One could tell fairly easily what most of the boys would become — modest employees, truck drivers or mechanics. I was gladder than ever to be a girl. It gave me a feeling of superiority. I knew in some secret way that I would have a big velvet hat like Didine's and sit one day to my heart's content on the terrace at Wexler's (202).

Even if what her future would look like was in no way clear to Madeleine, it was clear to her that it was not going to look like what she saw around her.

Imagining a different future and finding a way toward it recurs in these female stories of social mobility. Where the alternative vision came from varied; it could come simply from being put into a different setting — as a servant, a tutor, a summer visitor; it could come from books or stories told by mothers or friends; sometimes it followed a chance encounter with a stranger or stemmed from a friendship with someone whose world looked different, better, and reachable. The authors of success stories invariably recalled imagining themselves in a different future, in a different place from where they had grown up.[16] Their stories describe their journey and mark out the distance traveled from the point of origin, but often with only the vaguest allusion to the final destination.

The Distance Traveled

This act of imagination was imperative because of the degree to which authors of success stories deliberately had to forge for themselves not only a new class identity but also a credible account of their transformation. Militants, on the other hand, had to refashion a new *political* identity but had a stake in maintaining a sense of continuity in their social identity. They needed to continue to speak as workers. In the texts, these issues of refashioning one's life were often reflected in different literal and metaphorical uses of distancing from the family of origin.

Separation — both literal separation from parents and distancing from the culture of childhood that parents represent — figures in the plotting of workers' autobiographies and in their notions of destiny. But distance plays a varied role in these accounts.[17] The autobiographies suggest that the significance and degree of the break with parents varied not only by gender but also according to the kind of life story being told. Among militants, especially men, such a break, while often important, is rarely definitive for the plot. For the success stories, however, leaving home — putting geographic, cultural, and psychological distance between one's self and one's parents — seems more critical even if for them as well the break was never really complete. Finally, women, whatever path they followed, stuck closer to home.

Many of the autobiographers literally "left home" at an age we would see as precocious (see table 2). Boys, German boys in particular, often left home in early adolescence for apprenticeship or to search for employment, a practice that apparently continued until the early twentieth cen-

Table 2. Average Age at Which Autobiographers Reported Leaving Home*

	French Men	French Women	German Men	German Women
Authors born before 1870	14.8 (n=13)	17.5 (n=4)	16.0 (n=16)	18.5 (n=8)
Authors born after 1870	17.2 (n=9)	17.0 (n=4)	16.2 (n=15)	19.3 (n=7)

*Age was calculated as twenty when the autobiographer reported still being home at the end of the teen years.

tury. The French men's stories suggest a similar pattern early in the nineteenth century, but by the later century memoirists of both sexes stayed at or near home longer. German women authors were the least likely of all to remember leaving home in their teen years.

Authors recalled their actual physical departure from home in various ways. Sometimes, the departure was reported casually, as if undertaken as a matter of course. Some authors recalled looking eagerly toward their new situation. But others, especially the militants, recalled leaving as an economic necessity more than as a psychological emancipation. Such accounts suggest that the premature autonomy of working-class adolescents was another dimension of the overall deprivation they associated with growing up working class.

When Martin Nadaud recalled late in his life the tearfulness of his departure from home as a fourteen-year-old in the 1830s to go on the long, hard trip to Paris for work (a trip on which he was accompanied by his father), he was happy to report that such times were over. "To submit children of thirteen or fourteen years to such difficult conditions seems to me now the ultimate cruelty," he wrote. That such young migrant masons no longer traveled and worked under the hard conditions struck Nadaud as "a mark of the superiority of our civilization of today over that of the years in question" (88–89). Franz Rehbein recollected his departure from home when he was a teenager in the 1880s as an affront to working-class family life still common at the century's end. "I can still see her before me, my mother, how she took a deep breath and said, 'Well, go then. It's the fate of us poor people that we have to shove our children out into the world as soon as they can lift a finger.' And that's how it was in fact. For years people hadn't known anything different than that — that the children of poor people, as soon as they were let out of school, had to fend for themselves. The wind took them where it wanted to" (61–62).

In neither of these cases is the complaint a personal one. The hero's departure was premature and unfortunate; it did not really signal a major step forward in his life. Other kinds of distancing from parents — political or cultural — did figure into the plotting of quite a few accounts of developing militancy, but these departures, struggles, and other kinds of breaks with parents are usually less definitive than they are in success stories. Several of the militants told of having difficult relations with their families, of conflicts between the values represented by family life and those of activism. Jean-Baptiste Dumay dated his rebelliousness to his early teen years at Creusot. His parents wanted him to settle down and avoid trouble. They didn't want to let him leave home, and they only agreed when Jean-Baptiste was eighteen because he threatened to enlist in the army otherwise. Even after his marriage, his political activities continually complicated his family life, but he nevertheless repeatedly returned to his birthplace, which long remained the center of his political activities as well.

Alwin Ger described another process of distancing. He went off to the city near his mining village for his apprenticeship to a machine builder. For a while he visited his parents every Sunday, but once he set out on a plan of self-education, he stopped "since such an employment of my Sundays struck me now as wasted time, for which I had better uses" (134–35). His mother actually started coming to the town with his laundry because he didn't visit home as frequently, but Ger remembered that she could not understand what he was studying.

His relations with his parents were further strained because of a dispute over a new hat he bought. He discovered that city-born apprentices wore hats and asked his parents to help him buy one to replace the cap he wore, which marked him as a villager. To his parents this ambition represented his aspirations to act "above" his class; they advised modesty and humility more suitable to his position. For Alwin, the hat symbolized his desire and ability to improve himself and to change things. He finally managed to buy one from his own earnings and wore it "proud as a Spaniard" among the city youth. "Now I felt myself to be their equals for the first time, and nobody dared to make fun of me anymore" (145). (He did take it off and hide it, however, when he went home to visit.) City apprenticeship and all it stood for was a decisive moment in Ger's break with his parents, his village, and the culture of his childhood. Still, if Ger's adoption of socialism represented a similar rejection of his family's resigned outlook on life, it is significant that his first proselytizing effort at age sixteen was an anonymous article aimed at "reeducating" the youth of his own home village.

The fullest account of ongoing tension over leaving home exists in Charlotte Davy's autobiography. She had stayed with her widowed father through school-leaving and then went to live with an aunt. Her father asked her to return once he had remarried, but her relations with her stepmother were stormy. She held a series of jobs as a seamstress, earning sometimes as much as 2.50 francs a day, but the work was irregular. She did better when she got a job in a clothing manufactory: "I was happy to take home my pay. At least there was one reproach they could no longer direct at me: that of being fed for doing nothing" (37). But Charlotte continued to want to leave home and finally got an office job that made leaving possible. Her father was by this time retired, and her parents refused to let her leave. "My stepmother, furious with me, retorted that 'we've fed you while you were idle and you now refuse to help us, ingrate!' " (59) She finally did leave, but only at age twenty. And her departure from home is associated in her account with increased vulnerability rather than emancipation. Moreover, despite the tensions with her step-mother, Charlotte remained close to her father, who continued to be supportive as she took on a role in the emergent feminist movement. He was an encouraging presence when she gave her first speech.

For others among the militants, ties to home remained even stronger. Indeed, tales of intergenerational tension between militant youth and more conservative parents are strikingly rare. There were many cases of differences of opinion and struggles over power and contributions. One or two of the more bitter situations were resolved by an angry departure. But more often a clash of values led to an attempt like Ger's to "bring the message home." There are several stories of efforts to win over a mother whose moral authority and emotional importance remained very strong despite her "conservatism." Gaston Guiraud became a syndicalist without telling his grandmother, with whom he continued to live. She, he recalled, found out anyway and worried that he would be fired; besides, she believed, "There have to be the rich and the poor; there always have been and you're not the one to change that" (144). Franz Rehbein, who had to leave home for work at age fourteen, saw his mother again only after an absence of twenty years. She was antagonistic to his socialist politics, but she and Franz managed to arrive at a personal reconciliation. When she subsequently came to visit him and his family in Berlin, Rehbein noted, she was surprised to find his home clean and orderly, for that ran counter to her image of socialists (343–45). Anna Maier remembered having to read smuggled copies of socialist newspapers secretly at work because she didn't feel safe reading them at home in front of her mother. But she saw it as central to her task as a socialist woman "to win the mothers over" so that future generations of proletarian children would suffer less than she had (108–9). Betti Huber participated in her first strike around 1890 and remembered how "after much effort and the overcoming of many objections, I succeeded in winning my mother over to our ideas" (111).

Adelheid Popp's story is perhaps the most poignant. She remained very close to her mother despite their political disagreement. Adelheid promised her mother that she would never leave her and continued without success to try to earn her approval of political activities her mother found suspect: her mother would have preferred to see Adelheid simply marry like other girls. As Popp became increasingly involved in the socialist movement, she recalled, "My mother's opposition became an ever heavier burden to me. It inhibited my further development and I had to carry it around like a heavy weight" (91). Popp told Friedrich Engels, whom she met on one of his trips to the continent, about her difficulties at home. He and August Bebel agreed to visit Adelheid's mother at her tiny home in suburban Vienna in order to try to convince her that she should be proud of her daughter. Popp recalled that her mother, illiterate and politically uninformed, didn't understand who these important men were. Later her sole comment to Adelheid was, "Such *old* men you bring home!" (92) Her mother had evidently evaluated these leaders of the international socialist movement only as marital prospects for her daughter.

Far from rebelling against their families, many socialists, including those who like Popp had the bleakest memories of growing up, pursued political conversations with them. The deprivations of childhood offered personal motives for their political commitments, but activism also could provide a ground from which to attempt the resolution of interpersonal dilemmas as well as a reason to search for intergenerational solidarity. If militant autobiographers found much to disapprove of in the behavior of fellow workers and even parents, in the cultures from which they sprang, and in the homes they were born into, to cut themselves off would have been to deny elements of the very identity they took to be their own and championed. Much as they differed from their parents, and even suffered sometimes at their hands, they could not really find emancipation through a clean break with their past.

Telling a success story seems to have allowed or even required a more definitive break with origins. The break could take a number of forms; the simplest was departure from home for a new kind of surroundings. In true fairy-tale fashion, the earliest successes—Valentin Jamerey-Duval and Claude Genoux—left home as young boys (aged eleven and eight respectively) to seek their fortunes in the wider world. Each wrote his parents out of his story at an early point and returned home only for one brief visit later in life. Nikolaus Riggenbach went to Paris as a young apprentice to learn engineering and traveled widely thereafter. Georg Werner left home to attend a mining school. Marie Sans Gène took a series of servant jobs in upper-class households where her education in "how the other half lived" took her increasingly far from the culture of home. Her definitive departure from her native city Danzig—and from her family—led to her better future. Even after Marie's success was made, her mother continued to live out her years in the poorhouse in Danzig, refusing to join her daughter's more prosperous household. Jean Guehenno found a model for a different kind of life, and possible happiness, when he left his home in Brittany to take a position as a tutor in southern France. Angelina Bardin, an orphan who was emotionally attached to her rural foster parents, nevertheless had to return to Paris and "leave the fields behind" to change her story. Although she remained very close to her mother, Madeleine Henrey moved from Montmartre to England after her father's death; her mother eventually followed her there. Prosper Delafutry, who moved from the countryside to Paris, wrote the only other success story that explicitly mentions bringing his mother along.

The break was never clean, of course. The autobiographies themselves are often attempts to come to grips with the culture left behind—whether a sense of anger or nostalgia informs the account of the journey taken. A few of the authors went beyond nostalgia to voice doubts about whether their destinations were worth the trip. Two turn-of-the-century successes, in particular, were quite ambivalent about what taking the upward path entailed. Bruno Bürgel's interest in astronomy led him to a friendship with a university student who helped him establish a systematic program of studies. This work secured him a position at an astronomical society and eventually one at the university as well. But his story is far from the self-confident tale of the self-made man that Riggenbach and Delafutry were at least trying to tell. Bürgel, instead, returned continually to the incompleteness of his journey and his place "in-between." He saw in his daily life "workers who are suspicious of the bourgeoisie" and "bourgeois men who are condescending or hostile toward workers." His success was always tinged with his dissatisfaction at never quite belonging anywhere and the constant reminders of just how hard the road to success could be for someone not born to take it. And Jean Guehenno was acutely uncomfortable in his negotiation between the world of the educated classes and his shoemaker family. When he tried, in his autobiography, to "come to terms with this last man that I'd become, this seeker after wisdom, this man of books, seated in his easy chair," he doubted that he would ever completely succeed and felt "the dull anxiety of a sort of treason" (15).

Bürgel and Guehenno each registered the cultural and social distance they traveled at least in part as dislocation, as loss. Other successes evaluated their journey more complacently and looked back to the home they left behind with either disdain or nostalgia. But however they evaluated the trip, they told their stories from a different place than where they started — a place they once imagined and now inhabited. And because they are told from a position that is no longer working class, the success stories' transformations thus ironically serve as keen registers — perhaps keener even than the tales of the "class conscious" militants — of the differences that class made, of the palpable distance that they had to travel.

Grouped here are portraits of several of the autobiographers who did not include portraits in the original editions of their works. Some of these were included in later editions of the authors' autobiographies; some are from entirely different sources.

Claude Genoux. Contemporary portrait from the 1888 edition of his memoirs, reproduced in the 1983 edition, following p. 154. (Genoux, *Mémoires d'un enfant de la Savoie* [Montmelian: Gens de Savoie])

Claude Genoux as a boy in a troop of chimney sweeps. From the 1888
edition of his memoirs, reproduced in the 1983 edition, following p. 154.
(Genoux, *Mémoires d'un enfant de la Savoie* [Montmelian: Gens de Savoie])

Claude Genoux encountering a patron on the road. From the 1888 edition of his memoirs, reproduced in the 1983 edition, following p. 154. (Genoux, *Mémoires d'un enfant de la Savoie* [Montmelian: Gens de Savoie])

Ottilie Baader. From the cover of the 1979 edition of her autobiography. (Archiv der sozialen Demokratie der Friedrich-Ebert-Stiftung)

Marie Wegrainer [Marie Frank]. Frontispiece portrait from the 1979 edition of her memoirs. (Privatarchiv Charlotte Frank)

Jeanne Bouvier (front row, right) at an international conference of women workers, 1921. Cover photograph from the 1983 edition of her memoirs. (La Découverte)

Luise Zeitz. Sketch from Marie Juchacz, *Sie lebten für eine bessere Welt. Lebensbildern führender Frauen des 19. und 20. Jahrhunderts* (1958). (J. H. W. Dietz Nachfolger, Berlin/Bonn)

Adelheid Popp (seated, second from right) and Amalie Poelzer (standing, third from left) with members of the Frauenreichs- und N.Ö-Frauenlandes-kommittee, 1917. (J. H. W. Dietz Nachfolger, Berlin/Bonn)

I wanted . . . to realize a personal goal to which I have been attached for a long time . . . to put into relief the successive phases through which a worker's child must pass in order to become a militant and, simply, to become a man. (Georges Dumoulin, 11)

EIGHT

CONCLUSION

AUTOBIOGRAPHY AND HISTORY

These stories about the acquisition of class identity provide unique insights into the chronology of European class identity as a subjective experience. The testimonies began with the success story of Valentin Jamerey-Duval, an ironic self-portrait in the idiom of the Enlightenment. Jamerey-Duval was pretty much on his own, an anomalous peasant who became learned enough to publish his life story. Only decades later was he joined by a trickle, and then a stream, of fellow travelers, authors originating in the milieux of manual labor who came to leave a records of their lives—such artisans as Jacques-Louis Ménétra, Christian Döbel, and Agricol Perdiguier, or Utopians such as Suzanne Voilquin and Norbert Truquin. Political organization around the identity of worker added to the flow; Central European socialists such as Joseph Peukert, Adelheid Popp, and Nikolaus Osterroth told one set of stories while French syndicalists Möise Teyssandier, Georges Dumoulin, and Louis Lecoin told another. And theirs were not the only voices. As if to insist on another reality, men and women who had made it as entrepreneurs or academics, as good middle-class wives or as writers—Nikolaus Riggenbach, Marie Sans Gène, Prosper Delafutry, and Madeleine Henrey—added their distinctive accounts. More reluctant autobiographers—"Kathrin" and the anonymous authors of *Erinnerungen eines Waisenknaben* and *Im Kampf ums Dasein*—sounded discordant notes from the edge of the crowd.

Plots and Identities: National and Temporal Dimensions

E. P. Thompson long ago demonstrated the importance of examining the meanings that class relationships hold and how people construct such relationships through concrete historical experiences. By turning attention to the political-cultural dimensions of the English working-class identity, he not only challenged previous temporal and spatial landmarks of the history of class formation in England, but he also revolutionized historians' understanding of class.[1]

Workers' autobiography tracks not only changes in the experiences and categories people used to discuss class—the evolution from "people to proletariat"[2] and from proletariat to the more subtle and less culturally established identities of class in postwar and even postsocialist Europe—but something more as well. In addition to the insight they offer into the ways of earning livelihoods and reproducing the next generation of workers, the subjective and personal nature of these texts permit a view into the process of how working-class destiny, imagination, and self-understanding was nurtured and changed. Class identity, these texts make clear, had life-cyclical, familial, and gender dimensions along with its more familiar economic and political-cultural anchorings.

Temporalities differed, as one might expect, in the French and German proletarian milieux these texts describe. Different metaphors and stereotypes prevailed in them; different purposes structured them. Ways of telling the story of growing up working class were rooted in the different histories of politicization of working-class identity in France and

Central Europe. Conversely, these autobiographies strongly suggest that different memories and understandings of the growing-up experience — an experience already deeply marked by class long before the stories came to be told — also fed in different ways into the comparisons, resentments, or moments of nostalgia or anger that were later articulated in class identity. The cultural disappearance by the end of the nineteenth century of the French *gamin* — the poor and troublesome street urchin — and the contrasting centrality of the "bad childhood story" to German memoirs reflected the incorporation of working-class children into the mainstream institutions of childhood in France a generation or so earlier than in Central Europe. Experiencing childhood in a class-specific way certainly did not disappear (and still has not disappeared) in either place, but the sharpness of the contrasts between classes, and the role these contrasts played in political discourse diminished earlier in France. The somewhat more gradual character of French industrialization, which might have reduced somewhat its disruption of family economies, was thus echoed in autobiographical subjectivity.[3]

The stories often resorted for their narrative power to contrasts, either comparisons between expectations and experiences or between the author's own experiences and those of the more privileged. Childhood stories show this tendency most directly, but the narrative strategy persists through accounts of adolescence as well. Some episodes looked similar across the linguistic divide — in particular, the disappointments associated with the denial of intellectual ambitions at school-leaving. However, German adolescent boys are portrayed, even late in the nineteenth century, as cut loose from the family at age fourteen, living as apprentices or workers without proper supervision, on their own at an age when their counterparts in France (or England, for that matter) were still living at home. Again this image seems to have been institutionally based in the persistence in Central Europe of practices and expectations rooted in the artisanal life cycle. The boys portrayed in German autobiography grew up earlier and often with a more problematic relationship to the family; extrafamilial working-class institutions played a larger role in their stories.[4] The informal apprenticeship that persisted in Belle Epoque France did not separate boys from their families and no longer relegated them in quite the same way to the autonomy of the artisan subculture.[5]

This artisanal identity stamped on German boys at a fairly young age and persisting longer in Central Europe was connected to temporal and national differences. Historians of working-class political organization agree on the important role older artisanal traditions and organizations played in working-class formation even in the era of industrialization.[6] The French historian Gérard Noiriel has suggested, however, that there was a distinct rupture in France between the early nineteenth-century artisanal culture and the later wave of workers' organization around the turn of the century.[7] The memoirs echo this notion of rupture, drawn to date largely in terms of organizational and ideological discontinuities. The autobiographical evidence suggests an additional dimension that was familial and life-cyclical in character. The early French male memoirists set out from home young and recalled spending their adolescence in the all-male and organizationally based cryptofamilies of the *compagnonnages*, the migrant barracks, the café. The syndicalists of the later century more typically recounted living at home through the teen years and dividing their time (and income) among workplace, home, and neighborhood peer groups. This shift, of course, is a shift in preserved representations (autobiographies), not necessarily in lived experiences.

But representing the process of becoming working-class was, I have argued, connected to the project of organizing those identities politically. Representations of the connections between life course and class identity highlighted certain ways of becoming and being working class and suppressed others. Traveling artisans did not necessarily disappear from the French landscape earlier than in Central Europe (although they probably did), but the element of masculine class identity associated with leaving home in early adolescence and living without family during a formative stage of life seems to have disappeared earlier in France, along with the particular institutions that supported and emerged from this practice. Not only did the practices around apprenticeship and tramping last longer in Central Europe; they also continued longer to shape the politicized class identity of the worker.

Although the broader consequences of these differences for the character of class formation and political culture must remain speculative, they are suggestive. The autobiographies perhaps reveal the sociogenesis, even psychogenesis, of the somewhat different political programs organized workers eventually put forward. To mention one possibility, inherent in Central European socialist policy — both as formulated in discussions and eventually put into practice locally and nationally in the period leading up to and following World War I — was a sense of the state's responsibility to compensate for the inadequacies of working-class families. Where Social Democratic influence was strongest, such government-funded institutions as canteens, cooperatives, child-care facilities, housing complexes, festivals, and libraries provided what the family could not.[8] To be sure, this agenda mirrored distinctly bourgeois concerns about the nature of the working-class family, but to dismiss it in this way would be to overlook connections with the experiences of deprivation of adequate family life so characteristic of German militants' memoirs of childhood and adolescence.[9] These programs may well have been shaped by workers' demands for compensatory measures.

The socialist reorganization of everyday life that occurred so markedly in Central Europe in places where the Socialist Party gained power contrasted with the relegation of family welfare initiatives to the solidarist state in France. There, government programs focused on pronatalist measures centered around the mother-child pair. Typically, these were initiatives of middle-class reformers with state backing. It could be argued that this emphasis was at least in part the result of the relative inattention to or lower level of concern of the workers' movement for "private matters" involving the family.[10] There were relatively few localities in France where extensive experiments in redesign of working-class neighborhoods or institutions for the support of working-class family life — such as those put forward in Vienna, Berlin, and Frankfurt before and especially after the First World War — could be found. But another factor was also involved — namely, the starker gender polarization inherent in the syndicalist identity that was so central to working-class politics in France in the pre–World War I period. This polarization, which allowed for the politicization of working-class women primarily as mothers, only limited further the state's involvement in family matters to exclusively pronatalist policies initiated without significant worker input.

Plots and Identities: Gender Dimensions

In this regard and in others, the stories these people told about themselves demonstrate how different "working-class identity" was for men and for women. The stories differed not only, as expected, in content but in structure as well.

For male workers, life stories followed or deviated from one of several well-marked routes. German socialist men, whose politics provided them with a fairly clear idea of the problems inherent in growing up working class, recognized in their own lives the perils of childhood in a home where economic marginality brought alcoholism, paternal neglect or brutality, and the evils of child labor. In school, they had come to see, the teacher stood in for the state. And the state was single-minded in its agenda for working-class boys — to make them into obedient cannon fodder and to offer only limited education so as to deprive them of their full critical potential. Adolescence, once clearly demarcated by the transitions surrounding apprenticeship, was shifting by the turn of the twentieth century as industrialization undermined the economic promise of apprenticeship. Sometimes, instead of apprenticing formally at school-leaving, boys simply drifted into full-time labor in the local plantation, factory, or office or went on the road to pursue employment. Even if old routines no longer meant the same thing, the moment seems to have retained its life-cyclical significance. Then, through contacts at work or in the new location to which the search for employment brought him, the hero discovered new comrades or new ambitions. Either gradually or in a sudden moment of inspiration placed normatively in the late teen years or the early twenties, the young worker turned to socialism and found in it his mission in life.

For French militant men, childhood was not necessarily remembered as entirely miserable. Warm family lives provided some compensations even for the poorest, perhaps even looked good in comparison with the complaints they had read in middle-class memoirs.[11] In contrast with the German men's, school stories were sometimes tales of downright triumph. The roots of insurgency typically only sprouted later, in work life, even if injustices observed earlier were eventually integrated into the evolving vision.

Moreover, specifically syndicalist stories dominated French memoirs by the turn of the century and left their stamp on the identity of the militant. What had to happen for someone to "become a militant" if not "simply to become a man" occurred predominantly through interactions in workplaces and union halls. Of course this is in part an artifact of the sources. Few stories from this later period by French workers identified their authors primarily as socialists;[12] apparently the encouragement for publishing such stories was far weaker in France than in Central Europe. Arguably this scarcity is in some sense not accidental but rather a product of the institutions of the workers' movement itself. There is a strong likelihood that the relative marginality of the working-class socialist hero to French workers' autobiography reflects self-images then circulating in working-class culture. The stories do not exist now because they did not exist then.

In contrast to this political-cultural difference in the chronology of male militant life plots, male success stories do not exhibit the same sort of differences between French and German texts; their heroes, of course, were more international to begin with. They traveled, and so did the people into whose circles they moved. The similarities among these stories may also stem from institutional parallels across national divides — coming up by way of a technological or academic education, perhaps with help from a bourgeois self-help or popular education movement, left a similar cultural imprint wherever it occurred. Moreover, because these authors were rarely drawn from the most deprived of circumstances, the differences in working-class family life in France and Central Europe, felt most strongly in the most economically marginal families, may have been less significant to them.

For women, the plots were very different from those of men. Central European militant women shared the same miserable childhoods as their male counterparts, but the resemblances between their stories and the men's are few beyond that point. They did not, for the most part, recount suffering in school, so they could not trace their insurgency to early negative encounters with state authority. Adolescence did not represent for them such a clear break with childhood; no defining moment of leaving home and orienting themselves to a workplace or a new town opened new possibilities for them. They associated their initiation into sexuality almost exclusively with new modes of victimization; there is surprisingly little range of female sexual possibility over the time and space the stories document. They recalled remaining strikingly close to home, to their parents, including the mothers with whom they did not necessarily agree politically. If they were to find a political frame to shape their lives, they had to find it at home. This was a path to militancy that hardly matched the typical male model; only when the socialist subculture provided access through familial connections could women begin to imagine themselves becoming militants. It is hardly surprising, then, that most of the women who became activists in the Socialist Party and its affiliated unions initially did so as members of the families of male socialists.

If the German and Austrian women militants represented in autobiography had to struggle to provide themselves with models for female militancy, French women seem to have faced an even more difficult task. Not only did the state dominate family policy, of most concern to women, it also set the tone for representations of the working-class woman: she was first and foremost a suffering mother,[13] an expectable finding in view of state concerns with encouraging population growth. But because there was also little space for women in the syndicalist movement, there was not much of a basis from which to counter this state definition; probably there was not even much disagreement with the official imagery from within the workers' movement.[14] That the only autobiographies I have found in French of militant working-class women from the epoch of syndicalism (though others will no doubt eventually surface) are those of Davy and Bouvier — neither of whom had children — is in itself telling. There was such a separation between the image of militant and that of mother that combining the two must have been a trying task indeed. Here again, the scarcity of autobiographies suggests a lack of institutional support for certain — specifically female — patterns of becoming working class. And this scarcity underscores a deep-seated deprivation associated with gender. Not only did women suffer the deprivations that working-class men did; they seem even to have been deprived of the means men had to construct clear models that accounted for deprivation and promised paths out of it.

The autobiographies demonstrate how people found and used models for making sense of their lives, for adopting and rearranging their sense of themselves, for explaining how they came to be what they were. The plots that circulated, and the ones that could not or did not, make plain that self-images and ideas are tied to institutions: they emphasize the continual interaction between specific identities and specific social-institutional supports for those identities. The striking differences between the stories men and women told are perhaps the strongest demonstration of the social dimensions of constructing identities.

Making History: Autobiography and Agency

Autobiographies are typically plotted to answer a question of causal analysis: how did I become the kind of person I am today? The logic of autobiography requires at least an implicit answer to this question. Authors, in plotting their answers, have to decide how much to emphasize their own efforts and activities as opposed to resorting to the concepts of providence, or fate, or deterministic social forces outside their control.

Autobiographers tended to portray themselves as less in control in childhood than at later points in life, but they chose a variety of idioms and strategies for handling the complex question of agency. Authors such as Alwin Ger represented the transformative moment in their lives as an intellectual awakening for which their previous life had prepared them. For Marie Sans Gène, the plot more resembled a fairy tale: in her words, "my life took a completely different turn apparently through pure chance" (220). Such contrasts are significant, but they should not be exaggerated. Ger also talked of the "truly religious" mood that accompanied his moment of conversion to socialism. For him and others who recorded such conversions, the determined reading or study that often characterized the militant life story could still be accompanied by a sudden flash of insight or a chance encounter that made a critical difference. And the fairy-tale heroine Sans Gène had prepared herself for the moment of her deliverance by years of hard work. The "pure chance" was perhaps merely apparent. Both of these accounts, as is typical of the autobiographies in general, vacillate in their causal accounting between a focus on the author's intentional actions and the press of circumstances. Most writers emphasized their own agency, but there is always at least a subtextual role for chance. Only a few texts—not surprisingly those that do not clearly follow one of the standard plots of militant's life or success story—depict the hero or heroine primarily as a victim of circumstances. To use the metaphors developed by Norbert Ortmayr in his analysis of the life stories of Austrian rural farm servants, not one of these authors denied having been dealt a bad hand, but each offered evidence of having played that hand better than might have been predicted. Some even appeared to play it masterfully, and certainly better than many of their less fortunate class-fellows.[15]

Nearly all of these stories—militants' and success stories alike—share their authors' remembered determination to refashion their apparent destiny. They may not have wanted to tell the story that way, for they may have been intellectually committed to a contrary view of the limited power of human agency. Several of the socialist authors, for example, paid lip service to notions of destiny inherent in readings of Marx that they no doubt had encountered. Heinrich Lange began his autobiography with a disclaimer: "I don't believe in the saying: a man makes his own destiny. On the contrary, the individual is the product of the past through his ancestry, influenced by the environment and socialization in youth, and his actions are directed by his condition in life which he has to either come to terms with or confront" (3). Heinrich Holek, in a passage where he described and then forgave a transgression of his father,[16] wrote, "I don't reprove him for this. Because every person is a product of his conditions and his environment. They are the mold in which we are shaped and from which we emerge" (76–77). Dr. G. Braun's introduction to *Im Kampf ums Dasein* articulated the liberal variant on this theme: "These unfortunates . . . are the social victims of horrifying social abuses, which the state and all the parties have a great interest in correcting" (8). But the authors continually contradicted such deterministic visions in plotting their own lives. Very few claimed unambiguously to have forged their own path. The odds against it, as they all too well knew, were simply too high. Contingencies play a role in all the stories. Things might easily have turned out differently, but neither by their own account were these workers simply pushed along by fate or resigned to what was seemingly in store for them.

Certainly the nature of the source is important to consider here. People who choose to write autobiographies are no doubt self-selected for the strong egos our culture has come to identify with the active subject; an emphasis on the role of human action in their understandings of how the world works is thus hardly surprising. Moreover, the very project of autobiography is to impose a design, a logic, on a life. As such, it brings out in authors the tendency to find a causal logic that might have been less clear-cut had it not been for the literary need to create it.

But the overall presumption of the power of human agency is underscored by the contrast between the more conventionally plotted militants' lives and success stories and several of the texts that fit in neither of these categories. On the margins of the genre rests a tendency toward egolessness, fatalism, and impassivity, in particular among those "reluctant" or "accidental" autobiographers whose writings were solicited or encouraged by others or who wrote to describe their victimization. Weak egos are indeed apparent in some authors who seem never to have had it in them to take charge of their lives. Certainly two of the anonymous German texts fit this characterization, as does that of the French foundling Ida van de Leen. The authors wrote to bewail their destiny, to argue simply that they were victimized through no fault of their own. A similar aimlessness and even despair marks the stories by Carl Fischer and Marie Wegrainer.[17]

Perhaps the clearest example of a "victim" story is Lena Christ's. Christ, whose autobiography ends on a note of despair and whose life ended in suicide, presented herself as a victim of her abusive mother. Her decision to marry a man who would in turn brutalize her came not because she saw the marriage as desirable but rather because she saw no other way out of her unsatisfactory home life. The account of her moment of betrothal is itself distinctive when compared with the careful and self-directed marriage strategies of the women authors who wrote success stories. Unlike Marie Sans Gène, Madeleine Henrey, or Verena Conzett, Lena was something of a pawn in the transaction, confused about her role even though she had participated in the selection of her suitor. In the context of Lena's troubled relationship with her mother, stemming from her mother's shame at Lena's illegitimate birth and her subsequent efforts to make her life respectable, the daughter's marriage was swallowed into the mother's crusade. After her future husband presented her with a ring, Christ recalled:

> Because I had never experienced this sort of thing before, I had to ponder what I should now do or say. Luckily I recalled a scene in a novel, in which something similar happened and I behaved just like the heroine of this book: I blushed, looked confusedly toward the ground, and whispered: "Oh! how sweet!" then, falling back into my more usual natural manner, continued: "Listen, Benno, you shouldn't a spent so much money. My Mom will have a really hard time tryin' to match this."
>
> But then I approached my mother.
>
> "But what can you be thinkin' of me?" she cried with sparkling eyes. "Didn't you know I'd do what it took for you to be able to give your bridegroom a respectable present! Here, Herr Hasler, is your engagement ring; I hope I didn't make a bad deal at Thomas's" (223).[18]

After the marriage, Lena's life went from bad to worse. She was a victim of her husband's sexual passion, bore more children than she wanted to, was rejected by both families and eventually had to give up the children. Her story ends on this note of failure, this revelation of the extent of her incapacity.

Similar dynamics appear in others of these stories. The author of *Dulden*, who wrote from an asylum after being accused of infanticide, also presented herself as a victim of her mother. Specifically she suffered throughout her life from her mother's deathbed wish that she not marry the cousin she loved (the title of the book — *Dulden*, meaning patience or long suffering — came from the word printed on a ribbon on her mother's casket). Marie Wegrainer, who wrote to give her son a legacy because she had nothing else to give him, ended up where she did (in a common-law relationship and eventually bleak marriage with a poor man) in flight from her mother and her stepfather. Carl Fischer's story begins with his father's abuse of him and ends in loneliness and aimlessness.

Against the more centered accounts, the authors of these marginal texts told stories as victims of parental abuse; some fell early into adult relationships in which they were exploited, abused, or abandoned. It is impossible to generalize on the basis of these few stories about how the aimless and alienated became this way or why among them principally female voices resound. But can it be merely the failure to follow a typical plot that makes their stories stand out? These fates perhaps suggest the greater level of despair that might have emerged as a matter of course in working-class autobiography—given the level of poverty, abuse, and bleakness that often surrounded the poor as children—except for the selectivity that instead nurtured autobiographers who left a different collective portrait. If instead of the ego disorganization and despair that appear to exist on the margins of the genre resourcefulness and an ability to survive characterize the more common stories, is it because the social and institutional supports these authors found on their way to militancy or success distinguished them from these others? Are these voices from the margins indications of an aimlessness that was more typical of all of the lives that did not culminate in autobiography?

Such questions, are, of course, unanswerable and emphasize again the simultaneous richness and limitations of the texts (and our limitations as interpreters). Working-class autobiographers were both eloquent and extraordinary; despite levels of deprivation that were in some cases truly extreme, most workers who wrote autobiographies displayed not alienation and despair but a strong sense of their own efficacy as agents in their own lives and as makers of history. Telling a life story brought out the agent in them, to be sure. But more deeply, in all probability, the experiences that led them to see their lives as "worth telling" also encouraged them to see themselves as mattering, as making a difference. Most working-class autobiographers, however daunting the constraints of their lives, worked to plot their own destinies.

Autobiography, Agency, and the Discourse on Class

Moreover, for most of the authors, including some of the most despairing, writing autobiography was in its own way an effort to take control of their lives and to shape the historical record. Not only was writing autobiography usually a by-product of either individual social mobility or work on behalf of class improvement, it was also explicitly a contribution to the evolving discourse of class. Intervening in this discourse, in politically charged exchanges about the nature of class relations and the meaning of working-class birth, was part of the continuum of activities that reshaped the future of class relations and class conditions. Autobiographies, in fact, appeared as particularly compelling and "authentic" perspectives on working-class reality, and their authors spoke with authority about efforts to rethink and reorganize class relations. For their various audiences they carried models of how to be or warnings of what to watch out for.

The Dignity of Self-Representation

Regina Gagnier has argued that "autobiography is the arena of empower-ment to represent oneself in a discursive cultural field as well as the arena of subjective disempowerment by the 'subjecting' discourses of others."[19] In contributing their personal stories of "authentic" working-class iden-tity, autobiographers were also explicitly countering other versions of working-class reality that originated elsewhere in the social hierarchy or political spectrum. Sometimes the misinformation that workers felt the need to counter came from middle-class writers.[20] Roger Magraw has noted the particular example of Martin Nadaud, who saw himself as playing a role in the "struggle to reject bourgeois stereotyping of workers ... [the] refusal to be 'named' as 'savages' by the elites."[21] The climate of bourgeois condemnation and misrepresentation shaped decisively auto-biographers' insistence on their integrity, respectability, and authen-ticity. Moïse Teyssandier offered a clear illustration in his memoir, ad-dressed to the "mute" workers. "Stop and think a minute, Barbasse,[22] anonymous Barbasse, lost among the anonymous thousands of your spe-cies. Do you think there's a chance that your memories will be of interest to anyone? Haven't thousands and thousands of poor fellows, poor little urchins like yourself, had experiences at least as interesting as yours? They haven't said a word about them; they haven't sung them from the rooftops ... your fellow workers live and die silent about their existence" (21). Teyssandier went on to note that novels purported to portray working-class life, but they were written by "novelists who haven't lived [workers'] lives, [who are] very far from their feelings and aspirations" (21). Moreover, he noted, he had read success stories and wanted to sympathize with their authors, but in these works the act of pulling one-self up began with having had an education — through a lycée, collège, or a pastor's instruction. These stories angered him since they were not the stories of the typical poor, who were taxed for, but never saw the inside of, these institutions (22).

Such an urge to redefine came largely but not only from the militants. In her preface, Marie Sans Gène mentioned with irony that contempo-rary discussions of the plight of servant girls for the most part ignored their own testimony. Servants as such do not write; when they were no longer servants, "false shame" prevented their writing from the perspec-tive of their former identity (7).

Of course, some authors directed their words against the socialist ver-sion of class destiny. Writers of success stories in particular, who had invested themselves in assimilation into the middle class, often wrote to offer workers alternative visions to those that militants propounded. Prosper Delafutry was most explicit about this. He wrote "to show workers what can be accomplished by work, perseverance and economy adjoined with honesty . . . [and to show that our society] is better than those which have preceded it" (7). That he did so in the wake of the Communard insurrection and with the encouragement of a self-improvement association is hardly coincidental. His route offered ambitious workers an alternative to militancy, to define the plight of the worker not against a bourgeois misrepresentation but against what he saw as a socialist one.

These texts clearly entered into an increasingly urgent discussion of "the social question." Such historians as Rachel Fuchs and Joan Scott, for example, have discussed the reshaping of understandings of the plight of the woman worker in texts by middle-class authors in nineteenth-century France.[23] Fuchs has surveyed the wide range of opinions on the subject and has documented changes that occurred, both in cultural representation and in policy, toward the end of the century. But she has also pointed out how difficult it is to get at the actual opinions of "the poor and pregnant" themselves. Her evidence was hidden away in the dossiers of the charity hospitals and family courts. Middle-class women had come to express themselves in public by the century's end, but not so women workers.[24] In Germany, as Alfred Kelly, Ann Taylor Allen, and Joan Campbell have documented,[25] there was increasing public expression of concern about family life and mothering among the poor, about the changing characteristics of work life and its implications, and about the psychological profile of workers.

It was at least in part to counter and rectify this existing discourse on workers that autobiographers wrote from and claimed a position of authenticity. This authenticity was, of course, rhetorical rather than sociological.[26] Autobiographers, by virtue of having become autobiographers, were almost by definition no longer "typical" workers. They were boundary crossers, highly self-conscious because of their experiences as organizers or as movers up the social ladder. Their perceptions and claims were marked by these positions. They thus spoke with deep cultural and even moral ambiguity; in the name of class improvement, they rejected those aspects of their culture of origin that they deemed problematic. Their own position as products of this culture — in Bruno Bürgel's telling phrase, "the curse of proletarian birth" — was a precarious one; the emotional and intellectual deprivation they reported having suffered, had, they seemed to feel, made them "less" than they might otherwise have been. Their recognition of the costs of working-class origins echoes in both militants' accounts and many of the other stories as well, ranging from the intellectual anger of Alwin Ger through Jean Guehenno's unforgiving portrait of his mother and the self-doubts of Lena Christ. They sometimes saw a different potential embodied in people who had had it easier. Their envy of the middle-class child's easy access to toys and time to study, their anger at the general failure to recognize just how difficult it was for the worker to speak and write with confidence[27] also placed them in precarious situations. For, implicitly or explicitly, they came to understand their own deprivation through comparison with their class superiors; thus they could not avoid, even when they wanted to, internalizing some of that resentment in the form of wanting for workers what they had been deprived of instead of critiquing their desires.[28]

Nevertheless, as complicated as their position was, it was also in another sense epistemologically "privileged." These writers were astute observers of class dynamics precisely because of their marginality. In this they resemble other marginal types — for example, Europe's middle-class Jews upon whose experiences Naomi Scheman rests her notion of "privileged marginality."[29] As people who traversed class boundaries, working-class autobiographers were particularly attuned to the subtleties of class marking. Like actors who study every aspect of the characters they portray, those who crossed class boundaries became keenly aware of the ways in which class identity was not just about what work you did, it was about how you wrote and talked, dressed and behaved, felt and hoped as well.

Still, if their visions of a better future were influenced by the only alternatives they saw around them — those lived by their class superiors — they were also marked by their own experiences of coming from another reality. Thus their understandings of the problems inherent in "working-class culture" need to be seen as something more than the simple product of embourgeoisement. They are in this sense privileged insights, not merely evidence of cooptation. It is unfair to presume that whenever these authors wanted some of the things they had been deprived of, they did so only because in seeking to change the destinies of those of working-class origin, they had fallen from some hypothetical position of more authentic proletarian grace.

Endings

How do their stories end? Some autobiographers reflected back on a "whole life" as they wrote their memoirs. Some wrote as grandparents and even great-grandparents about a world they wished to describe and analyze for the young. Such militants as Ottilie Baader, Jeanne Bouvier, Julius Bruhns, and Georges Dumoulin addressed themselves to a younger generation of militants. Ludwig Richter and Nikolaus Riggenbach recalled their younger days as a self-conscious contribution to the history of a locality or a profession; they wrote as "old ones" at the end of their days. Older authors, whether they followed a militant or upwardly mobile path, often wrote with the complacency of a life well lived. Robert Köhler assured himself on the eve of publication in 1913 that "my only comfort is that I can tell myself that I haven't lived in vain" (3). Wilhelm Kaisen and Karl Grünberg, publishing late in life in the 1960s in West and East Germany, respectively, each felt that history had confirmed his particular brand of militancy. Even the anarchist-pacifist Louis Lecoin looked back from postwar France over his long life, much of which was spent in prison, with a certain optimism that the efforts of defenders of human life such as himself "could not continue to be in vain" (dedication).

Of course it helped if an older author also happened to be writing in an epoch of calm and apparent progress. The complacency of Lecoin's memoirs may well reflect postwar prosperity as much as the calm of his later life. It was harder for those writing late in life in, say, the 1920s or 1930s, to be so sure of the outcome of the struggle from which they were about to depart. For Baader or Bruhns, the struggle was still very much in progress. But even Bouvier could write from the "sweet quietude" of a retirement home.

Some stories end just on the verge of possibly better things, portending well for the unknown future. At the end of her story[30] Madeleine Henrey took a new job at the Savoy Hotel in London and wondered about her future as her mother dealt with a telegram informing her of her sister's death. Marie Sans Gène, Angelina Bardin, and René Bonnet also ended their stories with a voyage into an unknown fate.

Others ended on the verge of disaster — Franz Bergg wrote from prison, and an afterword tells the reader that he was not long to survive; Lena Christ ended with a lament about her superfluity, her failure, as a person. Moritz Bromme ended anticipating his impending death from tuberculosis, his wife's widowhood, his children's lives as orphans. Franz Rehbein, readers learn from an afterword, survived the publication of his memoirs by only two years and died at age thirty-two.

But most of the autobiographies followed none of these narrative strategies; most have an unfinished quality about them. Either they were written as stories of childhood and youth that end abruptly on the threshold of an active adulthood still being lived, or they continued the tale into adulthood and simply dissolve without much closure in the author's present. About a fifth of the texts were written before the author's fortieth birthday; most were written when the authors were in their forties or fifties. Only rarely does a sense of closure exist in them. No matter at which precise point in the life course the story was told (which did influence what was told and how it was told) rarely, except among the oldest authors, was a definitive ending described. For even as they wrote, the autobiographers were busy reconstructing themselves and their place in history. In Jean Guehenno's words, "Our memory is a very great artist . . . it contrives and arranges everything so that at each instant we will not be too discontented with ourselves, won't feel ashamed of ourselves, won't lack the necessary will to live on, face the future, this tomorrow which, barely lived, [the memory] reconstructs with its knowing and faithful hands until the day when model and artist disappear together" (13). Claude Genoux took a simple and direct route out of the dilemma of how to end his story: "Reader, I am stopping here. Still a worker like before, and that simply so that I can earn my bread honestly and help my family. I don't have the energy anymore to use my few moments of respite for work . . . my sixtieth year is at hand" (345).

In my rereading of these stories, I certainly can do no better at tying everything up neatly, but neither can I simply conclude the way Genoux or any other autobiographer did. So I will end where I might have begun — with a statement about my role in reviving these stories, my agenda in reading them into the history of class identity. Sometimes I suspect that I am just an updated Arthur Munby, or Dr. G. Braun, or Hedwig Bleuler-Wafer. Munby was a Victorian photographer who encouraged the maidservant Hannah Cullwick to write her memoirs. As Leonore Davidoff and Julia Swindells have argued, however, Munby's fascination with Cullwick as an embodiment of the "other" class and gender, the complicated relationship between the two, and Munby's role in Hannah's authorship, all call into question just whose voice readers hear in such a text as Cullwick's. Dr. G. Braun edited the anonymous memoir *Im Kampf ums Dasein* and reinterpreted her life as one of victimization even as the author herself saw in her life a decided integrity and perhaps wrote to defend her virtue. Bleuler-Wafer wrote the preface to *Dulden* and in so doing presented the author as authentic because she was simple-minded.

At the simplest level, my aim in undertaking this project was to find sources that would further democratize the historical record. Feminist scholarship opened up for me possibilities for using autobiography in historical inquiry that paralleled methodological innovations shaping oral history, social history, women's history, and labor history. As I began to collect workers' autobiographies, I noted the frequency with which authors expressed their desire to speak to the public, to become part of the historical record, to have their lives remembered. Ironically, the insistence of these workers on seizing the word in their lifetimes made their stories available to historians seeking to rediscover the subjective, but these writers could not control how their stories would be read. In the hands of some historians, the testimony of working-class writers is a tool with which to critique the authors' projects, or even to dismiss them, in the name of deconstructing the "Western personality." My aims lie more in the direction of querying, and perhaps recovering, certain aspects of these projects. They too intended to democratize the historical record, a project consistent with my own current political recognition of the need, more urgent now than ever, to nurture democracy in the institutions of everyday life and in culture, as well in economic and political organization. As a motivation, mine is certainly no less intrusive or directive than the aims of earlier editors who sought to reveal life in the depths or to capture workers for solidarism or socialism. I have certainly made judgments. As is no doubt apparent, I like some of these authors immensely; others among them I find pompous and self-serving. And while I find the optimism and smugness of such success stories as those of Prosper Delafutry or Nikolaus Riggenbach hard to take, I found myself taken despite myself by such others as Madeleine Henrey's or Jean Guehenno's. In addition I probably have more tolerance for the pieties of the self-educated than would historians who celebrate working-class popular culture and the counter-normative aspects of working-class family life more enthusiastically than I do. Some authors at times disappointed me keenly. That E. Unger-Winkelreid wrote his story to explain his conversion "from Bebel to Hitler" did not, I feel, throw my analysis into doubt; his text, after all, strikes out on its own and resembles neither in its ending nor in its beginning the stories of militants I freely admit to admiring, though not unreservedly.[31] But I was horrified to discover that one of the militants whose autobiography I found most compelling — Georges Dumoulin — in his later years (in a development that occurs after his story ends) advocated as the best possibility for French workers at that bleak historical moment collaboration with the Vichy regime.[32] But I hope that I have managed, despite my far from disinterested perspective on the history of class identities, to have been evenhanded in my reading of the texts. However I have judged particular texts and their authors, I have tried to give them a hearing and to understand their own assessments of their life and choices. As a historian, I believe it is crucial to contextualize these texts, but I've tried to avoid condescending through contextualization—to avoid dismissing their authors as simply deluded about their situation, their power, their level of cooptation. And I have tried to reconstruct a picture of the past that takes seriously, indeed is built from, accounts of living through and making history written by people whose stories are always at risk of being lost.

Chapter 1

1. Here and throughout the book, the autobiographical sources will be cited in the text in parenthetical form using the author's name and the page from which the quotation is drawn. Complete citations for the particular edition of the auto-biographical work from which the quotation is drawn are in the first section of the bibliography, arranged alphabetically by author's last name. The first section of the bibliography also includes basic biographical information on each author to make it easier for readers to keep track of the many authors cited. Except in the few cases where the cited work is an English-language edition, I have translated all of the quotations.

2. While the publication of autobiographies by commercial and socialist presses diminished, worker's life stories continued to be told in other forms. In Eastern Europe, for example, Communist Party–sponsored efforts to collect workers' testimonies brought together large numbers of generally unpublished texts. Privately written memoirs, of course, continued to be produced; in England, unpublished texts found in attics and other repositories of family memorabilia and dating from the nineteenth through the twentieth century form the basis of the collections of edited workers' memoirs published by John Burnett (1974). Some stories were captured in oral form in the United States in the 1930s by government-funded projects. The new interest in the genre of workers' autobiography in the wake of "history from below" since the 1960s is reflected in the numerous reprintings and anthologies cited in the first two sections of the bibliography.

3. See Bertaux (1981) and Geiger (1986).

4. See Passerini (1989). The ways in which this selectivity shapes the stories will emerge in more detail in successive chapters. Chapter 2 will examine the milieux of the autobiographers and the ways in which specific kinds of autobiographical writings were encouraged; see also chapter 8.

5. See Roche (1982) and Perrot (1986). There is an interesting comparison of two versions of a late eighteenth-century sailor's memoirs in the introduction by Richard and Sally Price (1988) to their new edition of this work.

6. A similar argument is made by William Sewell in the introduction to his study of the changing meaning of class identity in early nineteenth-century France (1980).

7. Passerini (1989).

8. A good example is the reinterpretation of the diaries of the maidservant Hannah Cullwick that resulted from revelations about Cullwick's relationship with the photographer Arthur Munby. For a full discussion see Davidoff (1979) and Swindells (1989).

9. For pertinent work on the theory, history, and interpretation of autobiographies, see Lejeune (1974, 1980).

10. Of course, what counts as "manual labor," the significance of such termi-

nology as "hands" as a way of referring to employees, and the weight carried by the distinction between manual labor and mental labor are themselves a product of the complex social history of industrial capitalism. The line between "skilled" and "unskilled" labor has a similarly charged history, one with particular salience for gender and ethnic division within the labor force and the labor movement. On this particular point, the work of Quataert (1985) and Rose (1992) is illuminating. As labor historians have pointed out, however, whatever the ideological function of the construct of "manual labor," images of workers' hands and arms (in particular male hands and arms) have also been central to the iconography of the labor movement. See, for example, Hobsbawm (1978), Faue (1991), Korff (1992), and Weitz (1991). My use of this notion as a defining characteristic of the occupational groups whose autobiographical works have been included in the study rests on the presumption that this has been a very meaningful historical division, even though it is clearly itself a historically created category, the meaning of which has shifted over time.

11. Joan Scott and Louise Tilly's *Women, Work and Family*, a pioneering study, was published in 1978. Since then, our understanding of European working-class history has been enriched by a large and growing historical literature on women and the working class. For recent works that synthesize from a variety of approaches the theoretical and substantive contributions of this literature, see Scott (1988), Tilly (1989), Canning (1992), and Rose (1992). Research on family history has also reshaped working-class history. See, for example, Ross's research on working-class motherhood in London (1982 and 1992). Analyses by McLaren (1983), Heywood (1987), Lynch (1988), and Fuchs (1984, 1992) address important aspects of the history of family life and reproduction among the French lower classes of the nineteenth century. Research on working-class families in Germany is also substantial. For a recent summary of works on the history of childhood in Germany, see Maynes and Taylor (1991); on the family more generally, the collections edited by Reulecke and Weber (1978), Schlumbohm (1983), and Evans and Lee (1981) provide a good grounding.

12. For a very useful discussion of feminist revisions of theories of class, especially in the context of working-class history, see Rose (1992) and Canning (1992). For provocative studies of the relationship between class and gender in European middle-class settings, see Smith (1981), Davidoff and Hall (1987), and Kaplan (1991).

13. E. P. Thompson's *The Making of the English Working Class*, first published in 1963, redefined the study of class relations for subsequent generations of historians of class relations. The study of the role of political and cultural factors in class formation in Europe has followed a variety of different directions since this work appeared. Roger Magraw's recent synthesis of French working-class history (1992) traces this historiography in the French context. For a general synthesis of works on the history of the working classes in Germany, see the volumes in the series edited by Gerhard A. Ritter, especially Ritter and Tenfelde (1992). Specific works that emphasize aspects of the general political context within which working-class formation occurred include Aminzade (1981, 1993), Merriman (1979, 1985), and Katznelson and Zolberg (1986). Cultural approaches to the history of working-class identity were sparked by Jacques Rancière's work (1989), first pub-

lished in French in 1981. On the German side, the *Alltagsgeschichte* tradition has brought anthropological approaches, cultural studies, and working-class history closer together. Pertinent examples of this approach, which aims at least in part at separating the history of "the working classes" in Germany from the history of the Social Democratic party, can be found in several collections edited or coedited by Richard Evans (1978, 1981, 1982), especially the studies by Alf Lüdtke, Michael Grüttner, and Stefan Bajohr, as well as in Evans (1990). Eley (1989) provides a summary of this historiographical development. For important work set in the Dutch context, see Kalb (1994). Interestingly enough, this same tendency toward recognizing the analytic distinction between the history of the working classes and that of organizations claiming to act as their political representation is noted by Noiriel (1990) in his analysis of French working-class historiography. See also Hanagan (1994).

14. For an introduction to life course analysis in sociology and history, see Elder (1987) and Hareven (1987). According to Hareven, life course approaches have added "a dynamic dimension to the historical study of the family. . . . The influence of the life-course approach on family history has been most powerful in understanding three areas of family behavior: the synchronization of individual life transitions with collective family changes; the interaction of individual and collective family changes with historical conditions; and the effect of earlier life transitions on later ones" (xi). Historians interested in life course have focused especially on the changes in the timing and meaning of different life phases and transitions between them. See, for example, Ariès (1962), Schlumbohn (1983a), and Heywood (1987) on the changing meaning and institutionalization of childhood or Modell, Furstenberg, and Hershberg (1978), Gillis (1981), Wegs (1987), and Taylor (1988a) on changing patterns of transition from childhood to adulthood. Most family history research on life cycle phases and life course has been based on the quantitative analysis of sources such as censuses that give information about individuals, households, or families at a single point in time (although family reconstitution studies follow the demographic history of a married couple over time); life course implications have been inferred from such cross-sectional data. Hareven points to the difficulties in developing historical methods for more direct life course analysis and to the dearth of longitudinal sources, that is, sources that follow individuals and/or families over long periods of time. Moreover, the typically demographic sources upon which much historical life course research has rested cannot provide insights into the meaning of life course developments to the individuals experiencing them. Autobiographies, although not available for broad populations, allow analysis of questions requiring sources offering subjective perspectives on long-term developments.

15. From the preface to the autobiography of Heinrich Lange (15).

16. Steedman (1991), p. 7. The texts discuss childhood in various ways. Some were first and foremost stories of growing up that ended with the hero's or heroine's early adulthood; in other texts, the childhood story was merely the first episode in a much longer life. As I will discuss below, I have limited my study to texts that include an account of childhood. In other words, these are autobiographers who by their very narrative strategy indicate that they believe there are important connections between childhood and later life.

17. For an English version, see Ariès (1962).

18. See C. Tilly (1973). More recently, Linda Pollock (1983) has argued that even the available descriptive literature, largely memoirs, was read by Ariès and many of his followers in the family history tradition in an unsystematic and unrepresentative manner.

19. See especially Kriedte et al. (1981) and Heywood (1987).

20. For analyses of the history of the British working-class family, see Levine (1987), Rose (1992), and Seccombe (1992a).

21. Spree (1981), pp. 54, 169.

22. For new evidence on changing class differentials in nutrition and health during the industrial revolution, as reflected in birth weights, see Ward (1993).

23. These are crude estimates from life tables. They are based on the proportion of adults alive at the mean age at maternity and paternity who survived fifteen years later, as indicated in life tables corresponding to regions and approximate mortality levels. Ages at maternity and paternity were estimated from evidence in Festy (1979), pp. 28–33, and Coale and Demeny (1966).

24. Spree (1981), p. 188, and Heywood (1987), pp. 162–63.

25. For a general survey of the social history of educational reform in late eighteenth- and early nineteenth-century Western Europe, see Maynes (1985). Works on specific aspects of this history are cited in subsequent notes here and in chapter 4.

26. On the role of schools in girls' vocational training, see Quataert (1985).

27. LaVopa (1980) offers an excellent analysis of the political influences shaping schoolteaching in *Vormärz* Prussia; Meyer (1976) and Bölling (1983) offer accounts of teachers over the course of the nineteenth century. Albisetti (1983) analyzes the campaign for secondary school reform that peaked in 1880s and 1890s. Lamberti (1989) offers an insightful analysis of the interrelationship between confessional and political issues in conflicts over schooling in Prussia in the Second Empire. She finds sentiment in favor of the removal of religious authority over the elementary schools effecting quiet reforms of practice at the local administrative level even as the more explicitly nationalist anti-Catholic policy at the state and imperial level was being debated. Conversely, the limits of school reform in Prussia were to some extent a result of the liberals' adoption of statist and anticlerical approaches.

28. See Reulecke (1978), p. 260. For a fuller treatment of the political order of Prussian classroom dynamics, see Meyer (1976).

29. Bölling (1983), p. 59. On Bavaria, see Blessing (1974).

30. See Bölling (1983) for a good discussion of regional and state variations in the political character of the teaching corps.

31. See Lamberti (1989).

32. On the ambiguous character of the Enlightenment discourse on popular education, see Chisick (1981).

33. Historical analyses of these debates and of subsequent educational policy have suggested discrepancies between hopes centered on schooling and social and political practice. On the one hand, some skeptics emphasize the ineffectiveness of the government interventions in education and argue that the gradual and constant pace of educational advance reflected its origins in "social demand"

in the marketplace. On the other hand, revisionist critics of the liberal educational policy of the Third Republic claim that the promise of schooling was a political ploy to create the consent of the underclasses to a new social, political, and economic order dominated by an industrial and technocratic bourgeoisie. But whatever retrospective analysis has to say about the realities that contradicted the Third Republic's dominant school mythology, it appears from the autobiographies, as chapter 4 will argue, to have been quite solid and extensively held. For a brief introduction to the political character of school reform in France in this period, see Maynes (1985). A broad overview of French political conflict in the nineteenth century can be found in Magraw (1983). For specific discussion of the Third Republic and the role of educational reform in Republican ideology, see Elwitt (1975) and Auspitz (1982). For discussion and critique of liberal claims about educational progress, see Furet and Ozouf (1982). For discussions of the place of girls' education in liberal and Republican educational thinking, see Mayeur (1979), Strumingher (1983), Clarke (1984), and Margadant (1990). For a discussion of conflicts and controversies in educational programs, see Frijhoff (1983).

34. On this, see especially Mayeur (1979), Strumingher (1983), and Clark (1984).

35. For a discussion of the historical literature on protoindustrialization and family history, see Rudolph (1992).

36. For a discussion of the general patterns of proletarianization, see C. Tilly (1979).

37. The articles in Zolberg and Katznelson (1986) provide analyses of national differences in the character of working-class formation.

38. Kaelble (1981), p. 120.

39. For analysis of connections between family economy and migration, see Moch (1983).

40. See, for example, Aminzade (1981), Johnson (1979), and Magraw (1992).

41. Kaelble (1986) provides a good summary of studies of aspects of social mobility in the era of industrialization.

42. See Shorter (1976), Evans (1976), Phayer (1977), Stone (1977), Gillis (1985), and Borscheid (1986). Shorter and Phayer both postulated that there was an earlier emergence of romantic attachments and spontaneous sexual behavior among proletarian youth less inhibited than their social betters by considerations of property and propriety. Borscheid finds contrary evidence in sources pertaining to marriage among people of modest classes in the nineteenth century. The highly charged discussion of prostitution has produced some formulations that also tend to "naturalize" sexuality among the poor. Richard Evans (1976), for example, points out in the German case that prostitution, because of its long embeddedness in popular traditions of economic makeshift, cannot have had the same moral stigma among the lower classes that it held for the upper.

43. See especially Sewell (1980) and Rancière (1989) on the cultural construction of class identity in France. For the role of historically specific notions of gender in constructs of working-class identity see Taylor (1983), Moses (1984), and Scott (1988).

44. Stearns (1978) and Blackbourn and Eley (1984).

45. On various aspects of the history of popular political organization in early nineteenth-century France, see Magraw (1992), Sewell (1980), Aminzade (1993), Johnson (1979), Merriman (1985), C. Tilly (1986c), Judt (1986), and T. Margadant (1979).

46. See Noiriel (1990) and Magraw (1992).

47. This notion that the reforms in Germany, in particular the emancipation of the serfs, was strictly the result of a "revolution from above" is challenged by research on agrarian social relations in Germany in the era of the French Revolution. See especially Hagen (1986).

48. Workers' organization in Germany prior to the unification of 1871 has not received as much historical attention as that in later epochs of German history or in contemporaneous France. For works in English, see Hamerow (1958), Noyes (1966), and Miller (1986). For an overview of German historical research on working-class conditions, see Kocka (1990).

49. There is a substantial literature on the history of the German Social Democratic Party and the workers' movement more generally, in both English and German. On the history of Social Democracy, see Roth (1963), Schorske (1983), Lidtke (1966, 1985), Nolan (1981), and Groh (1973). On the history of the trade union movement, see Schneider (1991). For a more general survey of German working-class history in the Second Empire, see Ritter and Tenfelde (1992). On women in the socialist movement, see Quataert (1979) and Niggemann (1981).

Chapter 2

1. The quotation is taken from a letter by Jamerey-Duval discussing his reluctance to publish his memoirs. It is included in Jean Marie Goulemot's edition of the *Mémoires*, p. 408–9.

2. My thinking about these texts has been strongly influenced by several recent literary historical studies of autobiography. The most important of these are a series of works by Philippe Lejeune, a French scholar who is currently involved in the analysis of the autobiographical series preserved in the Bibliothèque nationale in Paris. He has also written several important books on the autobiographical form which address such critical issues as authenticity, the role of audience and literary fashion in the shaping of autobiographical production, and narrative voice. For a complete listing of his pertinent works, see the bibliography. The works by Michael Vogtmeier, Susanna Egan and Estelle Jelinek listed in the bibliography and referred to in subsequent notes have also been extremely helpful. In addition, recent reprintings of several workers' autobiographies include helpful scholarship on individual texts and on the genre more generally. See especially introductions and supporting materials of the editions cited in the first section of the bibliography of the autobiographies of Valentin Jamerey-Duval, Jacques-Louis Ménétra, Ulrich Bräker, Jean-Baptiste Dumay, Marie Wegrainer, and Franz Rehbein, as well as introductions to the anthologies edited by Wolfgang Emmerich, Alfred Kelly, and Mark Traugott listed in the second section of the bibliography.

3. Rousseau's *Les Confessions* was first published in 1782; Goethe's *Aus meinem Leben. Dichtung und Wahrheit*, in 1811–13.

4. See Emmerich (1974), introduction, p. 14.

5. Jelinek (1980).

6. On the history of working-class autobiography in Germany, see Emmerich (1974), Vogtmeier (1984), and Frerichs (1980).

7. Emmerich (1974), especially pp. 14–22.

8. See Egan (1984) and Waltner (1989). For discussion of the role of narrative in the shaping of class identity in Europe, see Steinmetz (1992), Sommers (1992), and Hart (1992).

9. For example, Ménétra refers to *Le Contrat Social* and *L'Emile*, See also *Journal de ma vie*, introduction, p. 16. Several other autobiographers explicitly referred to the *Confessions*. Lucien Bourgeois rejected what he saw as the self-indulgence of Rousseau's text (p. 62); Ulrich Bräker clearly modeled his text on *The Confessions*, even if somewhat ironically; Jean Guehenno and Claude Genoux both wrote as scholars about Rousseau.

10. Burke (1978), pp. 6–22.

11. On plebeian culture and its evolution, see, for example, Thompson (1973), Jones (1974), Sewell (1980), Medick (1982), and Darnton (1985).

12. Dumoulin's title suggests the logbooks or records kept by a journeyman on his travels, for which the German equivalent would be the *Wanderbuch*. The closest English rendition of Baader's title would actually be "a rocky road," but, ironically, that term has taken on a distracting connotation in the contemporary American setting (it's the name of an ice cream flavor). The title for this book was suggested by Baader's.

13. Miguel de Cervantes's *Don Quixote de la Mancha* was first printed in 1605; Hans Grimmelshausen's *The Adventures of Simplicissimus* in 1668.

14. Most German men could read and write by the end of the eighteenth century. The *alphabetisation* of French men was accomplished by the middle of the nineteenth century. In both countries, women's literacy lagged behind that of men. For women, basic literacy skills were widely distributed in Germany by the middle of the nineteenth century, in France by the third quarter of that century. For a detailed analysis of the history of literacy and popular education in Western Europe, see Maynes (1985).

15. *Candide* was the French *philosophe* Voltaire's most popular work and emblematic of Enlightenment social criticism. It was written in novel form and published in 1759. Its hapless hero Candide travels through the world encountering its absurdities.

16. See pages 1, 26, and 60 of Henrey's autobiography for references to her mother's "gossip" and telling of family anecdotes.

17. Literally, "skinny Hans was our cook."

18. For discussion of the reading of fairy tales as cultural-historical documents, see Darnton (1985) and Zipes (1983).

19. For a provocative contemporary analysis of the ambiguous character of working-class "success stories," see Ryan and Sackrey (1984).

20. Langer (1913). This particular text, although it closely resembles several of the autobiographical success stories, has not been included in my study because of its fictional character. It would certainly be interesting eventually to compare fictional and autobiographical reconstructions of the sorts of trajectories I am

exploring here, but that goes beyond the scope of the current study. It is significant, however, that there was a definite audience in turn-of-the-century Germany not only for autobiographies but also for works of fiction and social criticism purporting to be autobiographies. It is not always easy to tell the difference, of course, and contemporaries debated the authenticity of several marginal texts. Several of the autobiographies I discuss, in particular the anonymous works and that of Franz Bergg, are similar in some regards to these fictional works.

21. There is a certain resonance here with patterns Susanna Egan (1983) noted in her analysis of European literary autobiographies. Although I would agree that "conversion" is a characteristic of some, but not all, Western autobiographies, a cross-cultural and well as cross-class comparison is in order here. On the role of religious motifs in militants' lives, see Spohn (1990).

22. Early examples include the texts by Menetra, Perdiguier, and Döbel. Former journeymen were still producing such works even in the twentieth century. See, for example, Lange. For discussion of the problematic gender relationships characteristic of the artisanal milieu in the late eighteenth and early nineteenth centuries, see Quataert (1985) and Clawson (1980).

23. For an interesting discussion of the history of militants' autobiographies in France, see Pierre Ponsot's introduction to the 1976 edition of Jean-Baptiste Dumay's memoirs.

24. For example the autobiographies of Jamerey-Duval, Bräker, Delafutry, Bürgel, and Riggenbach suggest such patronage.

25. Memoir authors who wrote while incarcerated include the political militants Bergg, Bruhns, Hoelz, and Lindner; the anonymous author of *Dulden* wrote in a mental asylum; Bromme was in a tuberculosis sanitorium; Karl Fischer also wrote when he was an invalid; René Bonnet may have written part of his memoir as a prisoner of war.

26. Upward marriages among the autobiographers include those of Henrey, Christ, and Sans Gène.

27. Birker (1973) provides a good history of the workers' education societies, including some discussion of their class character. On the French *Université populaire*, see Elwitt (1982), who points out the clear solidarist and often antisocialist strategy of these (even though they sometimes were closely connected with the syndicalist *Bourse de Travail*) as distinct from many contemporaneous German workers' education institutions.

28. See especially Rancière (1989).

29. For an analysis of workers' organization libraries in imperial Germany, see Steinberg (1976). While many workers' libraries were established by the Social Democratic Party, the majority were under the control of trade unions. The most popular book at the majority of the libraries was Bebel's *Die Frau und der Sozialismus*. Apart from this, of the "serious" socialist literature only Kautsky's popular version of *Das Kapital* was borrowed frequently. Records indicate a steady increase in the proportion of literary fiction among books borrowed, while the demand for works of social science and books on Marxism, socialism, and the history of the labor movement fell strikingly throughout the period. Dieter Langewiesche's studies of German workers' culture in this period also emphasize the popularity of mainstream fiction, political portraits, and the like and explore the complex

and changing relationship between "worker's culture" and "social-democratic culture." See Langewiesche (1976, 1978, 1987). The fullest study of "official" social-democratic culture is by Vernon Lidtke (1985).

30. Christian trade unionists adopted similar strategies for training their cadres, and their self-education also reveals itself in autobiography. They were involved in parallel but sometimes overlapping institutions. Franz Behrens arrived in Berlin at the end of the 1880s as a journeyman gardener and joined a gardeners' self-improvement society. Despite a winter of unemployment, he decided to remain in Berlin in order to avail himself of the possibilities that the city offered. Like Ottilie Baader, he was fed at the settlement house run by the middle-class reformer Lina Morgenstern. He also managed to attend lectures at the university and eventually joined the Christian and nationalist labor movement that was developing as an alternative to the socialist or "free" unions. Adam Stegerwald became a member of a Catholic Apprentices' Association in Stuttgart in the early 1890s. He found himself the victim of socialist teasing because he went to church even though he remembered outings that "red and white brothers" went on together. His dissatisfaction with the anticlericalism of the socialist unions led him into the Christian unions and also toward his first interest in further education since leaving elementary school. By the late 1890s he had become involved with the Center Party in Munich and through these new channels of access attended lectures by Lujo Brentano at the university there. Similarly, Karl Schirmer took evening classes in Munich as a journeyman, and he too "after overcoming many obstacles" attended lectures at the University of Munich (22–23).

31. See Rancière (1989) and Scheman (1993).

32. The work of Jürgen Habermas has provoked interesting interdisciplinary discussion on these issues. For a recent discussion of the implications and influence of Habermas's theory of the public spheres, see the collection of essays edited by Craig Calhoun (1992), and especially Calhoun's introduction and the essays by Geoff Eley and Mary Ryan.

33. See, for example, the work of Robert Darnton (1971) on popularizations of Enlightenment writings. Claire Goldberg Moses's history of feminism in France (1984) incorporates much fascinating information on the feminist publications that drew a readership that crossed gender and class boundaries.

34. See Eley (1980).

35. For discussion of this issue, see Lejeune (1980) and Vogtmeier (1984).

36. Vallés was the author of a series of autobiographical novels that recounted his youth and school years and his eventual political formation.

37. Biedenbach (1906), p. 2. This memoir has not been included in my set because of its probable fictional or fictionalized character. See note 20 above.

38. See Frank (1952).

39. For examples of autobiographical fiction by lower-class writers, see the second section of the bibliography.

Chapter 3

1. Among the fifty-four German texts, only ten describe childhoods in largely positive terms. Most of these were written by Christian trade unionists or upwardly

mobile workers. Franz Wieber, author of one of the relatively rare Christian-trade-unionist memoirs, even noted an implicit contrast between the childhoods of Christian as opposed to socialist militants — their birthplaces. "Like the cradles of so many Christian union leaders, mine stood as well in a small peasant village" (163). He went on to describe the site as "idyllic." Only five of the thirty-four socialist autobiographies recount happy childhoods. The bulk dwell on the hardships suffered by the author as a child or describe only exceptional aspects of or periods during childhood in positive terms.

2. See, for example, the happy childhoods of socialists Wilhelm Kaisen or Heinrich Lange, both of whom were raised by two parents. There are relatively few memoirs of Christian trade unionists, and, as most I have found were written for an anniversary collection, they tend to be brief. But none of the six I draw on here (Behrens, Giesberts, Schirmer, Stegerwald, Wieber, and Wiedeberg) describes childhood in largely negative terms, although some are mixed. The success stories, which also report childhood in largely positive or nostalgic or mixed terms, include those by Bürgel, Richter, Riggenbach, and Sans Gène.

3. For discussions of childrearing practices among middle-class Germans in the late eighteenth and nineteenth centuries, see Schlumbohm (1980, 1983), Weber-Kellermann (1974), and Elschenbroich (1977).

4. See Weber-Kellermann (1974), pp. 223–43.

5. Again, the tendency of the autobiographies can be specified more precisely. Only five of the thirty-six French autobiographers offer narratives of childhood dominated by excessive work and neglect. The greater number alternate between discussions of work demands and other pastimes, discipline, and affection. Even among militants, tales of unmitigated woe are a small minority of the narratives I've read — three of twenty-one.

6. It is important to note one German exception here. Wilhelm Kaisen, writing a decade or so later than Lecoin for a postwar West German audience, made arguments similar to those Lecoin advanced. As noted above, Kaisen's account is one of the handful of positive accounts of German working-class childhood.

7. Bardin's account reflects what was probably an exceptionally nurturant fostering situation. The account of Gabriel Jacques, published to expose the plight of the foundling, shows the opposite extreme. Nancy Fitch (1986) has explored the contours of the foundling experience in the Department of the Allier and suggests some plausible reasons for the quite varying experiences of foundlings.

8. See Coleman (1982) and Spree (1981).

9. Smaller families predominated among the French autobiographers, even those born in the period before 1870. When German families remained small, this seems to have been largely the consequence of parental death or abandonment, whereas deliberate fertility control was certainly more significant in creating the French pattern. Although several French autobiographers came from families of five or more children (e.g., Lecoin, Jamin, Truquin, Dumoulin, Perdiguier) it is the less common pattern, as indeed was the case in the French population as a whole. Moreover, among the families portrayed in the autobiographies, the connection between large family size and child labor was clear in both the French and German narratives. *All* autobiographers with five or more children in their families reported entering the workforce before school-leaving age.

Conversely, among the (predominantly French) autobiographers who reported not working prior to age fourteen, most were from families of one or two children. For a fuller discussion, see Maynes (1992).

10. Rosemary Beier (1983) has collected very interesting evidence about women who worked at home under sweated conditions in imperial Berlin. She discovered, ironically, that the children of these mothers tended to remember their mothers in a less favorable light than those whose mothers worked outside the home even though the former had chosen to stay home so as to be able to supervise their children. Her explanation centers on the fact that these mothers were so overworked that their time at home was spent on work; interactions with their children centered on disciplining them either for their interruptions or to get them to work harder.

11. See Elschenbroich (1977) and Schlumbohm (1980, 1983).

12. On this point, see Fuchs (1992) and Scott (1988a).

13. Here again, Carolyn Steedman's (1986) insights are informative; see especially pp. 72–78.

14. These accounts present an insoluble methodological dilemma. There do exist a few accounts by children abandoned by their mothers, so this group is not entirely unrepresented here (Bardin, van de Leen). But, for those abandoned by their mothers at birth, the most likely fate, at least until the end of the nineteenth century, was early death. Those abandoned by their fathers, either before or at birth or later in life, more often lived to tell the tale. Details on the fates of unmarried mothers and abandoned children in nineteenth-century France have been uncovered from other sources by Rachel Fuchs (1984, 1992).

15. Scott Haine makes a somewhat analogous point about adolescents in his discussion of the cultural and institutional evolution of working-class youth from *gamin* into *apache* in the course of the nineteenth century. He argues that the first construct centered around the large numbers of semiabandoned and impoverished young people in the streets of Paris in the early part of the century. By the Belle Epoque, *gamin* had taken on its more current meaning of preadolescent child; working-class youth life in the city centered on the new apolitical institutions of working-class leisure such as the café and dance-hall. *Apache* gangs were an expression of the search for leisure and cohort-identity among wage-earning youth. Among the autobiographical stories, Truquin's fits the *gamin* image most closely; Guiraud, that of *apache*. Madeleine Henrey described the *apache* subculture of Paris only to distance herself from it.

16. The portrayals often remind me of Carolyn Steedman's account of the "minimalist" mothering her own mother practiced. It was adequate to keep her children alive, but it was marginal in terms of the degree to which it assured that her daughters, in turn, would find mothering imaginable or desirable. Steedman suggests the extent to which working-class children suffered from this approach to mothering, but she is nevertheless sensitive to the material and emotional dynamics that produced it, as well as to how it perhaps served as a strategy for the working-class mother who rejected the role as selfless martyr to her children. See Steedman (1986), p. 83.

17. This *particular* context of the "bad childhood" story — the German Social Democratic emphasis on the misery of working-class family life as evidence of

class exploitation — also has broad political-cultural dimensions. It may help to explain, for example, the ambivalence about, if not downright hostility toward, certain aspects of working-class culture and institutions, starting with the family itself, so often noted by analysts of Social-Democratic culture of the imperial era. See, for example, Evans (1981, 1982, 1990) and Lidtke (1985).

Chapter 4

1. Michael Kohlhaas was the central figure in a well-known novella written in 1806 by Heinrich von Kleist. The story concerns a horse trader's search for justice after his horses were ruined by a nobleman. Denied justice through the usual means, Kohlhaas took the law into his own hands through a violent assault on the nobleman and the surrounding region. Eventually Kohlhaas's horses were restored, but he was executed for his illegal activities.

2. Margaret Flecken has come to similar conclusions about the character of teachers portrayed in German worker autobiographies she has surveyed, but she has argued that there is a consistent tendency for the urban schools to be portrayed more positively than the rural schools. I think that the state differences also need to be taken into account. There is evidence that in such cities as Bremen and Hamburg especially, which were not located in repressive states and where there were active workers' movements, teachers could be quite sympathetic to their working-class pupils, and some were among the earliest recruits into the Socialist Party. Conversely, Grünberg's Berlin experience suggests that not all cities provided such positive school environments. See Flecken (1981), especially pp. 138–56, and Bölling (1983), pp. 88–91.

3. Certainly freedom of movement of girls relative to boys was more restricted with sexual maturity. For a parallel discussion of the connections between staying at home and working-class respectability based on oral histories gathered from Viennese workers, see Robert Wegs (1987).

4. See Albisetti (1986), p. 97. In Prussia, according to Albisetti, the number of female elementary teachers increased nearly tenfold between 1878 and 1901, from around 1,500 to nearly 14,000. As R. Bölling (1983), p. 99, points out, roughly a fifth of the teachers of the German Empire were women by the turn of the century, with women being most common in the teaching corps of urban areas of the West and Catholic areas of the South.

5. A parallel account of a pupil rebellion on the occasion of a transfer of a well-liked teacher can be found in the anonymous orphan's autobiography *Erinnerungen eines Waisenknaben*, edited by A. Forel, pp. 25–29. For the negative portrait of a brothers' school at the turn of the century, see Valette, pp. 46–51. For a description of the elaborate method of classroom discipline maintained in the brothers' schools, see Zind (1970).

6. See Moch (1988) for a discussion of *institutrices* and Schaffer (1978) on French working-class girls' aspirations, some of which centered on becoming schoolteachers.

7. For a brief overview of educational policy in the German Socialist Party, see Maynes (1989), especially chap. 6. Particular aspects of the problem are ad-

dressed in Olson (1977), Schwarte (1980), Birker (1973), Wendorff (1978), and Lidtke (1985).

8. *Flachsmann als Erzieher* was a *Tendenzdrama* (political or topical play) first published by Otto Ernst (Schmidt) in 1901 in the context of continuing controversy over school reform. Interestingly enough, the playwright Ernst was the son of a Hamburg cigarmaker and also the author of a fictionalized autobiography, *Asmus Sempers Jugendland.* Julius Bruhns, another of the autobiographers in my set and also the son of a Hamburg cigar maker, was familiar with Ernst's more optimistic account of growing up in this milieu. Thanks to Gerhard Weiss for tracking down this reference.

9. For a full discussion of the place of women in the German Socialist movement, see Niggemann (1981).

Chapter 5

1. The phrase is borrowed from multiple sources and holds many resonances. Carolyn Steedman (1986) quotes the British working-class "success story" by Jeremy Seabrook, in which he recalled his Cambridge University days when he and his friends sat around "telling each other escape stories, in which we were all picaresque heroes of our own lives" (15); Linda Gordon (1988) more recently entitled her study of the tales of interaction between Italian immigrants in Boston and the social workers who kept their case record *Heroes of Their Own Lives* to suggest a stronger emphasis on agency that her analysis suggests; finally, Ann Waltner (1989) makes a provocative case for thinking about life course in terms of the kinds of heroes and heroines people imagine themselves to be in an analysis of Chinese fiction.

2. On the history of European youth in general, see Gillis (1981) and Mitterauer (1986). For an excellent study of the transformation of youth during the nineteenth century in a single locality in Germany, see Gestrich (1986).

3. For a comparative discussion of the organizational logic of European school systems in terms of their relationship to social mobility, see Kaelble (1986) and Müller et al. (1986). On particular institutions, see Tenfelde (1979), Koppenhöffer (1980), Kraul (1980), Harrigan (1980), and Albisetti (1983).

4. For an analysis of a pertinent survey of girls leaving school in late nineteenth-century Paris, see Shaffer (1978). On girls' schooling more generally, and on curriculum, teachers, and role models, see Strumingher (1983), Clark (1984), Mayeur (1979), Margadant (1990), and Albisetti (1982, 1988).

5. A clear exposition of the place of women in the European working-class family economy as well as of female wages can be found in Scott and Tilly (1978). See also Rose (1992). There is a very interesting discussion of the connections between kinship relationships and the paucity of female options for "independence" in the Mediterranean context in Palazzi (forthcoming).

6. In chapter 7, I will discuss the political significance of this "independence"; Poelzer saw it as allowing her to organize her time more freely, as well as to express herself without fear of reprisal. In this, she was in a similar situation to that of Ottilie Baader and Jeanne Bouvier.

7. Pertinent work on adolescent sociability includes, in addition to the general works cited in note 2, research on French adolescence by Haine (1992) and Alaimo (1992) and on Central Europe, by Medick (1984), Taylor (1988), Wegs (1988), and Linton (1991).

Chapter 6

1. Historical research on sexuality and sexual behavior that informs this account includes Foucault (1978), Gay (1984), and Mosse (1985), whose work has revised previous understandings of middle-class sexual mores in Victorian Europe, as well as Walkowitz (1980, 1992), Newton et al. (1983), Weeks (1981), McLaren (1983), Evans (1976, 1981), Fuchs (1984, 1992), Medick (1984), Ortmayr (forthcoming), Phayer (1977), and Schulte (1984), who have contributed studies on particular aspects of lower-class sexual behavior and the relations between sexuality, economic transformation, and class conflict.

2. On the politicization of concerns about sexual behavior see Taylor (1988b), Alaimo (1992), Offen (1984), and Fishman (1970).

3. For examples of this kind of argument, see Shorter (1973), Evans (1976), and Bajohr (1982).

4. See Steedman (1986), p. 10.

5. Darnton (1986), p. xv. François Rabelais was an early sixteenth-century French writer best known for his series of bawdy tales about Gargantua and Pantagruel, whose lives and travels were Rabelais's vehicle for social satire.

6. This is especially clear in Bräker's relationship with his first love, Annie. She treated him to drinks in the pubs when he was short of cash, and Bräker claimed she was known to be very forward even if he assured his readers that she was very able to defend her virtue against all challenges. Bräker's account is consonant with arguments about courtship behavior in protoindustrial villages as described in H. Medick (1984).

7. According to Edward Shorter (1976) and J. M. Phayer (1974), "traditional" peasant courtship, which was transformed between the late eighteenth and the early nineteenth centuries, was highly ritualized and empty of erotic content.

8. A number of recent social-historical case studies have documented different aspects of working-class sexual behavior in the nineteenth century. Most point to the association between extramarital intercourse or concubinage and higher rates of illegitimacy, on the one hand, and growing propertylessness, on the other. See, for example, Bajohr (1982), Berlanstein (1980), Gestrich (1986), Neuman (1972), Lee (1977), and Lynch (1988). Edward Shorter (1973) pointed out this association and inferred the occurrence of a dramatic revolution in sexual mores among women of the propertyless classes. Although there is some support for Shorter's claims in the studies cited here, most emphasized the costs of illegitimacy born by the mothers of illegitimate children and the desire for marriage that continued to motivate the women involved, a critique first formulated by L. Tilly, J. Scott, and M. Cohen in their response to Shorter (1976). See also Fuchs (1992).

9. Rachel Fuchs (1992), in her investigation of unmarried mothers in

nineteenth-century Paris, found evidence to indicate that women saw concubinage as a "failed" marriage rather than as a preferable alternative to it.

10. It is unusual to have knowledge of this sort outside of the autobiographical
text itself. We do in this case because of the eventual fame of Wegrainer's son,
Leonhard Frank. See the introduction to the 1979 edition of the memoir.

11. Note that this episode was not included in the body of the entire memoir
but was kept separate from it, perhaps because of its sensitive nature and Jamerey-
Duval's scruples about disclosure. See the editor's comments in the 1981 edition,
p. 393.

12. One other female autobiographer became a professional writer—Lena
Christ—but her autobiography cannot be characterized as a success story. It ends
on a note of despair; her future is never signaled. There is a better parallel in a
work of autobiographical fiction mentioned earlier—Angela Langer's *Stromaufwärts*.

13. Bardin, we know from the editor's preface, did "improve" her life. Her
autobiography's ending implies that her departure from the fields represented a
salvation of sorts from what had become a very sorry lot. But we do not actually
learn her specific destiny in the text itself.

14. On this, see B. Taylor (1983), especially p. 183, and Niggemann (1981),
p. 237.

15. The formulation within the socialist movement of an alternative sexual
vision is also explicit in several comments about the eventual marriages of socialist
militants. Several German socialist women remarked on their husband's support
for their political activities, and many were married to men they met through the
movement. Anna Altmann, for example, had married her husband in 1877 when
she was about twenty-five. He "had been in the ranks" since 1870 and "was
among those who considered women to be born equal with men and not as
creatures of a second species" (27). Wilhelm Kaisen met his future wife at the
party school in Berlin as a single man in his twenties and remained "thankful" for
this fifty years later (48). Fritz Pauk wrote the memoirs of the life that led him into
socialist propaganda work by the light of a feeble petroleum lamp while his wife
and children slept in a corner. He and his wife, he wrote, "lived together in peace
for our three children" (32). On socialists' views on marriage, see Niggemann
(1981).

16. Thomas Malthus was a British political economist who had published an
essay on population growth in 1798. His thesis was that because workers married
earlier in times of prosperity, and therefore had more children, population
growth counteracted the rise in prosperity and thus doomed workers to constant
poverty. He advocated sexual constraint as the solution, and his ideas were taken
up by many nineteenth-century reformers who felt that the only solution to
poverty was for the poor to have fewer children by restraining their sexual activities.

17. The sort of desperation Christ recounted, and her presentation of herself
as a victim of her husband's sexual appetites, echoes the reports of British
working-class women to the Women's Co-operative Guild on the eve of World War
I. See Davies (1978) and Seccombe (1992b). In different contexts, this claim

could thus lead to protest (as it did for the members of the guild) or despair (as for Christ).

18. Part of the explanation for this silence may lie in the political sensitivity of the issue of contraception around the turn of the century. Good discussions of this in the French and German contexts, respectively, can be found in McLaren (1983) and Niggemann (1981). There was considerable disagreement within workers' movements concerning contraception, and some politicized workers saw Malthusian campaigns as counterrevolutionary.

19. Note that texts like Popp's could simultaneously be an exposé and a militant's story and share some of the characteristics of both. Franz Bergg's was also a peculiar text in that, although Bergg identified himself as a socialist, he did not write with a socialist audience in mind, and his text was part "confessional" and part exposé rather than a more typical "coming-to-consciousness" account. Two additional texts are worth noting here. Both Karl Fischer's and Moritz Bromme's autobiographies were edited by Paul Göhre; Bromme was a socialist, Fischer was not. Fischer's, like the three women's texts discussed here, is lacking a clear agenda or structuring "plot." Bromme's is something of a hybrid between exposé and militant's tale.

Chapter 7

1. As Ann Waltner (1989) points out in her analysis of the influence of Chinese literary plots on the imaginations of readers and authors, people can draw upon literature for models in their exploration of imagined future for themselves.

2. For discussions of the history of recruitment into socialist and trade union movements, see the general studies by Katznelson and Zolberg (1986), Magraw (1992), Noiriel (1990), Ritter (1980), and Schneider (1991). For specific aspects of recruitment pertinent to the discussion here, see Loreck (1977), Hilden (1987), and Niggemann (1981).

3. The *Bourses de travail* were local workers' councils and usually included representatives of various trades. The CGT (*Confederation generale du travail*), founded in 1895, was a national organization bringing together workers of various political persuasions who were committed to syndicalist, or union, strategies for fighting economic injustice and for improving the conditions of labor.

4. On the Anti-Socialist Laws, see Lidtke (1966). On this same period in Hamburg, see Evans (1990), p. 61.

5. For discussions of the impact of the "outlaw period" on the long-term development of German socialism, see Roth (1963), Lidtke (1966, 1985), and Groh (1973). Older militants, of course, had this generational difference in mind in publishing their memoirs. This is made explicit, for example, in Julius Bruhns's comment that his friends urged him to write his memoirs because it would be useful "if our younger comrades could hear stories from the 'heroic age of Social Democracy' told by people who had experienced them." This was especially crucial, older socialists believed, in the years following World War I when party loyalties were in disarray, especially among young workers (5–6).

6. Amalie Seidl's memoir focuses on this strike. She does not discuss her child-

hood, and so her story was not included in the set on which the larger analysis rests. For reference to the text, see part 2 of the bibliography.

7. For further analysis of the place of women in the German working class and the workers' movement, see Quataert (1979), Niggemann (1981), and Canning (1992).

8. On various aspects of the relationship between women and socialism and trade unionism in France, see Sowervine (1983) and Hilden (1987). On the gendered dimensions of the imagery of the European worker's movement see Hobsbawm (1978), Scott (1988), and Weitz (1991).

9. It should be noted here that the stories by Austrian women socialists, with the exception of Popp's, were all published together in a collection (edited, in fact, by Popp). The existence of such a collection in some sense artificially inflates the number of texts in this category and makes them more cross-referential, but this is itself the product of a certain degree of institutional presence of women, however marginal, within the workers' movement in Austria. It is also not coincidental that feminine solidarity comes across here in comparison with a more isolated French text such as Bouvier's. This is just another demonstration of the degree to which the history of the genre and the history of the identity that I am using it to track are inextricable.

10. *Kapital* refers to Karl Marx's analysis of the history and logic of capitalism. The key text of socialist theory, the multivolume work was published between 1867 and 1894. Bebel's *Frau* refers to the book *Die Frau und der Sozialismus* (*Woman under Socialism*), a popular work of political and economic analysis first published in 1879.

11. Valette's grandfather was referring to language of the Revolutionary and post-Revolutionary era when the Whites (supporters of the conservative Restoration monarchy) instigated a counterrevolutionary suppression of the Reds, or supporters of the revolution.

12. For further exploration of these issues, see Spohn (1992), Berenson (1984), and B. Taylor (1983).

13. More subtly, several of the texts, when they allude to the problems with Bible-teaching in the elementary schools, single out the Old Testament for criticism in ways that reflect strains within this popular culture. In particular, authors such as Franz Bergg and Alwin Ger suggested that it was inappropriate to expose young children to the sexual knowledge and apparent immorality that the Old Testament stories described, evoking associations that were, however subtle and unconscious, intertwined with anti-Semitic stereotypes.

14. Genoux's text is really a mixed genre. It includes elements of both the success story (particularly its earlier episodes) and the militant's tale. It also was written fairly early on, when models themselves were more fluid.

15. Here Richter alluded to a phenomenon relating to bourgeois aspirations for upward mobility into the aristocracy. For a discussion of the political significance of this phenomenon, see the classic essay by Eckhart Kehr (1977).

16. It is also significant that such a strong control over the choice of marriage partners is missing from Lena Christ's story. Christ's decision not to write her autobiography as a success story, even though she, like the women discussed here,

did "marry up," is closely related to her inability to imagine a desirable future for herself and seek it. Her own agency is deemphasized, a point to which I will return in the concluding chapter. Instead, Lena's betrothal appears as a fulfillment of her mother's quest for respectability.

17. Theories of psychological development tend to associate the process of maturation with an increasing separation from parents. The autonomous individual is the desired end product of "growing up." Feminist critics of psychological development theory have pointed out how androcentric and even misogynist some versions of this understanding of development are. Maturation sometimes is defined as distancing from the mother and what she stands for, and imitation of the father and his world; it is a process that is therefore innately problematic for women. See, especially, Chodorow (1978). But such views that center on the equation between autonomy and adulthood have a class bias as well, even when applied to men. Carolyn Steedman (1986) points this out particularly clearly. See also Sacks (1989).

Chapter 8

1. See Thompson (1966).

2. The phrase is borrowed here from Werner Conze (1975), who pointed to the conceptual switch reflected in the language of class analysis in an early article on the subject.

3. For general discussion of the French pace of industrialization, see Katznelson and Zolberg (1979) and the introduction to Magraw (1992), vol. 1.

4. For discussion of the implications for solidarities generated by these patterns of adolescent socialization, see Schlumbohm (1980) and Clawson (1980).

5. On this point, see Haine (1992).

6. See, for example, Thompson (1966), Sewell (1980), and Aminzade (1981), who provide case studies. For more general discussion, see Magraw (1992) and the essays collected in Kaplan and Koepp (1986) and in Katznelson and Goldberg (1989).

7. Magraw (1992) argues that continuity may have been established through intergenerational contacts; nevertheless he too emphasizes the extent to which French working-class organization rested emphatically on older artisan traditions. For a somewhat different view, see Noiriel (1990). Whether or not these older organizational forms persisted into the late-century workers' movement, this chronology of organization was distinct from the Central European one. There, too, skilled workers played a major role, but they organized working-class opposition in the context of the emergent socialist movement rather than in advance of it.

8. For an important recent analysis of the history of social welfare programs in Germany, see Steinmetz (1993).

9. For an example of the discussion of the nature and direction of socialist reorganization of working-class life in the early twentieth century, see Gruber (1991) and the critique of it by Eric Weitz (forthcoming). See also Langewiesche (1987).

10. See Fuchs (1984, 1992) and Offen (1984). Of course, the contrast should

not be drawn too starkly. Socialists were not above using pronatalist rhetoric to serve their own ends. Some historians see continuities between the social welfare programs advocated by leftists during the Weimar era in the name of "social hygiene" and later racist programs of the Nazi state. On various aspects of this question, see Peukert (1992), Steinmetz (1993), Grossman (1984), and Mc-Laren (1983).

11. Several of the French autobiographers mentioned having read middle-class novels or autobiographies complaining about growing up bourgeois. While these authors generally mustered little sympathy for the "torments" of the bourgeoisie, they nevertheless occasionally registered awareness that all was not perfect in those circles. See, for example, Dumoulin, p. 11, or Bourgeois, p. 9, as well as the authors cited earlier (chapter 2, n. 10) who explicitly discussed Rousseau's life, which is pertinent as well. There is little reference to such accounts in the German texts despite the lively turn-of-the-century discussion of the problems of the (middle-class) adolescent. See, for example, Fishman (1979) and Taylor (1988b).

12. For an informative discussion of French workers' memoir literature, see Pierre Ponsot's introduction to Jean-Baptiste Dumay's *Mémoires*.

13. See Fuchs (1992), Scott (1988a), and McDougall (1983).

14. Again, it is important not to exaggerate the difference. In Germany, socialist representations of women were, at best, contradictory and subject to dispute. Women's roles as mothers and workers were often conflated. But the active socialist women's movement insisted on the identity of woman as worker even if there was a tendency on the part of many socialists and trade unionists to suppress or marginalize it. On different aspects of this contentious history, see Niggemann (1981), Canning (1992), and Weitz (1991).

15. See Ortmayr (1992), p. 20.

16. Paul Göhre had published Holek's father's autobiography in 1909 when Heinrich was in his mid-twenties. The particular context for the excerpt cited was Heinrich Holek's discussion of his father's autobiographical disclosure of Heinrich's mother's adultery with a boarder. It is apparent throughout the younger Holek's text that he had not forgiven his father for this, nor for a series of other tragedies that the family suffered, and for which he seemed to hold the father at least partially responsible despite the disclaimer. The older Holek was a disgraced manager of a socialist cooperative who considered suicide and perhaps even the murder of his children depending on whose version — father's or son's — is read.

17. It is worth making clear here that not all of the autobiographers who chose a nonconventional plot failed to develop a strong identity or sense of agency. Professional writers of working-class origin, for example, such as Anneliese Rüegg or René Bonnet, could, in writing for commercial presses, tell stories that were neither records of success nor calls to militancy and still emerge in distinctively plotted memoirs as having developed a firm sense of self.

18. Thanks to Uli Strasser here for help with the Bavarian dialect!

19. Gagnier (1990), p. 102.

20. Jacques Rancière (1989) noted the extent to which French workers who contributed to the construction of working-class identity through their political writing did so in collaboration with left-leaning middle-class intellectuals. Al-

though this leads him to question the identity so constructed it is worth pointing out how such epistemologically "marginal" constructions of otherwise unexpressed identities have been central to a whole range of movements against oppression. First-person accounts by somewhat atypical representatives have, for example, been central to the African American experience at crucial moments of emancipation, to Latin American liberation movements, to the second-wave feminist movement, the gay rights movements, and others. See, for example, Geiger (1986), the Personal Narratives Group (1989), McKay (1989), and Andrews (1986). For a discussion of the problematic connections between epistomology, identity, "experiences," and politics, see Scott (1991).

21. Magraw (1992), p. 89.

22. Barbasse was presumably the name with which Teyssandier was "rebaptised" by the *compagnonnage*. Like many of the French artisanal memoirists, he included this name in his title. Other such constructions can be found among the list of memoir titles in the bibliography.

23. See Fuchs (1992) and Scott (1988a).

24. See Fuchs (1992), especially chapters 2 and 3.

25. See Kelly's (1987) introduction, Campbell (1989), and Allen (1991).

26. On this point, see Scott (1991).

27. This feeling of inadequacy in the face of demands to speak in and write for the public is a recurrent theme of workers' autobiography. It often takes the form of remembering just how difficult it was to find a public voice. On this, see Maynes (1986). Another dimension of the problem was the emphasis in the texts on the hard work (often unappreciated by fellow workers) of self-education. For an especially forceful statement of this, see Georges Dumoulin's expression of anger at fellow workers' dismissal of his intellectual labor by reference to his "gift" of speech, p. 270.

28. Again, Steedman (1991) is eloquent on this subject.

29. See Scheman (1993).

30. Henrey's story would be taken up in further volumes. I have dealt here only with the story of her girlhood.

31. There is obviously room here for a deliberate comparison between socialist militancy tales and stories of recruits into the fascist movement. These stories were told primarily by a generation born later than the group of concern here, but the comparison would certainly be revealing. For an older analysis of the stories of German fascist recruits see Abel (1986).

32. On Dumoulin's fate, see Magraw (1992), 2:297–98. For German labor during the Third Reich, see Mason (1993).

BIBLIOGRAPHY

Autobiographies Used in This Study

This list includes information, arranged alphabetically by author, on the ninety autobiographies used in this study. Where other than the original edition was used, the original date of publication is indicated in square brackets following the date of the edition actually cited. The identification number that precedes each author's name is determined by the author's birthdate, 1 being the earliest- and 90 the latest-born. These numbers can be used to locate the author's birthplace on map 1 of chapter 1. The following information about each author and text is included where known:

1. author's dates of birth and death
2. author's place of birth (place-names are those in use at author's time of birth)
3. father's occupation; mother's occupation
4. author's occupations
5. information about the type and origins of the text and reference to any translations or translated excerpts

68. Anonymous. 1908. *Im Kampf ums Dasein! Wahrheitsgetreue Lebenserinnerungen eines Mädchens aus dem Volke als Fabrikarbeiterin, Dienstmädchen und Kellnerin.* Mit einem Vorwort von Dr. G. Braun. Stuttgart: Verlag von Karl Weber & Co.
    1. ca. 1880–?
    2. not specified
    3. cigar worker; homeworker
    4. homeworker, factory worker, servant, waitress, hairdresser
    5. anonymous text presented by reformist editor as account of poor woman's victimization; this perspective is countered by author's own view of her relative success; Excerpts translated in Kelly (1987)

82. Anonymous. 1910. *Erinnerungen eines Waisenknaben. von ihm selbst erzählt.* Foreword by Prof. A. Forel. Munich: Ernst Reinhardt.
    1. ca. 1890–?
    2. unknown
    3. died in reserves; unspecified but unable to keep him
    4. apprentice engraver
    5. anonymous text solicited by the editor, a psychologist interested in working-class mentality, when the author was in his late teens

36. Anonymous ["Kathrin"]. 1910. *Dulden. Aus der Lebensbeschreibung einer Armen.* Edited by Prof. G. Bleuler, Director of the Mental Asylum Burghölzi in Zürich. Munich: Ernst Reinhardt Verlag.
    1. 1860–?
    2. unknown
    3. factory weaver; not specified

4. factory worker

5. anonymous exposé by woman accused twice of infanticide written under pressure from doctor in asylum where author was incarcerated

24. Altmann, Anna. 1912. "Blätter und Blüten." In A. Popp, ed. *Gedenkbuch. 20 Jahre österreichische Arbeiterinnenbewegung.* Vienna: Kommissionsverlag der Wiener Volksbuchhandlung. 23–34.

    1. 1852–?

    2. Laipa in Bohemia

    3. not specified

    4. textile worker

    5. militant's life published in a collection of memoirs of women involved in the socialist women's movement

23. Baader, Ottilie. 1979 [1921]. *Ein Steiniger Weg. Lebenserinnerungen einer Sozialisten.* New edition edited by Marie Juhacz. Berlin: J. H. W. Dietz Nachf.

    1. 1847–1925

    2. Frankfurt/Oder

    3. factory worker; homeworker

    4. seamstress, socialist organizer

    5. militant's life published by socialist-affiliated press; excerpts translated in Kelly (1987)

87. Bardin, Angelina. 1956. *Angelina. Une fille des champs.* Paris: Editions Andre Bonne.

    1. 1901–?

    2. unknown (Paris foundling)

    3. unknown

    4. foundling, farm servant, household servant, eventually nurse

    5. exposé written by a foundling in 1935, covering her first seventeen years, not published until 1956

51. "Batard," A[ugust]-R. [Nantais la Belle Conduite]. 1956. *A l'école du courage et du savoir. Souvenirs d'un apprenti Bourrelier-harnacheur, Compagnon du Tour de France, 1887–1891.* Nantes: Union compagnonnique.

    1. ca. 1870–?

    2. Nantes

    3. café owners

    4. saddle maker, organizer

    5. largely nostalgic recollection of artisan life of the old days, although syndicalist activity formed part of the story

57. Behrens, Franz. 1924. "Franz Behrens." In *25 Jahre Christliche Gewerkschaftsbewegung (1899–1924).* Berlin: Christlicher Gerwerkschaftsverlag.

    1. 1872–?

    2. Stargard in Mecklenburg-Strelitz

    3. brickworks owner; assistant to husband

    4. gardener, trade unionist

    5. militant's life published in a collection of memoirs of Christian trade unionists

48. Bergg, Franz. 1913. *Franz Bergg. Ein Proletarierleben.* Bearbeitet und her-

ausgegeben von Nikolaus Welter. 2ter Auflage. Frankfurt/Main: Neuer Frank-
furter Verlag.

    1. 1866–1913?

    2. Mosberg an der Alle (East Prussia)

    3. coachman, railroad worker, porter; junk dealer, laundress, charwoman

    4. waiter, cigar maker, poet

    5. text requested by the director of the prison in which Bergg was incarcer-
ated; excerpts translated in Kelly (1987)

64. Beutelmeyer, Marie. 1912. "Aus Oberösterreich." In A. Popp, ed.
Gedenkbuch. 20 Jahre österreichische Arbeiterinnenbewegung. Vienna: Kommissionsverlag der Wiener Volksbuchhandlung. 70–75.

    1. ca. 1877–?

    2. Upper Austria

    3. died early; rural servant

    4. factory worker

    5. militant's life published in a collection of memoirs of women involved in
the socialist women's movement

29. Blanc, Elise. 1953. "Madame Elise Blanc. L'ombre Court." In *Paysans par
Eux-Mêmes.* Edited by Emile Guillaumin. Paris: Librairie Stock, Delamain and
Boutelleau. 248–70.

    1. ca. 1855–?

    2. region around Moulins

    3. peasant and domestic on a château farm, vigneron, tenant farmer; peasant

    4. domestic servant

    5. text given to editor by a village notable who told him it had been written by
an old woman; it was "a bundle of large sheets of paper of unequal sizes, yel-
lowed, frayed — sheets without empty spots or margins covered front and back
with a cramped writing" (248)

22. Bock, Wilhelm. 1927. *Im Dienste der Freiheit. Freud und Leid aus sechs Jahrzehn-
ten Kampf und Aufstieg.* Berlin: J. H. W. Dietz Nachf.

    1. 1846–1931

    2. Grossbreitenbach (Thuringia)

    3. political refugee; day laborer

    4. field-worker, porcelain factory worker

    5. militant's life published by socialist-affiliated press

89. Bonnet, Marcelin René. 1954. *Enfance Limousin.* Paris.

    1. 1905–?

    2. Champeaux in Limousin

    3. peasants and seasonal migrants to factory work

    4. carpenter, foreman, writer

    5. writer's story of his early life, begun in the mid-1930s and apparently writ-
ten in part when author was a prisoner of war

73. Bourgeois, Lucien. 1925. *L'ascension.* Paris: F. Rieder et Cie.

    1. 1882–

    2. Crepy-en-Valois

    3. station inspector; seamstress, factory worker

    4. factory worker, secretary, writer

5. story of an autodidact with experience in both solidarist and militant movements published with the encouragement of a literary friend

43. Bouvier, Jeanne. 1983 [1936]. *Mes mèmoires ou 59 anneés d'activité industrielle, sociale et intellectuelle d'une ouvrière*. Paris: La Decouverté / Maspero.

   1. 1865–1964

   2. Isère

   3. railroad worker, cooper, peasant, unemployed; servant, charwoman

   4. factory worker, domestic, hatmaker, seamstress, trade unionist, writer

   5. autodidact and militant's life first published in era of the Popular Front by L'Action Intellectuelle

2. Bräker, Ulrich. 1970 [1789]. *The Life Story and Real Adventures of the Poor Man of Toggenburg*. Translated by Derek Bowman. Edinburgh: University Press.

   1. 1735–98

   2. near Wattweil, Switzerland

   3. peasant, saltpeter burner, weaver; spinner

   4. farmhand, servant, soldier, weaver

   5. story of intellectual ascent, though not material success, originally published with support of local learned society

18. B[rocher], Victorine. 1977 [1909]. *Souvenirs d'une morte vivante*. Paris: François Maspero.

   1. 1838–1921

   2. Paris

   3. shoemaker, political organizer and exile; unspecified worker

   4. intermittent work, Communard

   5. militant's life written with encouragement of Communard comrades

59. Bromme, Moritz, Th. W. 1905. *Lebensgeschichte eines modernen Fabrikarbeiters*. Edited by Paul Göhre. Jena: Eugen Diederichs Verlag.

   1. 1873–1926

   2. Leipzig

   3. farm worker, brickworker, railroad worker; tailoress

   4. wood and metalworker, factory worker

   5. text solicited by reformist editor Paul Göhre and written when author was in a tuberculosis asylum; excerpts translated in Kelly (1987)

37. Bruhns, Julius. 1921. *"Es klingt im Sturm ein altes Lied!" Aus der Jugendzeit der Sozialdemokratie*. Stuttgart: J. H. W. Dietz Nachf.; Berlin: Buchhandlung Vorwärts.

   1. 1860–?

   2. Hamburg suburb

   3. cigar maker; laundress

   4. cigar worker, organizer, socialist journalist

   5. militant's life, initially written in prison and published by socialist-affiliated press

61. Bürgel, Bruno. 1919. *Vom Arbeiter zum Astronomen. Die Lebensgeschichte eines Arbeiters*. Berlin: Verlag Ullstein & Co.

   1. 1875–1948

   2. Berlin suburb

3. orphan; foster parents were artisans

4. apprentice, factory worker, astronomer's assistant

5. success story but aimed at class reconciliation; published by a commercial press

71. Christ, Lena. 1921 [1912]. *Erinnerungen.* Munich: Albert Langen.

1. 1881–1920

2. rural Bavaria

3. unknown; servant, innkeeper

4. waitress, writer

5. professional writer's story of her early life

15. Commissaire, Sebastien. 1888. *Mémoires et souvenirs de Sebastien Commissaire. Ancien représentant du peuple.* Lyon: Meton.

1. 1822–1900

2. Dole

3. weaver, dyer; servant, weaver

4. weaver, organizer, elected official

5. militant's life apparently written in the 1870s and including both record of political activities and details of personal life

38. Conzett, Verena. 1929. *Erlebtes und Erstrebtes. Ein Stück Zeitgeschichte.* Zurich: Manesse Verlag.

1. ca. 1860–?

2. Melikon in Switzerland

3. factory worker and foreman; homeworker

4. factory worker, shop girl, wife of socialist journalist

5. text begins as autobiography documenting author's successful marriage, but it also documents the career of her husband, a middle-class socialist journalist

12. Courmeaux, Eugene. *Notes, souvenirs et impressions d'un vieux Reimois.* Première série, de 1817 à 1825. Reims.

1. 1817–1902

2. Reims

3. wine grower then shopkeeper; shopgirl then shopkeeper

4. librarian, elected official

5. mix of success story and local history written late in author's life

74. Davy, Charlotte. 1927. *Une Femme . . . .* Paris: Eugene Figuiere.

1. ca. 1885–?

2. Melun suburb

3. railroad employee; invalid

4. seamstress, office worker, feminist organizer, writer

5. exposé and militant's life; though noted in the preface that the text reads like a novel, it is autobiographical except for the author's decision to change the names

4. de Beranger, Pierre-Jean. (1913) [?]. "Ma Biographie." In *P.-J. de Beranger. Texts Choisis et Commentés.* Edited by S. Strowski. Paris: Librairie Plon.

1. 1780–?

2. Paris

3. unclear; dressmaker

4. printer, songwriter, and poet

5. life of an early political songwriter

33. Delafutry, Prosper. 1887 [1886]. *Les mémoires d'un travailleur.* 3d ed. Paris: L. Sauvaitre.

  1. 1858–?

  2. Merard (Oise)

  3. peasant, day laborer; servant, factory worker

  4. day laborer, teacher, writer

  5. success story written when the author was in his twenties and distributed by the reformist/self-help groups Cercle Parisien de la Ligue Française de l'Enseignement and the Société Franklin through their popular libraries

44. Dikreiter, Heinrich Georg. N.d. (ca. 1914). *Vom Waisenhaus zur Fabrik. Geschichte einer Proletarierjugend.* Berlin: Vorwärts Verlag.

  1. 1865–1947

  2. Strassburg

  3. lithographer; died early

  4. shepherd, factory worker, eventually editor of socialist newspaper.

  5. militant's life published by the socialist press

8. Döbel, Christian. N.d. *Ein deutscher Handwerksbursch der Biedermeierzeit. Auf der Walze durch den Balkan & Orient.* Edited by O. Woehle. Stuttgart.

  1. 1805–?

  2. Berterode near Eisenach

  3. peasants

  4. wagon maker

  5. artisan's life and travels

19. Dumay, Jean-Baptiste. 1976. *Mémoires d'un militant ouvrier du Creusot, 1841–1905.* Grenoble: François Maspero.

  1. 1841–1926

  2. Creusot

  3. miner, killed in accident before author's birth; seamstress

  4. factory worker, organizer, trade unionist, and socialist

  5. militant's life written in retirement and published in its entirety only recently; excerpts translated in Traugott (1993)

65. Dumoulin, Georges. 1938. *Carnets de Route. (Quarante anneés de vie militante).* Lille: Editions de L'Avenir.

  1. 1877–1963

  2. Ardres-en-Calaisis (Pas-de-Calais)

  3. petty retailer, day laborer; textile worker

  4. day laborer, miner, trade unionist

  5. militant's life, written in context of the Popular Front of the 1930s

20. Fischer, Carl. 1904. *Denkwürdigkeiten und Erinnerungen eines Arbeiters.* Edited by Paul Göhre. Leipzig: Eugen Diedrichs.

  1. 1841–1906

  2. Grünberg in Silesia

  3. baker; assistant to husband

  4. baker's apprentice, factory worker, day laborer

5. text found by reformist editor Paul Göhre; in some aspects resembles an artisan's tale but only part of it is centered on apprenticeship and journeyman's life

30. Fischer, F. L. 1906. *Arbeiterschicksale*. Edited by Fr. Naumann. Berlin-Schöneberg: Buchverlag der "Hilfe."

   1. 1855–?

   2. Zwickau

   3. miner, bankrupt mine owner, suicide; servant, day laborer, factory worker

   4. shepherd, factory worker, miner

   5. solicited by the editor to help bring about middle-class sympathy for workers' plight and published by reformist press

10. Genoux, Claude. 1983 [1870]. *Mémoires d'un enfant de la Savoie*. Paris: Gens de Savoie.

   1. 1811–74

   2. Albertville (Savoie)

   3. not mentioned

   4. chimney sweep, street entertainer, petty retailer, printer, writer, Republican socialist organizer

   5. autodidact scholar and militant's life written at several moments in the author's middle age and later life

32. Ger[isch], Alwin. 1918. *Erzgebirgisches Volk. Erinnerung von A. Ger.* Berlin: Vorwärts Bibliothek.

   1. 1857–1922

   2. mining village in the Erzgebirge in Saxony

   3. miner; homeworker

   4. machinist, socialist propagandist

   5. militant's life set in context of critique of mining communities and published by the socialist press, begins as a local history and evolves into autobiography

45. Giesberts, Johannes. 1924. "Aus meinem Leben." In *25 Jahre Christliche Gewerkschaftsbewegung (1899–1924)*. Berlin: Christlicher Gerwerkschaftsverlag.

   1. ca. 1865–?

   2. Ströhlen in the Lower Rhine

   3. baker; none mentioned

   4. baker, brewer, railroad worker, trade unionist

   5. militant's life published in a collection of memoirs of Christian trade unionists

84. Grünberg, Karl. 1969 [1964]. *Episoden. Sechs Jahrzehnte Kampf um den Sozialismus.* Berlin: Dietz.

   1. 1891–1972

   2. Berlin suburb

   3. shoemaker; unspecified

   4. factory worker, office worker, socialist youth organizer, writer

   5. militant's life written in postwar East Germany

83. Guehenno, Jean. 1961. *Changer la vie. Mon enfance et ma jeunesse.* Paris: Bernard Grasset Editeur.

    1. ca. 1890–?

    2. Fougères

    3. shoemaker, shoe salesman; shoe factory worker

    4. shoe factory employee, professor, writer

    5. success story with motive of class reconciliation

72. Guiraud, Gaston. 1938. *P'tite Guèle*. Paris.

    1. 1881–1954

    2. Paris

    3. unknown; died at author's birth

    4. office boy, factory worker, trade unionist, writer

    5. writer's story of early life that includes militant's tale

90. Henrey, Mrs. Robert. 1950. *The Little Madeleine. The Autobiography of a Young Girl in Montmartre*. New York: Dutton.

    1. 1906–

    2. Paris

    3. construction worker: seamstress, lace maker

    4. seamstress, office worker, shop girl, beautician, eventually writer

    5. writer's story of early life, published originally in English and later translated into French

5. Henri, Pierre dit La Rigueur. 1856. *Confessions d'un Ouvrier*. Originally published by Emile Souvestre. 3d ed. Paris: Michel Levy Frères.

    1. ca. 1796–

    2. Paris

    3. mason; servant when widowed

    4. mason

    5. artisan's life written in three large blue notebooks; given to publisher by a friend who came across them in author's shop

81. Hoelz, Max. 1930. *From White Cross to Red Flag*. Translated by F. A. Voigt. London: Jonathan Cape.

    1. 1889–1933

    2. Moritz, near Riesa

    3. sawmill worker, farmhand, brewery worker; day laborer

    4. farmhand, domestic, apprentice engineer, revolutionary leader

    5. militant's life written in prison

75. Holek, Heinrich. 1927. *Unterwegs. Eine Selbstbiographie*. Vienna: Bugra.

    1. 1885–1934

    2. Aussig in Bohemia

    3. factory worker, manager of cooperative; dockworker

    4. brickyard worker, eventually socialist journalist

    5. militant's life by the son of a socialist autobiographer

52. Huber, Betti. 1912. "Wie wir anfingen." In A. Popp, ed. *Gedenkbuch. 20 Jahre österreichische Arbeiterinnenbewegung*. Vienna: Kommissionsverlag der Wiener Volksbuchhandlung. 110–12.

    1. ca. 1870–?

    2. Vienna

    3. owners of a small shop

    4. tailoress

5. militant's life published in a collection of memoirs of women involved in the socialist women's movement

1. Jamerey-Duval, Valentin. 1981 [1784]. *Mémoires. Enfance et education d'un paysan au XVIIIe siècle.* Paris: Editions le Sycamore.
  1. 1695–1775
  2. Arthonnay (Yonne)
  3. wheelwright; peasant
  4. shepherd, farm servant, librarian
  5. story of intellectual ascent of a peasant; written between 1733 and 1747 and published in various stages with encouragment of author's patrons

69. Jamin, Leon. 1912. *Petit-Pierre. Histoires et souvenirs d'un apprenti.* Paris: Niclous Frères.
  1. ca. 1880–?
  2. unknown
  3. sailmaker; no occupation
  4. carpenter, mechanic, member of Paris Chamber of Commerce
  5. autodidact and militant's life but also modest success story framed in preface as "exemplary" — a third-person account wherein identity between author and hero is not clearly stated, but the text includes details and documentation that suggest it to be autobiographical

66. Jobst, Sophie. 1912. "Erlebnisse auf der Agitation." In A. Popp, ed. *Gedenkbuch. 20 Jahre österreichische Arbeiterinnenbewegung.* Vienna: Kommissionsverlag der Wiener Volksbuchhandlung. 82–87.
  1. ca. 1878–?
  2. western Bohemia
  3. not specified
  4. factory seamstress, homeworker, socialist organizer
  5. militant's life published in a collection of memoirs of women involved in the socialist women's movement

76. Kaisen, Wilhelm. 1967. *Meine Arbeit. Mein Leben.* Munich: List.
  1. 1887–?
  2. Hamburg suburb
  3. bricklayer, factory worker; charwoman
  4. factory worker, craftsman, trade unionist
  5. militant's life written in postwar West Germany

21. Köhler, Robert. 1913. *Erinnerungen aus dem Leben eines Proletariers.* Reichenberg: Runge & Co.
  1. 1841–?
  2. Bohemia
  3. unknown; mother left author with grandparents
  4. bindery worker, factory worker
  5. militant's life

39. Lange, Heinrich. N.d. *Aus einer alten Handwerksburschen Mappe. Eine Geschichte von Heimat, Werden and Wirken.* Leipzig.
  1. ca. 1860–?
  2. Schmarbeck in Hanover
  3. shepherd; shepherdess

4. shepherd, turner

5. militant's life set in context of local history

79. Lecoin, Louis. 1965. *Le cours d'une vie*. Paris: chez l'auteur.

1. 1888–?

2. Saint-Armand-Montrond

3. day laborers

4. day laborer, gardener, employee, trade unionist, pacifist

5. militant's life published in association with political journal the author edited

77. Lindner, Alois. 1924. *Abenteurfahrten eines revolutionären Arbeiters*. Berlin: Neuer Deutscher Verlag.

1. 1887–?

2. Kelheim

3. canal worker, junk dealer; assistant to husband

4. junk dealer, apprentice butcher, factory worker, sailor

5. militant's life written when author was in prison for a political assassination

53. Lüth, Franz. N.d. [1908]. *Aus der Jugendzeit eines Tagelöhners*. Edited by W. H. Michaelis. Berlin: Verlag von Fritz Kater.

1. ca. 1870–1907

2. Mecklenburg

3. parents both tenant farmers and day laborers

4. farm servant, road worker, propagandist

5. militant's life written in third person

54. Maier, Anna. 1912. "Wie Ich Reif Wurde." In A. Popp, ed. *Gedenkbuch. 20 Jahren österreichische Arbeiterinnenbewegung*. Vienna: Kommissionsverlag der Wiener Volksbuchhandlung. 107–9.

1. ca. 1870–?

2. near Sternberg

3. weaver; spooler

4. tobacco worker

5. militant's life published in a collection of memoirs of women involved in the socialist women's movement

3. Ménétra, Jacques-Louis. 1982. *Journal de ma vie. Jacques-Louis Ménétra. Compagnon vitrier au 18e siècle*. Presented by Daniel Roche. Paris: Montalba.

1. 1738–?

2. Paris

3. window maker; not mentioned

4. window maker

5. artisan's life written between 1764 and 1802 but not published until 1982; available in translation

86. Michaud, René. 1983 [1963]. *J'avais vingt ans. Un jeune ouvrier au début de siècle*. Paris: Syros.

1. 1900–1979

2. Paris suburb

3. railroad worker; laundress, seamstress

4. factory worker, trade unionist, socialist organizer, writer

5. militant's early life originally published with syndicalist encouragement

16. Mistral, Frederic. 1906. *Moun Espelido. Memori e Raconte. Mes Origines. Mémoires et Recits.* Paris: Plon-Nourrit et Cie.

  1. 1830–1914

  2. Maillan (Vaucluse)

  3. prosperous peasant; day laborer, peasant

  4. writer

  5. well-known memoir of Provençal author who brought Provençal literature to national attention; provides a nostalgic account of a comfortable peasant childhood

11. Nadaud, Martin. 1976 [1895]. *Mémoires de Leonard, ancien garçon maçon.* Paris: Librairie Hachette.

  1. 1815–98

  2. La Martineche (Creuse)

  3. mason, peasant; peasant

  4. mason, instructor, Republican socialist organizer and politician

  5. militant's life; author calls these the memoirs of Leonard, his father's name, but the story centers on his own life; excerpts translated in Traugott (1993)

49. Noske, Gustav. 1919. *Wie Ich Wurde. Selbstbiographien von volkstümlicher Personalichkeiten. Noske.* Berlin: Kultur-Verlag.

  1. 1868–

  2. Brandenburg am Havel

  3. Russian immigrant weaver; weaver

  4. basket weaver, factory worker, government military post after Revolution of 1918

  5. success story and militant's life written shortly after the author, a moderate socialist, had coordinated the military forces that defeated the socialist movement's left wing

14. Ortillon, Antoine. 1857. *Vie privée d'un orphelin. Ecrite par lui-meme.* Paris: Imprimerie Boisseau et Augros.

  1. 1818–?

  2. village in Champagne

  3. unknown

  4. field worker, servant

  5. text, with unclear origins or auspices of publication, written to complain of injustice of author's abandonment by reason of illegitimate birth

62. Osterroth, Nikolaus. 1920. *Vom Beter zum Kämpfer.* Berlin: Vorwärts Verlag.

  1. 1875–1933

  2. Baden

  3. butcher, bankrupted farmer; shop assistant

  4. brickyard worker, miner, organizer, and socialist journalist

  5. militant's life published by the socialist press; excerpts translated in Kelly (1987)

80. Pauk, Fritz. 1930. *Jugendjahre eines Tabakarbeiters.* Bearbeitet von Roamer. Jena: Karl Zwing Verlag.

  1. 1888–?

  2. market town in the Lipperland

  3. carpenter who did not marry mother; farm laborer, flax spinner

4. agricultural laborer, tobacco worker, socialist organizer

5. militant's life; excerpts translated in Kelly (1987)

9. Perdiguier, Agricol. 1914 [1854]. *Mémoires d'un compagnon.* Moulins: Edition des Cahiers du Centre.

    1. 1805–75

    2. Morières (Vaucluse)

    3. carpenter/farmer; seamstress

    4. carpenter, artisanal organizer

    5. classic memoir on the boundaries between artisan and militant's life published with encouragement of artisanal organizations; excerpts translated in Traugott (1993)

40. Perthen, Anna. 1912. "Der Anfang in Bodenbach." In A. Popp, ed. *Gedenkbuch. 20 Jahren österreichische Arbeiterinnenbewegung.* Vienna: Kommissionsverlag der Wiener Volksbuchhandlung. 113–16.

    1. ca. 1860–?

    2. Bodenbach

    3. textile worker; textile worker

    4. homeworker, textile worker

    5. militant's life published in a collection of memoirs of women involved in the socialist women's movement

31. Peukert, Josef. 1913. *Erinnerun gen eines Proletariers aus der revolutionären Arbeiterbewegung.* Berlin: Verlag des Sozialistischen Bundes.

    1. 1855–1910

    2. Albrechtsdorf, Austrian Iserthal

    3. parents both glassworkers

    4. glassworker, painter, traveling salesman, organizer, and propagandist

    5. militant's life written in part to defend the author's political activities

55. Poelzer, Amalie. "Erinnerungen." In A. Popp, ed. *Gedenkbuch. 20 Jahre österreichische Arbeiterinnenbewegung.* Vienna: Kommissionsverlag der Wiener Volksbuchhandlung. 103–6.

    1. ca. 1870–?

    2. Vienna

    3. not specified

    4. seamstress

    5. militant's life published in a collection of memoirs of women involved in the socialist women's movement

50. Anonymous [Popp, Adelheid]. 1909. *Die Jugendgeschichte einer Arbeiterin. Von ihr selbst erzählt.* Foreword by August Bebel. Munich: Ernst Reinhardt Verlag.

    1. 1869–1939

    2. village near Vienna

    3. home weaver; home weaver, factory weaver

    4. servant, weaver, factory worker, socialist organizer

    5. militant's early life originally published anonymously but later editions under author's name; available in translation

63. Rehbein, Franz. 1985 [1911]. *Das Leben eines Landarbeiters.* Edited by Urs J. Diederichs and Holger Rüdel. Hamburg: Hans Christians Verlag. Original version edited by Paul Göhre and published by Eugen Diedrichs Verlag.

1. ca. 1870–1910

2. Pomerania

3. tailor; assistant to husband, washerwoman, day laborer

4. farm laborer, socialist journalist

5. militant's life originally published with encouragement of reformist editor Paul Göhre; excerpts translated in Kelly (1987)

25. Richter, Prof. Dr. Otto. 1919. *Lebensfreuden eines Arbeiterkindes*. Dresden: Oskar Laube Verlag.

1. 1852–?

2. Meissen

3. farm servant, porcelain factory worker; cook, laundress

4. factory worker, secretary, eventually professor

5. success story with local history dimension

13. Riggenbach, Nikolaus. 1900 [1886]. *Erinnerungen eines alten Mechanikers*. Basel: R. Reich.

1. 1817–?

2. Gebweiler in Alsace

3. failed entrepreneur; none mentioned

4. office worker, apprentice turner, factory foreman, mechanic, railroad engineer

5. success story written with the encouragement of settlement house movement

46. Roth, Aurelia. 1912. "Eine Glasschleiferin." In A. Popp, ed. *Gedenkbuch. 20 Jahre österreichische Arbeiterinnenbewegung*. Vienna: Kommissionsverlag der Wiener Volksbuchhandlung. 52–61.

1. ca. 1865–?

2. Isergebirg region of Austria

3. glass polisher; jewelry worker

4. homeworker, factory glassworker

5. militant's life published in a collection of memoirs of women involved in the socialist women's movement; excerpts translated in Kelly (1987)

67. Rüegg, Anneliese. 1914. *Erlebnisse einer Serviertochter. Bilder aus der Hotelindustrie*. Zurich: Buchhandlung des Schweiz. Grütliverein.

1. 1879–

2. Switzerland

3. mechanic; silk winder

4. factory worker, servant, hotel worker, writer

5. exposé of hotel industry and its workers' conditions

28. Sans Gène, Marie [Anna Hill]. N.d. (1908?) [1906]. *Jugenderinnerungen eines armen Dienstmädchen*. New edition with an afterword by Dr. C. Meyer. Bremen: Verlag Friedrich Roever.

1. 1853–?

2. Danzig

3. horse trader, coachman; laundress, petty retailer

4. servant, laborer, eventually wife of a Berlin art critic

5. text, written with encouragement of author's husband and under a pseudonym, is both a success story and an evocation of the exoticism of working-class Danzig

42. Schirmer, Karl. 1924. *50 Jahre Arbeiter*. Berlin: Bücher der Arbeit.
  1. 1864–?
  2. Winterstetten in Swabia
  3. smith; none mentioned
  4. shepherd, metalworker, machine factory worker, trade union organizer
  5. militant's life

56. Sponer, Marie. 1912. "Aus Nordböhmen." In A. Popp, ed. *Gedenkbuch. 20 Jahren österreichischen Arbeiterinnenbewegung*. Vienna: Kommissionsverlag der Wiener Volksbuchhandlung. 140–45.
  1. ca. 1870–?
  2. northern Bohemia
  3. carter; not specified
  4. factory worker
  5. militant's life published in a collection of memoirs of women involved in the socialist women's movement

60. Stegerwald, Adam. 1924. "Aus meinem Leben." In *25 Jahre Christliche Gewerkschaftsbewegung (1899–1924)*. Berlin: Christlicher Gerwerkschaftsverlag.
  1. 1874–
  2. Greussenheim near Wurzburg
  3. peasants
  4. carpenter, trade union organizer
  5. militant's life published in a collection of memoirs of Christian trade unionists

41. Teyssandier, Moïse. 1928. *Barbasse. Souvenirs d'un ouvrier perigourdin*. Perigieux.
  1. ca. 1860–
  2. countryside around Perigord
  3. farm worker; farm worker
  4. shepherd, farm worker, baker, sailor, trade unionist
  5. militant's life written with motive of making "real" worker's life known

26. Tricot, Henri. 1898. *Confessions d'un anarchiste*. Lyon.
  1. 1852–?
  2. Condes near Chaumont
  3. unknown
  4. artisan, monk, anarchist activist
  5. militant's life recounting author's trajectory through Catholicism, anarchism, Christian socialism

17. Truquin, Norbert. 1977 [1888]. *Mémoires et aventures d'un prolétaire à travers la revolution*. Paris: François Maspero.
  1. 1833–?
  2. Rozieres (Sommes)
  3. bankrupt factory director, artisan; no occupation
  4. wool comber, servant, porter, brick-maker, factory worker, trader, farmer, silk weaver, socialist organizer
  5. militant's life punctuated by global travels; excerpts translated in Traugott (1993)

85. Turek, Ludwig. 1980 [1925]. *Ein Prolet Erzählt. Lebensschilderung eines deutschen Arbeiters.* Munich: Damnitz Verlag.

    1. 1898–1975

    2. Stehdhal near Magdeburg

    3. died early; factory worker, day laborer

    4. farm worker, baker, cigar worker, typesetter, writer

    5. militant's life but with much emphasis on personal life written during Weimar outpouring of worker memoirs; excerpts translated in Kelly (1987)

70. Unger-Winkelried, E. 1934. *Von Bebel zu Hitler. Vom Zukunftsstaat zum Dritten Reich.* Berlin-Schöneberg: Verlag Deutsche Kultur-Wacht.

    1. ca. 1880–?

    2. Weissenburg in Alsace

    3. shepherd, butcher worker; farm worker, servant

    4. apprentice, factory worker, socialist journalist, Nazi propagandist

    5. militant's story including conversion to Nazism written with aim of bringing workers into the fascist fold

78. Valette, Philippe. 1947. *Mon Village. Recit.* Paris.

    1. 1887–

    2. Chalons region (Allier)

    3. day laborer; cook

    4. day laborer, office boy, waiter, writer

    5. writer's story of early life

88. Van de Leen, Ida. 1950. *La Hulotte. Roman Veçu.* Paris: Imprimerie Artisanale.

    1. ca. 1902–?

    2. Paris

    3. unknown

    4. unwed mother at sixteen, eventual destiny unknown

    5. third person exposé; the author called this a "lived novel" and dedicated it to her two children and to the memory of Pierre and Sophie (the names of her two foster parents in the book)

6. Vincard, aîné (Jules). 1878. *Mémoires épisodiques d'un vieux chansonnier Saint-simonien.* Paris: E. Dentu.

    1. 1796–1879

    2. Paris

    3. manufacturer of measuring instruments; laundress

    4. worker in father's shop, artisan, singer, poet

    5. militant's life centered on Saint-Simonien movement.

7. Voilquin, Suzanne. 1978 [1865]. *Souvenirs d'une fille du peuple. ou la Saint-simonienne en Egypt.* Paris: Maspero.

    1. 1801–

    2. Paris

    3. hatmaker; none mentioned

    4. embroiderer, midwife, socialist organizer

    5. militant's memoir and history of Saint-Simonien movement; excerpts translated in Traugott (1993)

34. Voisin, Joseph dit Angoumois. 1931. *Histoire de ma vie et 55 ans de compagnonnage.* Tours: Imprimerie du Progrés.

1. 1858–?

2. Mulon (Charente)

3. agricultural day laborers

4. carpenter, artisanal organizer

5. militant's life written in 1931 as part of a requested history of the Compagnons Charpentiers

27. Wegrainer, Marie [Marie Frank]. 1979 [1914]. *Der Lebensroman einer Arbeiterfrau. von ihr selbst geschrieben.* Frankfurt/Main: Campus Verlag.

1. 1852–1924

2. "Lipprichshausen near Wurzburg" (actually Bamberg)

3. smith; servant

4. servant

5. text written under a pseudonym and with names disguised, with aim of commercial success, by mother of soon-to-be-famous working-class writer Leonhard Frank

35. Wieber, Franz. 1924. "Aus meinem Leben." In *25 Jahre Christliche Gewerkschaftsbewegung (1899–1924).* Berlin: Christlicher Gerwerkschaftsverlag.

1. 1858–?

2. Hunhau near Fulda

3. peasant/weaver; not mentioned

4. herder, spooler, factory worker, trade union organizer

5. militant's life published in a collection of memoirs of Christian trade unionists

58. Wiedeberg, Josef. 1924. "Josef Wiedeberg." In *25 Jahre Christliche Gewerkschaftsbewegung (1899–1924).* Berlin: Christlicher Gerwerkschaftsverlag.

1. 1872–?

2. Kleinitz in Lower Silesia

3. carpenter; not specified

4. spooler, mason

5. militant's life published in a collection of memoirs of Christian trade unionists

47. Zietz, Luise. 1919. "Aus meinem Leben." *Die Kämpferin, Zeitschrift für Frauen und Mädchen des werktätigen Volkes.* 1:2 Beilage, 1.

1. 1865–1922

2. Holstein

3. wool weavers

4. homeworker, kindergarten teacher, socialist organizer

5. militant's life in very brief form published in socialist women's newspaper

Additional Autobiographies, Anthologies, and Autobiographical Fiction

This list includes works of autobiography or autobiographical fiction used or mentioned in the book but not included in the set used in the analysis and documented above. This section also includes anthologies of working-class autobiography.

Anonymous. 1906. *Mieze Biedenbachs Erlebnisse. Erinnerungen einer Kellnerin.* Berlin: F. Fontane & Co.

Böhme, Margarete, ed. 1905. *Tagebuch einer Verlorenen. von einer Toten.* Berlin: F. Fontane & Co.

Burnett, John, ed. 1974. *The Annals of Labor: Autobiographies of British Working-Class People, 1820–1920.* Bloomington: Indiana University Press.

——, ed. 1982. *Destiny Obscure: Autobiographies of Childhood, Education and the Family from the 1820s to the 1920s.* London: A. Lane.

Burnett, John, David Vincent, and David Mayall, eds. 1984–89. *The Autobiography of the Working Class. An Annotated, Critical Bibliography, 1790–1900.* New York: New York University Press.

Davies, Margaret L., ed. 1975. *Life as We Have Known It.* New York: Norton.

Depresle, Gaston. 1925. *Anthologie des écrivains ouvriers.* Paris: Editions Aujourd'hui.

Deutscher Textilarbeiterverband, ed. 1930. *Mein Arbeitstag — mein Wochenende. 150 Berichten von Textilarbeiterinnen.* Berlin: Verlagsgesellschaft des Allgemeinen deutschen Gewerkschaftsbundes g.m.b.h.

Emmerich, Wolfgang, ed. 1974. *Proletarische Lebensläufe. Autobiographische Dokumente zur Entstehung der Zweiten Kultur in Deutschland*, 2 vols. Reinbek bei Hamburg: Rowohlt.

Ernst [Schmidt], Otto. 1904. *Asmus Sempers Jugendland. Der Roman einer Kindheit.* Leipzig.

Feller, Paul. 1960. *Nécessité, adolescence, poésie. Ebauché d'un catalogue bibliographique universel des auteurs ayant, des l'adolescence, gagné leur vie du travail de leurs mains.* Callaiz: La Musée du Soir.

Frank, Leonhard. 1952. *Links Wo das Herz ist.* Munich: Nymphenburger Verlagshandlung.

Guillaumin, Emile, ed. 1953. *Paysans, par eux-mêmes.* Paris: Librairie Stock, Delamain and Boutelleau.

Juchacz, Marie. 1958. *Sie lebten für eine bessere Welt. Lebensbilder führender Frauen des 19. und 20. Jahrhunderts.* Berlin: Dietz Verlag.

Kelly, Alfred, ed. 1987. *The German Worker: Working-Class Autobiographies from the Age of Industrialzation.* Berkeley: University of California Press.

Kempf, Rosa. 1911. *Das Leben junger Fabrikmädchen in München. Verein für Sozialpolitik.* Vol. 135, pt. 2.

Klucsarits, Richard, and F. G. Kürbisch. 1975. *Arbeiterinnen Kämpfen um Ihr Recht.* Wuppertal: Hammer.

Langer, Angela. 1913. *Stromaufwärts. Aus einem Frauenleben.* Berlin: C. Fischer Verlag.

Levenstein, Adolf, ed. 1909. *Aus der Tiefe. Beiträge zur Seelenanalyse moderner Arbeiter.* Berlin: Frowein Verlag.

Maitron, Jean. 1967–93. *Dictionnaire biographique du mouvement ouvrier français.* Paris: Editions Ouvrières.

Münchow, Ursula, ed. 1976. *Arbeiter über ihr Leben.* Berlin: Dietz Verlag.

Ortmayr, Norbert, ed. 1992. *Knechte: Autobiographische Dokumente und sozialhistorische Skizzen.* Vienna: Böhlau Verlag.

Ozouf, Jacques. 1967. *Nous les maîtres d'école. Autobiographies d'instituteurs de la belle epoque.* Paris: Julliard.

Peneff, Jean, ed. 1979. *Autobiographies de militants CGTU-CGT.* Nantes: Université de Nantes; C.N.R.S. Les Cahiers du L.E.R.S.C.O.

Seidl, Amalie. 1912. "Der erste Arbeiterinnenstreik in Wien." In A. Popp, ed. *Gedenkbuch. 20 Jahren österreichische Arbeiterinnenbewegung.* Vienna: Kommissionsverlag der Wiener Volksbuchhandlung. 66–69.

Traugott, Mark, ed. 1993. *The French Worker: Autobiographies from the Early Industrial Era.* Berkeley: University of California Press.

Weber, Therese, ed. 1985. *Mägde. Lebenserinnerungen an die Dienstbotenzeit bei Bauern.* Vienna: Böhlau Verlag.

Secondary Literature

Abel, Theodore. 1986. *Why Hitler Came to Power.* Cambridge: Harvard University Press.

Abrams, Philip. 1982. *Historical Sociology.* Ithaca: Cornell University Press.

Alaimo, Kathleen. 1992. "Shaping Adolescence in the Popular Milieu: Social Policy, Reformers, and French Youth 1870–1920." *The Journal of Family History* 17:419–38.

Albisetti, James C. 1982. "Could Separate be Equal? Helene Lange and Women's Education in Imperial Germany." *History of Education Quarterly* 22:301–17.

———. 1983. *Secondary School Reform in Imperial Germany.* Princeton: Princeton University Press.

———. 1986. "Women and the Professions in Imperial Germany." In *German Women in the Eighteenth and Nineteenth Centuries: A Social and Literary History,* edited by Ruth-Ellen B. Joeres and Mary Jo Maynes. Bloomington: Indiana University Press.

———. 1988. *Schooling German Girls and Women.* Princeton: Princeton University Press.

Allen, Ann Taylor. 1991. *Feminism and Motherhood in Germany.* New Brunswick: Rutgers University Press.

Aminzade, Ronald. 1981. *Class, Politics and Early Industrial Capitalism: A Study of Mid-Nineteenth-Century Toulouse.* Albany: State University of New York Press.

———. 1993. *Ballots and Barricades.* Princeton: Princeton University Press.

Andrews, William L. 1986. *To Tell a Free Story: The First Century of Afro-American Autobiography, 1760–1865.* Urbana: University of Illinois Press.

Ariès, Philippe. 1962. *Centuries of Childhood.* Translated by Robert Baldick. New York: Knopf.

Auspitz, Katherine. 1982. *The Radical Bourgeoisie: The Ligue de l'enseignement and the Origins of the Third Republic, 1866–1885.* Cambridge: Cambridge University Press.

Bajohr, Steven. 1982. "Illegitimacy and the Working Class: Illegitimate Mothers in Brunswick, 1900–1933." In *The German Working Class, 1888–1933,* edited by Richard J. Evans. London: Croom Helm.

Beier, Rosemarie. 1983. *Frauenarbeit und Frauenalltag im Deutschen Kaiserreich: Heimarbeiterinnen in der Berliner Bekleidungs-industrie, 1880–1914.* Frankfurt/Main: Campus Verlag.

Bendele, Ulrich. 1979. *Sozialdemokratische Schulpolitik.* Frankfurt.

Berenson, Edgar. 1984. *Populist Religion and Left-wing Politics in France, 1830–1852.* Princeton: Princeton University Press.

Berlanstein, Lenard. 1980. "Illegitimacy, Concubinage and Proletarianization in a French Town, 1760–1914." *Journal of Family History* 5:360–74.

———. 1984. *The Working People of Paris, 1871–1914*. Baltimore: Johns Hopkins University Press.

Bernold, Monika. 1994. "Darstellungsmuster des Anfangs. Spuren geschlechtsspezifischer Identitätsbildung in Eröffnungserzählungen geschriebener Lebens-Geschichten." *In Frauen in Österreich. Beiträge zu ihrer Situation im 19. und 20. Jahrhundert*, edited by David Good, Margarete Grandner, and Mary Jo Maynes. Vienna: Böhlau Verlag.

Bertaux, Daniel. 1981. "From the Life-History Approach to the Transformation of Sociological Practice." In *Biography and Society*, edited by Daniel Bertaux. Beverly Hills: Sage.

———. 1984. "The Life Story Approach: A Continental View." *Annual Review of Sociology* 10:215–37.

Birker, Karl. 1973. *Die deutschen Arbeiterbildungsvereine 1840–70*. Berlin: Colloquium Verlag.

Blackbourn, David and Geoff Eley. 1984. *The Peculiarities of German History*. Oxford: Oxford University Press.

Blessing, Werner K. 1974. "Allgemeine Volksschulbildung und politische Indoktrination in bayerischen Vormärz," *Zeitschrift für bayerischen Landesgeschichte* 37:479–568.

Bollenbeck, Georg. 1976. *Zur Theorie und Geschichte der frühen Arbeiterlebenserinnungen*. Kronbach: Scriptor Verlag.

Bölling, Rainer. 1983. *Sozialgeschichte der deutschen Lehrer. Ein Überblick von 1800 bis zur Gegenwart*. Göttingen: Vandenhoeck & Ruprecht.

———. 1985. "Schule, Staat und Gesellschaft in Deutschland. Neuere Literatur zur Sozialgeschichte der Bildung im 19. und 20. Jahrhundert." *Archiv für Sozialgeschichte* 25:670–86.

Borscheid, Peter. 1986. "Romantic Love or Material Interest: Choosing Partners in Nineteenth-Century Germany." *Journal of Family History* 11:157–68.

Borscheid, Peter and H. J. Teuteberg, eds. 1983. *Ehe, Liebe, Tod. Zum Wandel der Familie, der Geschlechts- und Generationsbeziehungen in der Neuzeit*. Münster: F. Coppenrath-Verlag.

Bowman, Derek. 1970. "Introduction." In *The Life Story and Real Adventures of the Poor Man of Toggenburg*. By Ulrich Bräker, translated by Derek Bowman. Edinburgh: Edinburgh University Press.

Burke, Peter. 1978. *Popular Culture in Early Modern Europe*. New York: Harper and Row.

Campbell, Joan. 1989. *Joy in Work, German Work: The National Debate, 1800–1945*. Princeton: Princeton University Press.

Canning, Kathleen. 1992. "Gender and the Politics of Class Formation: Rethinking German Labor History." *American Historical Review* 97:736–68.

———. 1994. "Feminist History after the Linguistic Turn: Historicizing Discourse and Experience." *Signs* 19:368–404.

Chartier, Roger. 1991. *Les Usages de la Lecture*. Paris: Fayard.

Chisick, Harvey. 1981. *The Limits of Reform in the Enlightenment: Attitudes toward the Education of the Lower Classes in Eighteenth-Century France*. Princeton: Princeton University Press.

Chodorow, Nancy. 1978. *The Reproduction of Mothering.* Berkeley: University of California Press.

Clark, Linda. 1984. *Schooling the Daughters of Marianne: Textbooks and the Socialization of Girls in Modern French Primary Schools.* Albany: State University of New York Press.

Clawson, Mary Ann. 1980. "Early Modern Fraternalism and the Patriarchal Family." *Feminist Studies* 6:368–91.

Coale, Ansley, and Paul Demeny. 1966. *Model Life Tables and Stable Populations.* Princeton: Princeton University Press.

Coe, Richard N. 1984. *Reminiscences of Childhood. An Approach to a Comparative Methodology.* Leeds: Leeds Philosophical and Literary Society.

Coleman, William. 1982. *Death Is a Social Disease: Public Health and Political Economy in Early Industrial France.* Madison: University of Wisconsin Press.

Conze, Werner. 1975. "Vom 'Pöbel' zum 'Proletariat.' Sozialgeschichtliche Vorraussetzungen für den Sozialismus in Deutschland." In *Moderne deutsche Sozialgeschichte,* edited by Hans-Ulrich Wehler. Cologne/Berlin: Kiepenheur und Witsch.

Conze, Werner, and Ulrich Engelhardt, eds. 1981. *Arbeiterexistenz im 19. Jahrhundert.* Stuttgart: Klett-Cotta.

Crew, David F. 1979. *Town in the Ruhr: A Social History of Bochum, 1860–1914.* New York: Columbia University Press.

Crubellier, Maurice. 1983. "Genealogie d'une morale: La morale de l'école republicaine." *L'offre d'école. Éléments pour une étude comparée des politiques éducatives au XIXè siècle,* edited by Willem Frijhoff. Paris: Publications de la Sorbonne.

Darnton, Robert. 1971. "The High Enlightenment and the Low-Life of Literature in Pre-revolutionary France." *Past and Present* 51:81–115.

———. 1985. *The Great Cat Massacre and Other Episodes in French Cultural History.* New York: Vintage.

———. 1986. "Foreword." In *Journal of My Life.* By Jacques-Louis Menetra, introduced by Daniel Roche. New York: Columbia University Press.

Davidoff, Leonore. 1979. "Class and Gender in Victorian England: The Diaries of Arthur J. Munby and Hannah Cullwick." *Feminist Studies* 87–141.

Davidoff, Leonore, and Catherine Hall. 1987. *Family Fortunes: Men and Women of the English Middles Class, 1780–1850.* Chicago: University of Chicago Press.

Dowe, Dieter. 1978. "The Workingmen's Choral Movement in Germany before the First World War." *Journal of Contemporary History* 13:269–96.

Egan, Susanna. 1984. *Patterns of Experience in Autobiography.* Chapel Hill: University of North Carolina Press.

Elder, Glen H. 1987. "Families and Lives: Some Developments in Life-Course Studies." In *Family History at the Crossroads,* edited by Tamara Hareven and Andrejs Plakans. Princeton: Princeton University Press.

Eley, Geoff. 1980. *Reshaping the German Right: Radical Nationalism and Political Change after Bismarck.* New Haven: Yale University Press.

———. 1989. "Labor History, Social History, *Alltagsgeschichte:* Experience, Culture and the Politics of the Everyday—a New Direction for German Social History?" *Journal of Modern History* 61:297–343.

Elschenbroich, Donata. 1977. *Kinder werden nicht geboren. Studien zur Entstehung der Kindheit.* Frankfurt/Main.

Elwitt, Sanford. 1975. *The Making of the Third Republic: Class and Politics in France, 1869–1884.* Baton Rouge: Louisiana State University Press.

———. 1982. "Education and the Social Questions: The *Universités Populaires* in Late Nineteenth Century France." *History of Education Quarterly* 22:55–72.

———. 1986. *The Third Republic Defended: Bourgeois Reform in France, 1880–1914.* Baton Rouge: Louisiana State University Press.

Evans, Richard. 1976. "Prostitution, State and Society in Imperial Germany." *Past and Present* 70:106–31.

———. 1981. "Politics and the Family: Social Democracy and the Working-Class Family in Theory and Practice before 1914." In *The German Family. Essays on the Social History of the Family in Nineteenth- and Twentieth-Century Germany.* Edited by Richard J. Evans and W. R. Lee. London: Croom Helm.

———. 1982. *The German Working Class, 1888–1933: The Politics of Everyday Life.* London: Croom Helm.

———. 1990. *Proletarians and Politics: Socialism, Protest and the Working Class in Germany before the First World War.* New York: Harvester.

Fassbinder, Horant, et al. 1975. *Berliner Arbeiterviertel 1800–1918.* Berlin: Verlag für das Studium der Arbeiterbewegung.

Faue, Elizabeth. 1991. *Community of Suffering and Struggle: Women, Men, and the Labor Movement in Minneapolis, 1915–1945.* Chapel Hill: University of North Carolina Press.

Festy, Patrick. 1979. *La fecondité des pays occidentaux de 1870 à 1970.* Paris: Presses Universitaires de France.

Fishman, Sterling. 1970. "Suicide, Sex and the Discovery of the German Adolescent." *History of Education Quarterly* 10:170–88.

Fitch, Nancy. 1986. " 'Les petits Parisians en province': The Silent Revolution in the Allier, 1860–1900." *The Journal of Family History* 11:131–55.

Flandrin, Jean-Luis. 1979. *Families in Former Times: Kinship, Household and Sexuality.* Cambridge: Cambridge University Press.

Flecken, Margarete. 1981. *Arbeiterkinder im 19. Jahrhundert. Eine sozialgeschichtliche Untersuchung ihrer Lebenswelt.* Weinheim: Beltz Verlag.

Foucault, Michel. 1977. *Discipline and Punish: The Birth of the Prison.* Translated by Alan Sheridan. New York: Pantheon.

———. 1978. *The History of Sexuality.* Vol. 1. Translated by Robert Hurley. New York: Pantheon.

Frerichs, Petra. 1980. *Bürgerliche Autobiographie und proletarische Selbstdarstellung.* Frankfurt/Main: Haag-Herchen.

Frevert, Ute, ed. 1988. *Bürgerinnen und Bürger. Geschlechterverhältnisse im neunzehnten Jahrhundert.* Göttingen: Vandenhoeck und Ruprecht.

Frijhoff, Willem, ed. 1983. *L'offre d'école. Éléments pour une étude comparée des politiques éducatives au XIXè siècle.* Paris: Publications de la Sorbonne.

Fuchs, Rachel G. 1984. *Abandoned Children: Foundlings and Child Welfare in Nineteenth-Century France.* Albany: State University of New York Press.

———. 1992. *Poor and Pregnant in Paris: Strategies for Survival in the Nineteenth Century.* New Brunswick: Rutgers University Press.

Fullerton, Ronald A. 1977. "Creating a Mass Book Market in Germany: The Story of the 'Colpoteur Novel,' 1870–1890." *Journal of Social History* 10:265–83.

Furet, François, and Jacques Ozouf. 1982. *Reading and Writing: Literacy in France from Calvin to Jules Ferry.* Cambridge: Cambridge University Press.

Gagnier, Regenia. 1990. "The Literary Standard, Working-Class Autobiography, and Gender." In *Revealing Lives: Autobiography, Biography and Gender,* edited by Susan Groag Bell and Marilyn Yalom. Albany: State University of New York Press.

Gay, Peter. 1984. *The Bourgeois Experience. Victorian to Freud.* Vol. 1, *Education of the Senses.* New York: Oxford University Press.

Geiger, Susan. 1986. "Women's Life Histories: Method and Content." *Signs* 11:334–51.

Gestrich, Andreas. 1986. *Traditionelle Jugendkultur und Industrialisierung.* Göttingen: Vandenhoeck und Ruprecht.

Gildea, Robert. 1980. "Education and the *Classes Moyennes* in the Nineteenth Century." In *The Making of Frenchmen. Current Directions in the History of Education in France, 1679–1979,* edited by Donald N. Baker and Patrick J. Harrigan. Waterloo: University of Waterloo Press.

Gillis, John. 1981. *Youth and History: Tradition and Change in European Age Relations.* 2d ed. New York: Academic Press.

———. 1985. *For Better or for Worse: British Marriage, 1600 to the Present.* New York: Oxford University Press.

Gordon, Linda. 1988. *Heroes of Their Own Lives.* New York: Viking.

Graff, Harvey. 1991. *The Literacy Myth.* New Brunswick: Transaction Press.

Grew, Raymond, and Patrick J. Harrigan with James Whitney. 1983. "The Availability of Schooling in Nineteenth-Century France." *Journal of Interdisciplinary History* 14:25–63.

Grew, Raymond, Patrick J. Harrigan, and James B. Whitney. 1984. "La scolarisation en France, 1829–1906." *Annales, E.S.C.* 39 (1984): 116–57.

Groh, Dieter. 1973. *Negative Integration und revolutionärer Attentismus: die deutsche Sozialdemokratie am Vorabend des ersten Weltkriegs.* Frankfurt / Main.: Propylaen.

Grossmann, Atina. 1984. "Abortion and Economic Crisis: The 1931 Campaign against Paragraph 218." In *When Biology became Destiny: Women in Weimar and Nazi Germany,* edited by Renate Bridenthal, Atina Grossmann, and Marion Kaplan. New York: Monthly Review Press.

Gruber, Helmut. 1991. *Red Vienna: Experiment in Working-Class Culture.* New York: Oxford University Press.

Gutmann, Myron P., and René Leboutte. 1984. "Rethinking Protoindustrialization and the Family." *Journal of Interdisciplinary History* 14:587–607.

Hagen, William. 1986. "The Junker's Faithless Servant: Peasant Insubordination and the Breakdown of Serfdom in Brandenburg-Prussia, 1763–1811." In *The German Peasantry,* edited by Richard J. Evans and W. R. Lee. New York: St. Martin's Press.

Haine, W. Scott. 1992. "The Development of Leisure and the Transformation of Working-Class Adolescence, Paris, 1830–1940." *Journal of Family History* 17:451–78.

Hall, Alex. 1977. *Scandal, Sensation and Social Democracy: The SPD-Press and Wilhelmine Germany, 1890–1914*. Cambridge: Cambridge University Press.

———. 1978. "Youth in Rebellion: The Beginnings of the Socialist Youth Movement, 1904–1914." In *Society and Politics in Wilhelmine Germany*, edited by Richard J. Evans. London: Croom Helm.

Hamerow, Theodore. 1958. *Restoration, Revolution, Reaction: Economics and Politics in Germany, 1815–1871*. Princeton: Princeton University Press.

Hanagan, Michael. 1989. *Nascent Proletarians: Class Formation in Postrevolutionary France, 1840–1880*. Oxford: Basil Blackwell.

———. 1992. "Population Change, Labor Markets, and Working-Class Militancy: The Regions around Birmingham and Saint-Etienne, 1840–1880." In *The European Experience of Declining Fertility, 1850–1970: The Quiet Revolution*, edited by John R. Gillis, Louise A. Tilly, and David Levine. Oxford: Basil Blackwell.

———. 1994. "New Perspectives on Class Formation: Culture, Reproduction and Agency." *Social Science History* 16:77–94.

Hareven, Tamara. 1987. "Family History at the Crossroads." In *Family History at the Crossroads*, edited by Tamara Hareven and Andrejs Plakans. Princeton: Princeton University Press.

Harrigan, Patrick J. 1980. *Mobility, Elites and Education in French Society of the Second Empire*. Waterloo: Wilfred Laurier University Press.

Harsin, Jill. 1985. *Policing Prostitution in Nineteenth-Century France*. Princeton: Princeton University Press.

Hart, Janet. 1992. "Cracking the Code: Narrative and Political Mobilization in the Greek Resistance." *Social Science History* 16:631–68.

Haumann, Keiko, ed. 1982. *Arbeiteralltag in Stadt und Land: Neue Wege der Geschichtsschreibung*. Berlin: Argument-Verlag.

Hawes, Joseph M., and N. Ray Hiner, eds. 1991. *Children in Historical and Comparative Perspective: An International Handbook and Research Guide*. New York: Greenwood Press.

Heinemann, Manfred. "Economic Foundations for the Development of Schools in Prussia." In *L'offre d'école. Éléments pour une étude comparée des politiques éducatives au XIXè siècle*, edited by Willem Frijhoff. Paris: Publications de la Sorbonne.

Hermann, Ulrich, Andreas Gestrich, and Susanna Mutschler. 1983. "Kindheit, Jugendalter und Familienleben in einem schwabischen Dorf im 19. und 20. Jahrhundert bis zum ersten Weltkrieg." In *Ehe, Liebe, Tod, Zum Wandel der Familie, der Geschlechts- und Generations beziehungen in der Neuzeit*, edited by Peter Borscheid und H. J. Teuteberg. Münster: F. Coppenrath-Verlag.

Heywood, Christopher. 1987. *Childhood in Nineteenth-Century France*. Cambridge: Cambridge University Press.

Hickey, Stephan. 1985. *Workers in Imperial Germany: The Miners of the Ruhr*. Oxford: Clarendon Press.

Hilden, Patricia. 1987. "Re-writing the History of Socialism: Working Women and the Parti Ouvrier Français." *European History Quarterly* 17:285–306.

Hobsbawm, Eric. 1978. "Man and Woman in Socialist Iconography." *History Workshop Journal* 6:121–38.

Hohorst, Gerd, Jürgen Kocka, and Gerhard A. Ritter. 1978. *Sozialgeschichtliches*

Arbeitsbuch Bd. 2. *Materialen zur Statistik des Kaiserreichs.* Munich: Verlag C. H. Beck.

Hufton, Olwen. 1974. *The Poor in Eighteenth-Century France.* Oxford: Oxford University Press.

Imhof, Arthur E. 1981. "Women, Family and Death: Excess Mortality of Women in Childbearing Age in Four Communities in Nineteenth-Century Germany." In *The German Family: Essays on the Social History of the Family in Nineteenth- and Twentieth-Century Germany,* edited by Richard J. Evans and W. R. Lee. London: Croom Helm.

Jackson, James H. 1981. "Overcrowding and Family Life: Working-Class Families and the Housing Crisis in Late Nineteenth-Century Duisberg." In *The German Family: Essays on the Social History of the Family in Nineteenth- and Twentieth-Century Germany,* edited by Richard J. Evans and W. R. Lee. London: Croom Helm.

Jelinek, Estelle, ed. 1980. *Women's Autobiography.* Bloomington: Indiana University Press.

Johnson, Christopher. 1979. "Patterns of Proletarianization: Parisian Tailors and Lodève Woolens Workers." In *Consciousness and Class Experience in Nineteenth-century Europe.* Edited by John Merriman. New York: Holmes and Meier.

Jones, Gareth Stedman. 1974. "Working-Class Culture and Working-Class Politics in London, 1870–1900: Notes on the Remaking of a Working Class." *Journal of Social History* 7:460–508.

Kaelble, Hartmut. 1981. "Abweichung oder Konvergenz? Soziale Mobilität in Frankreich und Deutschland während des 19. und 20. Jahrhundert." In *Aspekte der historischen Forschung in Frankreich und Deutschland,* edited by Gerhardt A. Ritter and Rudolf Vierhaus. Göttingen: Vandenhoeck and Ruprecht.

———. 1986. *Industrialization and Social Inequality in Nineteenth-Century Europe.* Leamington Spa: Berg Publishers.

Kalb, Don. 1994. "On Class, the Logic of Solidarity, and the Civilizing Process: Workers, Priests and Alcohol in Dutch Shoemaking Communities, 1900–1920." *Social Science History* 18:127–52.

Kaplan, Marion A. 1991. *The Making of the Jewish Middle Class: Women, Family and Identity in Imperial Germany.* New York: Oxford University Press.

Kaplan, Steven, and Cynthia Koepp. *Work in France.* Cambridge: Cambridge University Press.

Katznelson, Ira, and Aristide Zolberg, eds. 1986. *Working-Class Formation.* Princeton: Princeton University Press.

Kehr, Eckhart. 1977. "The Genesis of the Royal Prussian Reserve Officer." In *Economics, Militarism and Foreign Policy: Essays on German History,* edited by Gordon A. Craig. Berkeley: University of California Press.

Kelly, Alfred. 1987. "Introduction." In *The German Worker: Working-Class Autobiographies from the Age of Industrialization,* edited by Alfred Kelly. Berkeley: University of California Press.

Knodel, John. 1968. "Law, Marriage and Illegitimacy in Nineteenth-Century Germany." *Population Studies* 22:297–318.

Kocka, Jürgen. 1983. *Lohnarbeit und Klassenbildung. Arbeiter und Arbeiterbewegung in Deutschland, 1800–1870.* Berlin and Bonn: J. H. W. Dietz Nachf.

————. 1990. *Arbeiterverhältnisse und Arbeiterexistenzen: Grundlagen der Klassenbildung im 19. Jahrhundert.* Bonn: Verlag J. H. W. Dietz Nachf.

Koomen, Willem. 1974. "A Note on the Authoritarian German Family." *Journal of Marriage and the Family* 36:634–36.

Koppenhöffer, Peter. 1980. *Bildung und Auslese. Untersuchungen zur sozialen Herkunft der höheren Schüler Badens, 1834/36–1890.* Weinheim: Beltz Verlag.

Korff, Gottfried. 1992. "Fraternal Hands and Workers' Fists: On Political Metaphors of the Hand." Paper presented at the joint ILWCH/Mouvement Social conference, Paris, October 24–25.

Kraul, Margaret. 1980. *Gymnasium und Gesellschaft im Vormärz.* Göttingen: Vandenhoeck und Ruprocht.

Kriedte, Peter, Hans Medick, and Jürgen Schlumbohm. 1981. *Industrialization before Industrialization: Rural Industry in the Genesis of Capitalism.* Translated by Beate Schempp. Cambridge: Cambridge University Press.

Kuczynski, Jürgen. 1968. *Studien zur Geschichte der Lage des arbeitenden Kinder in Deutschland von 1700 bis zur Gegenwart.* Berlin.

Lamberti, Marjorie. 1989. *State, Society and the Elementary School in Imperial Germany.* New York: Oxford University Press.

Langewiesche, Dieter. 1978. "The Cult of Monarchy, Political Loyalty and the Workers' Movement in Imperial Germany." *Journal of Contemporary History* 13:357–75.

————. 1981a. "Arbeiterbildung in Deutschland und Österreich." In *Arbeiter im Industrialisierungsprozess,* edited by Werner Conze and Ulrich Engelhardt. Stuttgart: Klett-Cotta.

————. 1981b. "Zur Lebensweise von Arbeitern in Deutschland im Zeitalter der Industrialisierung." In *Arbeiter in Deutschland,* edited by Dieter Langewiesche and Klaus Schonhoven. Paderborn: Schöningh.

————. 1987. "The Impact of the German Labor Movement on Workers' Culture." *Journal of Modern History* 59:506–23.

Langewiesche, Dieter, and Klaus Schönhoven. 1976. "Arbeiterbibliotheken und Arbeiterlekture im Wilhelminischen Deutschland." *Archiv für Sozialgeschichte* 16:135–204.

LaVopa, Anthony. 1980. *Prussian Schoolteachers: Profession and Office, 1763–1848.* Chapel Hill: University of North Carolina Press.

Lee, W. R. 1977. "Bastardy and the Socio-Economic Structure of Southern Germany." *Journal of Interdisciplinary History* 7:403–25.

————. 1981a. "The German Family: A Critical Survey of the Current State of Historical Research." In *The German Family: Essays on the Social History of the Family in Nineteenth- and Twentieth-Century Germany,* edited by Richard J. Evans and W. R. Lee. London: Croom Helm.

————. 1981b. "Family and 'Modernisation': The Peasant Family and Social Change in Nineteenth-Century Bavaria." In *The German Family: Essays on the Social History of the Family in Nineteenth- and Twentieth-Century Germany,* edited by Richard J. Evans and W. R. Lee. London: Croom Helm.

Lehman, A. 1983. *Erzählstruktur und Lebenslauf. Autobiographische Untersuchungen.* Frankfurt/Main: Campus Verlag.

Lejeune, Philippe. 1971. *L'autobiographie en France*. Paris: A. Colin.

———. 1975. *Le pacte autobiographique*. Paris: Editions du Seuil.

———. 1980. *Je est un autre*. Paris: Editions du Seuil.

———. 1985. "Répertoire des autobiographies écrites en France au XIXè siècle." Paper presented at a roundtable on the theme of "Les autobiographies des gens ordinaires au XIXè siècle," Paris, October 22, 1985.

———. 1986. "Crime et Testament: les Autobiographies de Criminels au XIXe Siècle." In *Récits de Vie et Institutions*, edited by Philippe Lejeune. Cahiers de Sémiotique Textuelle 8–9. Paris: Université Paris X.

———. 1989. *On Autobiography*. Minneapolis: University of Minnesota Press.

Levine, David. 1987. *Reproducing Families*. Cambridge: Cambridge University Press.

Lidtke, Vernon. 1966. *The Outlawed Party: Social Democracy in Germany, 1878–1890*. Princeton: Princeton University Press.

———. 1985. *The Alternative Culture. Socialist Labor in Imperial Germany*. New York: Oxford University Press.

Linton, Derek. 1987. "Industrialization and Intergenerational Social Mobility in a Rhenish Textile Town." *Journal of Interdisciplinary History* 18:107–26.

———. 1991. *Who Has the Youth, Has the Future: The Campaign to Save Young Workers in Imperial Germany*. New York: Cambridge University Press.

Lipp, Carola. 1986. "Sexualität und Heirat." In *Die Arbeiter: Lebensformen, Alltag und Kultur von der Frühindustrialisierung bis zur "Wirtschaftswunder,"* edited by Wolfgand Ruppert. Munich: Verlag C. H. Beck.

Loreck, Jürgen. 1977. *Wie man früher Sozialdemokrat wurde. Das Kommunikationsverhalten in der deutschen Arbeiterbewegung und die Konzeption der sozialistischen Parteipublizistik durch August Bebel*. Bonn-Bad Godesberg: Verlag Neue Gesellschaft Gmbh.

Lüdtke, Alf. 1981. "Erfahrung von Industriearbeitern — Thesen zu einer vernachlässigten Dimension der Arbeitergeschichte." In *Arbeiter im Industrialisierungsprozess*, edited by Werner Conze and Ulrich Engelhardt. Stuttgart: Klett-Cotta.

———. 1986. "Cash, Coffee-Breaks, Horseplay: *Eigensinn* and Politics among Factory Workers in Germany c. 1900." In *Confrontation, Class Consciousness and the Labour Process: Studies in Proletaian Class Formation*, edited by Michael Hanagan and Charles Stephenson. Westport, Conn: Greenwood Press.

Lundgreen, Peter. 1980–81. *Sozialgeschichte der deutschen Schule im Überblick*. 2 vols. Göttingen.: Vandenhoeck & Ruprecht.

———. 1981. "Bildung und Besitz — Einheit oder Inkongruenz in der europäischen Sozialgeschichte." *Geschichte und Gesellschaft* 7:262–75.

Lundgreen, Peter, M. Kraul, and K. Ditt. 1988. *Bildungschancen und soziale Mobilität in der städtischen Gesellschaft des 19. Jahrhunderts*. Göttingen: Vandenhoeck & Ruprecht.

Lynch, Kathryn. 1986. "Marriage Age among French Factory Workers: An Alsatian Example." *Journal of Interdisciplinary History* 14:405–29.

———. 1988. *Family, Class and Ideology in Early Industrial France*. Madison: University of Wisconsin Press.

Magraw, Roger. 1983. *France, 1815–1914. The Bourgeois Century.* London: Fontana.

———. 1992. *A History of the French Working Class.* 2 vols. Oxford: Basil Blackwell.

Margadant, Jo Burr. 1990. *Madame le Professeur.* Princeton, N.J.: Princeton University Press.

Margadant, Ted. 1979. *French Peasants in Revolt: The Insurrection of 1851.* Princeton: Princeton University Press.

Mayeur, Françoise. 1979. *L'education des filles en France au XIXe siècle.* Paris: Hachette.

Maynes, Mary Jo. 1985. *Schooling in Western Europe: A Social History.* Albany: State University of New York Press.

———. 1992a. "The Contours of Childhood: Demography, Strategy and Mythology of Childhood in French and German Lower-class Autobiographies." In *The European Experience of Declining Fertility. A Quiet Revolution, 1850–1970,* edited by John Gillis, Louise Tilly, and David Levine. Oxford: Basil Blackwell.

———. 1992b. "Adolescent Sexuality and Social Identity in French and German Lower-Class Autobiography." *Journal of Family History* 17:397–418.

———. 1992c. "Autobiography and Class Formation in Nineteenth-Century Europe: Methodological Considerations." *Social Science History* 16:517–37.

Maynes, Mary Jo, and Tom Taylor. 1991. "Children in German History." In *Children in Historical and Comparative Perspective: An International Handbook,* edited by Ray Hiner and Joseph Hawes. New York: Greenwood Press.

McDougall, Mary Lynn. 1983. "Protecting Infants: The French Campaign for Maternity Leaves, 1890–1913." *French Historical Studies* 13:79–105.

McKay, Nellie. 1989. "Nineteenth-Century Black Women's Spiritual Autobiographies." In *Interpreting Women's Lives: Feminist Theory and Personal Narratives,* edited by the Personal Narratives Group. Bloomington: Indiana University Press.

McLaren, Angus. 1983. *Sexuality and the Social Order: The Debate over the Fertility of Women and Workers in France, 17701920.* New York: Holmes and Meier.

Medick, Hans. 1982. "Plebeian Culture in the Transition to Capitalism." In *Culture, Ideology and Politics,* edited by R. Samuels and G. S. Jones. London: Routledge.

———. 1984. "Village Spinning Bees: Sexual Culture and Free Time among Rural Village Youth in Early Modern Germany." In *Interest and Emotion: Essays on the Study of Family and Kinship,* edited by Hans Medick and David Sabean. Cambridge: Cambridge University Press.

Merriman, John, ed. 1979. *Consciousness and Class Experience in Nineteenth-Century Europe.* New York: Holmes and Meier.

———. 1985. *The Red City: Limoges and the French Nineteenth Century.* New York: Oxford University Press.

Meyer, Alfred G. 1985. *The Feminism and Socialism of Lily Braun.* Bloomington: Indiana University Press.

Meyer, Folkert. 1976. *Schule der Untertanen. Lehrer und Politik in Preussen, 1848–1900.* Hamburg: Hoffmann und Campe.

Miller, Susanne. 1986. *A History of German Social Democracy from 1848 to the Present.* Translated by J. A. Underwood. Leamington Spa: Berg.

Mitterauer, Michael. 1992. *A History of Youth*. Oxford: Basil Blackwell.

Mitterauer, Michael, and Reinhard Sieder. 1982. *The European Family: Patriarchy and Partnership from the Middle Ages to the Present*. Chicago: University of Chicago Press.

Moch, Leslie Page. 1983. *Paths to the City: Regional Migration in Nineteenth-Century France*. Beverly Hills: Sage.

——. 1988. "Government Policy and Women's Experiences: The Case of Teachers in France." *Feminist Studies* 14:301–24.

Modell, John, Frank F. Furstenberg, Jr. and Theodore Hershberg. 1978. "Social Change and the Transition to Adulthood in Historical Perspective." In *The American Family in Social-Historical Perspective*, edited by Michael Gordon. New York: St. Martin's Press.

Moses, Claire Goldberg. 1984. *French Feminism in the Nineteenth Century*. Albany: State University of New York Press.

Mosse, George. 1985. *Nationalism and Sexuality*. Madison: University of Wisconsin Press.

Müller, Detlef K., Fritz K. Ringer, and Brian Simon, eds. 1986. *The Rise of the Modern Educational System: Structural Change and Social Reproduction, 1820–1920*. Cambridge: Cambridge University Press.

Münchow, Ursula. 1973. *Frühe deutsche Arbeiterautobiographien*. Berlin: Akademie Verlag.

——. 1976. *Arbeiter über ihr Leben: Von den Anfangen der Arbeiterbewegung bis zum Ende der Weimarer Republik*. Berlin: Dietz Verlag.

Neuman, R. P. 1972. "Industrialization and Sexual Behavior: Some Aspects of Working-Class Life in Imperial Germany." In *Modern European Social History*, edited by Robert Bezucha. Lexington, Mass.: D. C. Heath.

Niethammer, Lutz, in collaboration with Franz Bruggemeier. 1976. "Wie wohnten Arbeiter im Kaiserreich?" *Archiv für Sozialgeschichte* 16:61–134.

Niggemann, Heinz. 1981. *Emanzipation zwischen Sozialismus und Feminismus*. Wuppertal: Peter Hammer Verlag.

Noiriel, Gérard. 1990. *Workers in French Society in the 19th and 20th Centuries*. New York: Berg.

Nolan, Mary. 1981. *Social Democracy and Society: Working-Class Radicalism in Dusseldorf, 1890–1920*. Cambridge: Cambridge University Press.

Offen, Karen. 1984. "Depopulation, Nationalism and Feminism in Fin-de-siècle France." *American Historical Review* 89:648–67.

Olson, James. 1977. "Radical Social Democracy and School Reform in Wilhelmine Germany." *History of Education Quarterly* 17:3–16.

Ortmayr, Norbert. 1992. "Sozialhistorische Skizzen zur Geschichte des ländlichen Gesindes in Österreich." In *Knechte: Autobiographische Dokumente und sozialhistorische Skizzen*, edited by Norbert Ortmayr. Vienna: Böhlau Verlag.

——. Forthcoming. "Illegitimacy and Low-Wage Economy in Highland Austria and Jamaica." In *Gender, Kinship, Power*, edited by Mary Jo Maynes, Ann Waltner, Birgitte Soland, and Ulrike Strasser.

Palazzi, Maura. Forthcoming. "Single Women's Work and Residence in the Context of a Patrilineal System (18th- and 19th-century Northern Italy)." In *Gen-*

der, Kinship, Power, edited by Mary Jo Maynes, Ann Waltner, Birgitte Soland, and Ulrike Strasser.

Passerini, Luisa. 1989. "Women's Personal Narratives: Myths, Experiences and Emotions." In *Interpreting Women's Lives,* edited by Personal Narratives Group. Bloomington: Indiana University Press.

Perrot, Michelle. 1986. "A Nineteenth-Century Worker's Experiences as Related in a Worker's Autobiography: Norbert Truquin." In *Work in France,* edited by Steven Kaplan and Cynthia Koepp. Ithaca: Cornell University Press.

Peukert, Detlef. 1992. *The Weimar Republic: The Crisis of Classical Modernity.* New York: Hill and Wang.

Phayer, J. M. 1974. "Lower-class Morality: The Case of Bavaria." *Journal of Social History* 8:79–95.

———. 1977. *Sexual Liberation and Religion in 19th Century Europe.* London: Croom Helm.

Pollock, Linda. 1983. *Forgotten Children.* Cambridge: Cambridge University Press.

Price, Richard, and Sally Price, eds. 1988. *Narrative of a Five Years' Expedition against the Revolted Negroes of Surinam.* Baltimore: Johns Hopkins University Press.

Prost, Antoine, and Gérard Vincent, eds. 1991. *A History of Private Life.* Vol. 5. *Riddles of Identity in Modern Life.* Cambridge: Harvard University Press.

Quataert, Jean. 1985. "The Shaping of Women's Work in Manufacturing Guilds, Households and the State in Central Europe, 1648–1870." *American Historical Review* 90:1127–48.

———. 1979. *Reluctant Feminists in German Social Democracy, 1885–1917.* Princeton: Princeton University Press.

Rancière, Jacques. 1989. *The Nights of Labor: The Workers' Dream in Nineteenth-Century France.* Translated by John Drury. Philadelphia: Temple University Press.

Reulecke, Jürgen. 1976. "Vom blauen Montag zum Arbeiterurlaub. Vorgeschichte und Entstehung des Erholungsurlaubs für Arbeiter vor dem Ersten Weltkrieg." *Archiv für Sozialgeschichte* 16:205–48.

———. 1978. "Von der Dorfschule zum Schulsystem." In *Fabrik. Familie. Feierabend. Beiträge zur Sozialgeschichte des Alltags im Industriezeitalter,* edited by Jürgen Reulecke and Wolfhard Weber. Wuppertal: Peter Hammer Verlag.

Ringer, Fritz. 1979. *Education and Society in Modern Europe.* Bloomington: Indiana University Press.

Ritter, Gerhard A. 1978. "Workers' Culture in Imperial Germany: Problems and Points of Departure for Research." *Journal of Contemporary History* 13:165–89.

———. 1979. *Arbeiterkultur.* Königstein: Athenaeum.

Ritter, Gerhard A., and Klaus Tenfelde. 1992. *Arbeiter im Deutschen Kaiserreich 1871 bis 1914.* Bonn: J. H. W. Dietz Verlag Nachf.

Roberts, James S. 1984. *Drink, Temperance and the Working-Class in Nineteenth-Century Germany.* Boston: George Allen and Unwin.

Roche, Daniel. 1981. *Le peuple de Paris: Essai sur la culture populaire au XVIIIè siècle.* Paris: Aubier Montagne.

———. 1982. "L'autobiographie d'un homme du peuple." and "Jacques-Louis

Ménétra: Une manière de vivre au XVIIIe siècle." In *Journal de ma vie. Jacques-Louis Méétra. Compagnon vitrier au 18e siècle*, presented by Daniel Roche. Paris: Montalba.

Rose, Sonya. 1992. *Limited Livelihoods: Gender and Class in Nineteenth-Century England*. Berkeley: University of California Press.

Rosenbaum, Heidi, ed. 1978. *Seminär. Familie und Gesellschaftsstruktur. Materiellen zu den sozio-ökonomischen Bedingungen von Familieformen*. Frankfurt/Main.: Suhrkamp.

Ross, Ellen. 1982. "Fierce Questions and Taunts: Married Life in Working-Class London, 1880–1914." *Feminist Studies* 8:575–602.

———. 1992. "Motherhood and the State in Britain, 1904–1914." In *The European Experience of Declining Fertiliuty: A Quiet Revolution, 1850–1970*, edited by John R. Gillis, Louise A. Tilly, and David Levine. Oxford: Basil Blackwell.

Roth, Günther. 1963. *The Social Democrats in Imperial Germany: A Study in Working Class Isolation and National Integration*. Totowa, N.J.: Bedminster Press.

Roth, Lothar. 1982. *Die Erfindung des Jugendlichen*. Munchen.

Rudolph, Richard. 1992. "The European Peasant Family and Economy: Central Themes and Issues." *The Journal of Family History* 17:119–38.

Ruppert, Wolfgang, ed. 1986. *Die Arbeiter: Lebensformen, Alltag und Kultur von der Frühindustrialisierung bis zur "Wirtschaftswunder"*. Munich: Verlag C. H. Beck.

Ryan, J., and C. Sackrey. 1984. *Strangers in Paradise. Academics from the Working Class*. Boston: South End Press.

Sabean, David. 1990. *Property, Production and Family in Neckarhausen, 1700–1870*. Cambridge: Cambridge University Press.

Sacks, Karen. 1989. "What's a Life Story Got to Do With It?" In *Interpreting Women's Lives. Feminist Theory and Personal Narratives*, edited by the Personal Narratives Group. Bloomington: Indiana University Press.

Saul, Klaus. 1971. "Der Kampf um die Jugend zwischen Volksschule und Kaserne." *Militargeschichtliche Mitteilungen* 1:97–143.

———. 1979. "Der Traum von einer besseren Welt. Anfänge einer sozialistischen Kinderliteratur im kaiserlichen Deutschland." *Journal für Geschichte* 1:2–11.

Saul, Klaus, et al., eds. 1982. *Arbeiterfamilien im Kaiserreich. Materielen zur Sozialgeschichte in Deutschland, 1871–1914*. Düsseldorf: Droste.

Scheman, Naomi. 1993. "Who Is That Masked Woman? Reflections on Power, Privilege and Home-ophobia." In *Engenderings: Construction of Authority, Knowledge and Privilege*. New York: Routledge.

Schenda, Rudolph. 1970. *Volk Ohne Buch. Studien zur Sozialgeschichte der populären Lesestoffe, 1770–1910*. Frankfurt/Main.: Verlag Klostermann.

Schlumbohm, Jürgen. 1980. " 'Traditional' Collectivity and 'Modern' Individuality: Some Questions and Suggestions for the Historical Study of Socialization. The Examples of the German Lower and Upper Bourgeoisies around 1800." *Social History* 5:71–103.

———. 1983a. *Kinderstuben. Wie Kinder zu Bauern, Bürgern, Aristokraten wurden, 1700–1850*. Munich: DTV.

———. 1983b. "Geschichte der Kindheit—Fragen und Kontroversen." *Geschichtsdidatik* 8:305–15.

Schneider, Michael. 1991. *A Brief History of the German Trade Unions.* Translated by Barrie Selman. Bonn: Verlag J. H. W. Dietz Nachf.

Schomerus, Heilweg. 1981. "The Family Life-Cycle: A Study of Factory Workers in Nineteenth-Century Württemberg." In *The German Family: Essays on the Social History of the Family in Nineteenth- and Twentieth-Century Germany,* edited by Richard J. Evans and W. R. Lee. London: Croom Helm.

Schönert, Joerg. 1983. "Kriminalgeschichten in der deutschen Literatur zwischen 1770 und 1890." *Geschichte un Gesellschaft* 9:49–68.

Schorske, Carl. 1983. *German Social Democracy, 1905–1917.* Cambridge: Harvard University Press.

Schulte, Regine. 1984. "Infanticide in Rural Bavaria in the Nineteenth Century." In *Interest and Emotion: Essays on the Study of Family and Kinship,* edited by Hans Medick and David Sabean. Cambridge: Cambridge University Press.

Schwarte, N. 1980. *Schulpolitik und Pädagogik der deutschen Sozialdemokratie.* Cologne: Böhlau Verlag.

Scott, Joan. 1988a. " 'L'ouvrière! Mot impie, sordide . . .': Women Workers in the Discourse of French Political Economy, 1840–1860." In *Gender and the Politics of History.* New York: Columbia University Press.

———. 1988b. "Women in *The Making of the English Working Class.*" In *Gender and the Politics of History.* New York: Columbia University Press.

———. 1991. "The Evidence of Experience." *Critical Inquiry* 17:773–97.

Seccombe, Wally. 1986. "Patriarchy Stabilized: The Construction of the Male Breadwinner Wage Norm in Nineteenth-Century Britain." *Social History* 2:53–76.

———. 1992a. *A Millenium in Family Change: Feudalism to Capitalism in Northwestern Europe.* London: Verso.

———. 1992b. "Men's 'Marital Rights' and Women's 'Wifely Duties': Changing Conjugal Relations in the Fertility Decline." In *The European Experience of Declining Fertility. A Quiet Revolution, 1850–1970,* edited by John Gillis, Louise Tilly, and David Levine. Oxford: Basil Blackwell.

Sewell, William. 1980. *Work and Revolution in France.* Cambridge: Cambridge University Press.

Shaffer, John. 1978. "Family, Class and Young Women's Occupational Expectations." *Journal of Family History* 3:62–77.

Shorter, Edward. 1973. "Female Emancipation, Birth Control and Fertility in European History." *American Historical Review* 78:447–76.

———. 1976. *The Making of the Modern Family.* New York: Basic Books.

Smith, Bonnie. 1981. *Ladies of the Leisure Class: The Bourgeoises of Northern France in the Nineteenth Century.* Princeton, N.J.: Princeton University Press.

Somers, Margaret. 1992. "Narrativity, Narrative Identity, and Social Action: Rethinking English Working-Class Formation." *Social Science History* 16:591–630.

Sowerwine, Charles. 1982. *Sisters or Citizens? Women and Socialism in France since 1876.* Cambridge: Cambridge University Press.

———. 1983. "Workers and Women in France before 1914: The Debate over the Couriau Affair." *Journal of Modern History* 55:411–41.

Sperber, Jonathan. 1984. *Popular Catholicism in Nineteenth-Century Germany.* Princeton: Princeton University Press.

Spohn, Wilfried. 1990. "Piety, Secularism, Socialism — On Religion and Working-Class Formation in Imperial Germany, 1871–1914." Paper presented at "What's Next for the Kaiserreich?" conference, Philadelphia, January 1990.

Spree, Reinhard. 1981. *Soziale Ungleichheit vor Krankheit und Tod*. Göttingen: Vandenhoeck und Ruprecht.

Stack, Carol. 1974. *All Our Kin*. New York: Harper and Row.

Stadelmann, Rudolf, and Wolfram Fischer. 1955. *Die Bildungswelt des deutschen Handwerkers um 1800*. Berlin: Duncker & Humblot.

Stearns, Peter. 1970. "Adaptation to Industrialization: German Workers as a Test Case." *Central European History* 3:303–31.

———. 1978. *Paths to Authority: The Middle Class and the Industrial Labor Force in France, 1820–1848*. Urbana: University of Illinois Press.

Steedman, Carolyn. 1991. *Landscape for a Good Woman: The Story of Two Lives*. New Brunswick: Rutgers University Press.

———. 1992. *Past Tenses: Essays on Writing, Autobiographys and History*. London: Rivers Oram Press.

Steinberg, Hans-Josef. 1976. "Workers' Libraries in Germany before 1914." *History Workshop* 1:166–80.

Steinmetz, George. 1992. "Reflections on the Role of Social Narratives in Working-Class Formation: Narrative Theory in the Social Sciences." *Social Science History* 16:489–517.

———. 1993. *Regulating the Social: The Welfare State and Local Politics in Imperial Germany*. Princeton: Princeton University Press.

Stone, Lawrence. 1977. *The Family, Sex and Marriage, 1500–1800*. New York: Harper and Row.

Struminger, Laura S. 1983. *What Were Little Girls and Boys Made Of? Primary Education in Rural France, 1830–1880*. Albany: State University of New York Press.

Swindells, Julia. 1989. "Liberating the Subject? Autobiography and 'Women's History': A Reading of *The Diaries of Hannah Cullwick*." In *Interpreting Women's Lives: Feminist Theory and Personal Narratives*, edited by the Personal Narratives Group. Bloomington: Indiana University Press.

Taylor, Barbara. 1983. *Eve and the New Jerusalem: Socialism and Feminism in the Nineteenth Century*. New York: Pantheon.

Taylor, Tom. 1988a. "The Transition to Adulthood in Comparative Perspective: Professional Males in Germany and the United States at the Turn of the Century." *Journal of Social History* 21:635–58.

———. 1988b. "The Crisis of Youth in Wilhelmine Germany." Ph.D. diss., University of Minnesota.

Tenfelde, Klaus. 1977a. "Arbeiterhaushalt und Arbeiterbewegung 1850–1914." *Sozialwissenschaftliche Informationen für Unterricht und Studium* 6:160–65.

———. 1977b. *Sozialgeschichte der Bergarbeiterschaft an der Ruhr im 19. Jahrhundert*. Bonn-Bad Godesberg: Verlag Neue Gesellschaft.

———. 1981. "Bildung und sozialer Aufstieg im Ruhrbergbau vor 1914." In *Arbeiter im Industrialisierungsprozess*, edited by Werner Conze and Ulrich Engelhardt. Stuttgart: Klett-Cotta.

———. 1984. "Schwierigkeiten mit dem Alltag." *Geschichte und Gesellschaft* 10:376–94.

Teuteberg, Hans Jürgen, and Annagret Bernhard. 1978. "Wandel der Kindernahrung in der Zeit der Industrialisierung." In *Fabrik. Familie. Feierabend. Beiträge zur Sozialgeschichte des Alltags im Industriezeitalter,* edited by Jürgen Reulecke und Wolfhard Weber. Wuppertal: Peter Hammer Verlag.

Thompson, Edward P. 1966. *The Making of the English Working Class.* New York: Vintage.

———. 1967. "Time and Work Discipline." *Past and Present* 38:59–96.

———. 1973. "Patrician Society, Plebeian Culture." *Journal of Social History* 7:382–405.

Tilly, Charles. 1973. "Population and Pedagogy in France." *History of Education Quarterly* 13:113–27.

———. 1979. "Did the Cake of Custom Break?" In *Consciousness and Class Experience in Nineteenth-century Europe,* edited by John Merriman. New York: Holmes and Meier. 17–44.

———. 1986a. "Putting Demography into History and *Vice Versa.*" The New School for Social Research. The Working Paper Series, #30.

———. 1986b. "Family History, Social History and Social Change." New School for Social Research. The Working Paper Series, #24.

———. 1986c. *The Contentious French.* Cambridge, Mass.: Belknap Press.

Tilly, Louise. 1989. "Gender, Women's History and Social History." *Social Science History* 13:439–62.

Tilly, Louise, and Joan Scott. 1978. *Women, Work and Family.* New York: Holt.

Tilly, Louise, Joan Scott, and Miriam Cohen. 1976. "Women's Work and European Fertility Patterns." *Journal of Interdisciplinary History* 6:447–76.

Vincent, David. 1981. *Bread, Knowledge and Freedom: A Study of Nineteenth-Century Working-Class Autobiography.* London: Europa.

Vogtmeier, Michael. 1984. *Die proletarische Autobiographie, 1903–1914: Studien zur Gattungs- und Funktionsgeschichte der Autobiographie.* Frankfurt/Main: Peter Lang.

Walkowitz, Judith. 1980. *Prostitution and Victorian Society: Women, Class and the State.* New York: Cambridge University Press.

———. 1992. *City of Dreadful Delights: Narratives of Sexual Danger in Late-Victorian London.* Chicago: University of Chicago Press.

Waltner, Ann. 1989. "On Not Becoming a Heroine: Lin Dai-yu and Cui Ying-ying." *Signs* 15:61–78.

Ward, W. Peter. 1993. *Birth Weight and Economic Growth.* Chicago: University of Chicago Press.

Watkins, Susan. 1991. *From Provinces into Nations: The Demographic Integration of Western Europe, 1870–1960.* Princeton, N.J.: Princeton University Press.

Weber-Kellermann, Ingeborg. 1974. *Die deutsche Familie.* Frankfurt/Main: Suhrkamp.

———. 1979. *Die Kindheit. Kleidung und Wohnung, Arbeit und Spiel.* Frankfurt/Main.

Weeks, Jeffrey. 1981. *Sex, Politics and Society. The Regulation of Sexuality since 1800.* London: Longman.

Wegs, Robert. 1987. "Adolescence and Working-Class Youth in Vienna, 1890–1938." Paper presented at the Social Science History Association meeting, New Orleans, November 1, 1987.

———. 1992. "Working-Class 'Adolescence' in Austria, 1890–1930." *Journal of Family History* 17:439–50.

Weissbach, Lee Shai. 1989. *Child Labor in Nineteenth-Century France: Assuring the Future Harvest.* Baton Rouge: Louisiana State University Press.

Weitz, Eric. 1991. "The Communist Party and the Construction of Gender: The German, French, and Italian Cases, 1919–1948." Paper presented at the Social Science History Association annual meeting, New Orleans, October 1991.

———. 1992. "Popular Communism: Political Strategies and Social Histories in the Formation of the German, French and Italian Communist Parties, 1919–1948." Western Societies Program Occasional Papers #31. Ithaca, N.Y.: Center for International Studies.

———. Forthcoming. Review of Helmut Gruber's *Red Vienna. Internationale Wissentschaftliche Korrespondenz.*

Wendorff, W. 1978. *Schule und Bildung in der Politik von Wilhelm Liebknecht.* Berlin: Colloquium-Verlag.

Wheeler, Robert F. 1978. "Organized Sport and Organized Labour: The Workers' Sports Movement." *Journal of Contemporary History* 13:191–210.

Wuthnow, Robert. 1989. *Communities of Discourse: Ideology and Social Structure in the Reformation, the Enlightenment and European Socialism.* Cambridge: Harvard University Press.

Zind, Pierre. 1970. "La methode pédagogoque de Jean-Baptiste de la Salle au debut du XVIIIè siècle." In *Histoire de l'enseignement de 1610 à nos jours.* Actes du 95è Congrés des Sociétés Savantes. Reims.

Zipes, Jack. 1983. *Fairytales and the Art of the Subversive.* London: Heinemann.